Great EASY Meals

250 Fun & Fast Recipes

HYPERION
New York

Food Network Magazine
Editor in Chief Maile Carpenter
Design Director Deirdre Koribanick
Associate Art Director Shira Gordon
Managing Editor Maria Baugh
Food Editor Liz Sgroi
Photo Director Alice Albert
Deputy Photo Editor Kathleen E. Bednarek

Food Network Kitchens
Senior Vice President,
Culinary Production Susan Stockton
Vice President, Test Kitchen
Katherine Alford
Executive Culinary Producer Jill Novatt
Recipe Developers Andrea Albin,
Leah Brickley, Sarah Copeland, Bob Hoebee,
Claudia Sidoti, Amy Stevenson

Hearst Communications
Editorial Director Ellen Levine
Vice President,
Publisher Hearst Books Jacqueline Deval

Project Editor Marisa Bulzone

Food Network Magazine and the Food
Network Magazine logo are trademarks of
Food Network Magazine, LLC.

Foodnetwork.com/magazine

Library of Congress Cataloging-in-Publication Data

Food Network Magazine Great
Easy Meals / Food Network Magazine.
p. cm.
ISBN 978-1-4013-2419-3
1. Quick and easy cooking. I. Food Network
(Firm) II. Food Network Magazine. III. Title:
Great Easy Meals.
TX833.5.F667 2010
641.5'55—dc22

                                                    2010028513

Hyperion books are available for special promotions,
premiums, or corporate training. For details, contact the
HarperCollins Special Markets Department in the New
York office at 212-207-7528, fax 212-207-7222, or e-mail
spsales@harpercollins.com.

FIRST EDITION

10 9 8 7 6 5 4 3

Photography Credits:
All food photography by Antonis Achilleos, except:
Pages iii and xviii-xix: Marko Metzinger/Studio D;
page iv: Lara Robby/Studio D; page vii (left to right):
courtesy Food Network (5), Peter Ross (far right); Charles
Masters: pages xx, 40, 44, 90, 94, 154, 158, 216, 220,
262, 266, 324, 328, 354, 356; page 42: James Baigrie;
page 92: Dave Lauridsen; page 156: Miki Duisterhof;
pages 218, 264, and 326: David A. Land; pages 380–383:
Jeffrey Westbrook/Studio D; page 384: Con Poulos.

All food styling by Jamie Kimm, except:
Heidi Johannsen: pages 17, 21, 26, 27, 100, 103, 136, 164,
199, 222, 242, 243, 268, 272, 274, 275, 276, 279, 331,
340, 345, 347 (top left and right), 351 (bottom right),
352 (top right, bottom left and right); Stephana Bottom:
pages 356–379.

All prop styling for food photography by Marina Malchin.

To our readers,
for loving food as
much as we do.

ACKNOWLEDGMENTS

Huge thanks to everyone who made this book happen, most of all to the chefs in Food Network Kitchens, led by Susan Stockton, senior vice president, culinary production; and Katherine Alford, vice president, test kitchen. Susan and Katherine's incredible team created every dish in this book, and they continue dreaming up ingenious recipes for Food Network Magazine month after month. Thanks to all of these chefs for their endless supply of ideas—Claudia Sidoti, Bob Hoebee, Leah Brickley, Andrea Albin, Sarah Copeland and Amy Stevenson; to the Kitchens' ace purchasing team—Cedric Council, Jake Schiffman and Dave Mechlowicz; and to recipe tester Treva Chadwell, along with all of the folks in Food Network Kitchens for their contributions and invaluable feedback.

Thanks, too, to the magazine's editorial food team—Erin Phraner, Carolyn Coppersmith and especially our tireless food editor, Liz Sgroi, who spent countless hours on this book, making sure every page was inspiring and fun, just like her stories in the magazine. And thanks to Managing Editor Maria Baugh and Jacqueline Deval, Vice President, Publisher, Hearst Books, who coordinated this entire project, along with editor Marisa Bulzone; and to our great partners at Hyperion, led by President and Publisher Ellen Archer.

We are grateful, as always, to Design Director Deirdre Koribanick and her hugely talented art and photo team—Art Director Ian Doherty, Associate Art Director Shira Gordon, Digital Imaging Specialist Hans Lee, Photo Director Alice Albert and Deputy Photo Editor Kate Bednarek—who made this book as bright, colorful and energetic as every issue of the magazine. And we're thankful for the brilliant artists they hired to style and photograph the dishes, including photographers Antonis Achilleos and Charles Masters, food stylists Jamie Kimm and Stephana Bottom, and prop stylist Marina Malchin. Thanks, too, to the dedicated copy team who pored over every page: Copy Chief Joy Sanchez and Copy Editor Paula Sevenbergen.

Of course, this book wouldn't exist without the leaders at Hearst Magazines and Food Network, who partnered to create Food Network Magazine. Thanks to Food Network President Brooke Johnson; Sergei Kuharsky, General Manager, New Enterprises; and Amanda Melnick, Vice President, New Business and Integrated Marketing. Thanks, also, to Hearst Chairman Cathie Black; President David Carey; President, Marketing and Publishing Director Michael Clinton; Executive Vice President and General Manager John Loughlin, and especially to Editorial Director Ellen Levine, who mentors and inspires the magazine staff every day.

Contents

Papardelle with
Snap Peas,
page 318

Meet the Stars

Melissa d'Arabian
page 42

Guy Fieri
page 92

Pat and Gina Neely
page 156

Michael Symon
page 218

Ellie Krieger
page 265

Ted Allen
page 326

Recipes

Soups & Stews

Sandwiches & Pizza

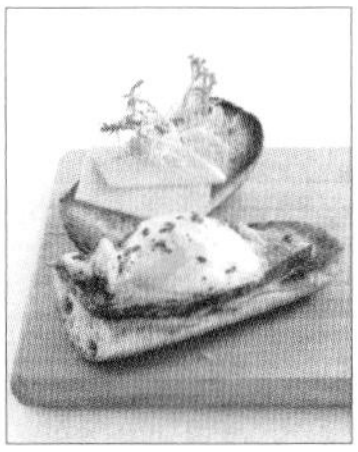
47 Bistro Egg Sandwiches

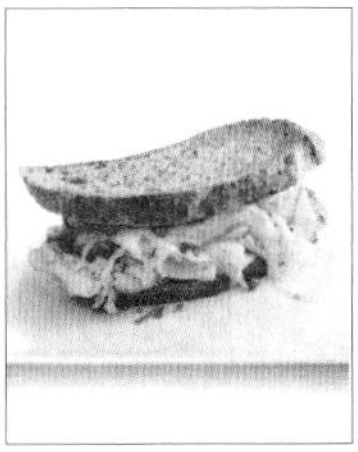
48 Turkey Reubens

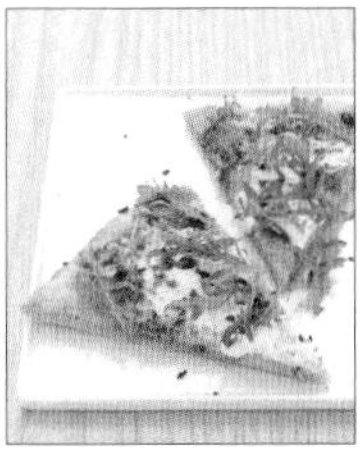
51 White Clam Pizza

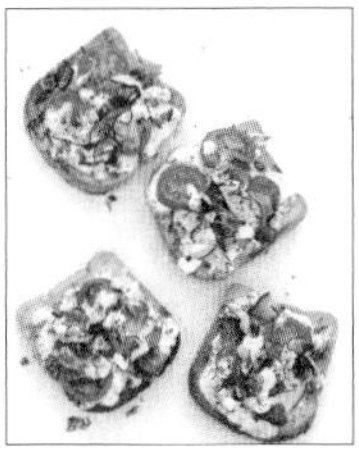
52 Bacon-Tomato Cheese Toasts

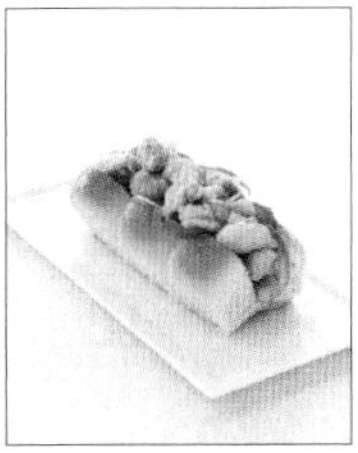
55 Fried Catfish Rolls

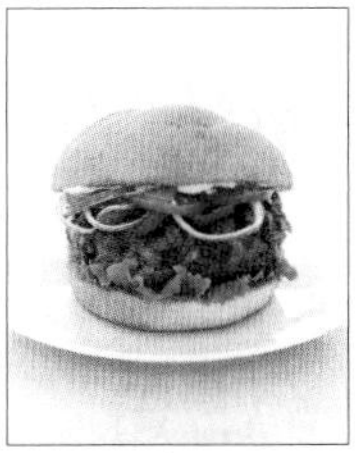
56 Manchego-Stuffed Pork Burgers

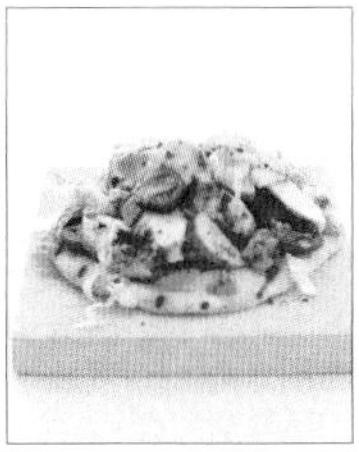
59 Chicken Salad Pita with Baba Ghanoush

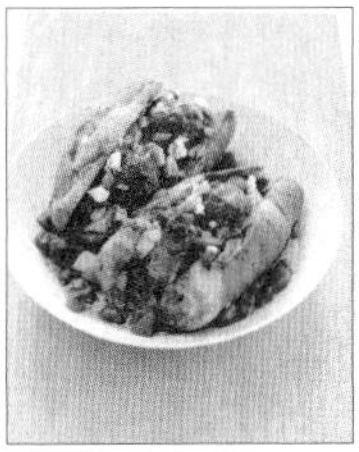
60 Mexican Meatball Subs

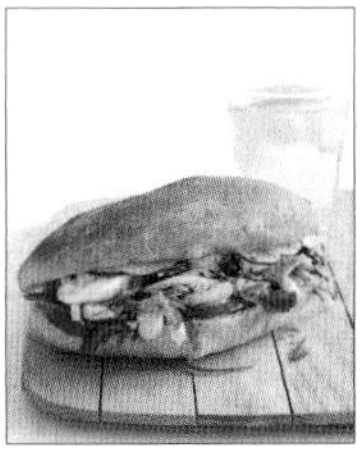
63 Parisian Tuna Sandwiches

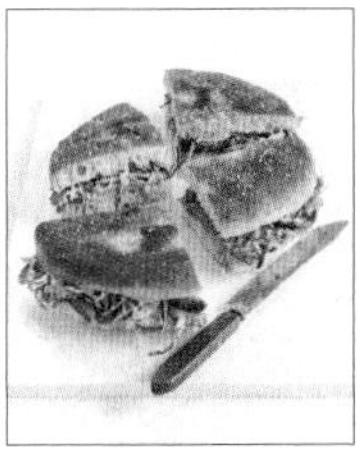
64 Sesame Beef Sandwiches

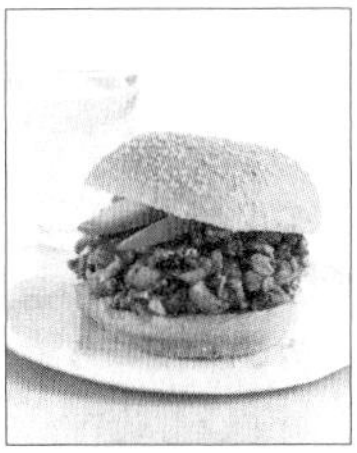
67 Turkey Picadillo Sandwiches

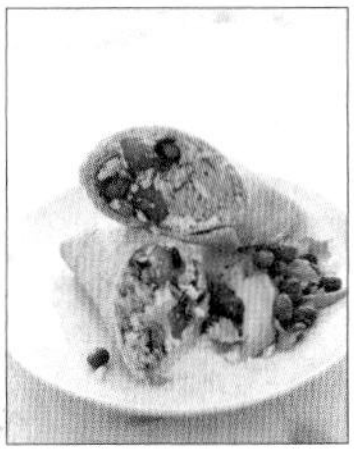
68 Chicken and Bean Burritos

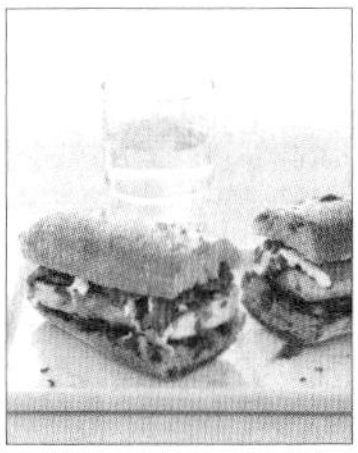
71 Tofu Parmesan Subs

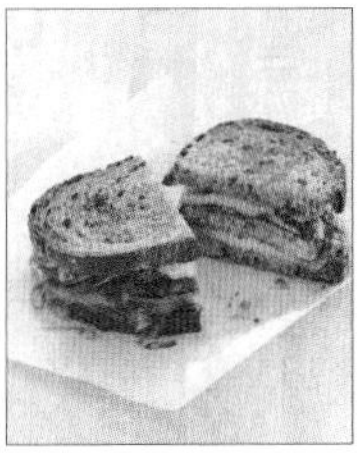
72 Patty Melts

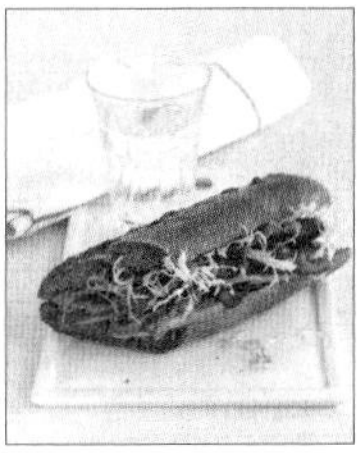
75 Avocado BLTs

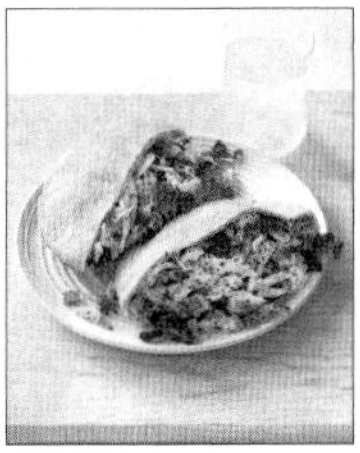
76 Poppy Seed-Chicken Pitas

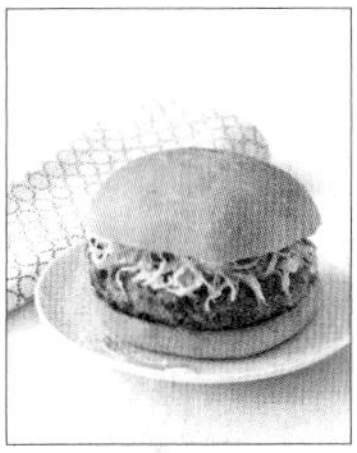
79 Jerk Turkey Burgers with Mango Slaw

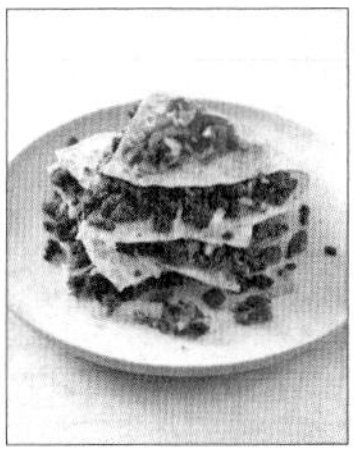
80 Meaty Quesadillas

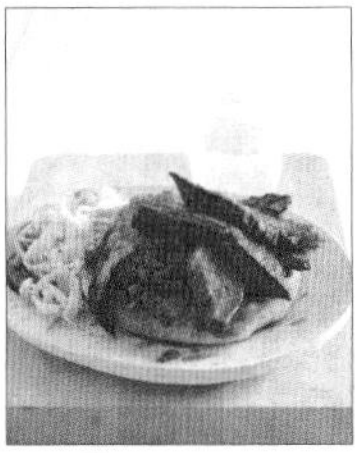
83 Slow-Cooker Brisket Sandwiches

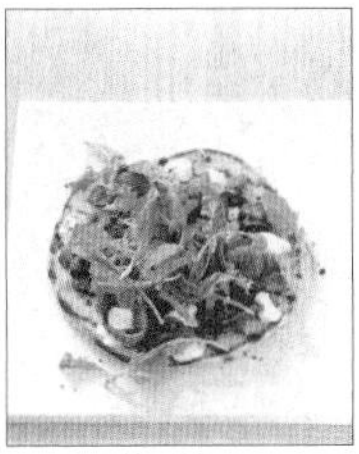
84 Grilled Pita Pizzas

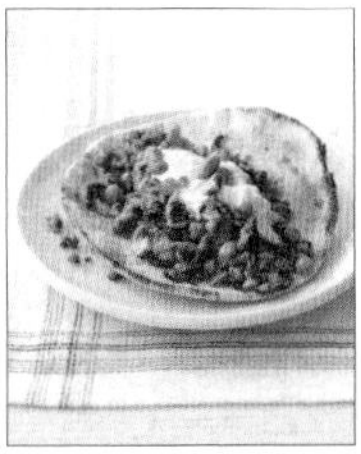
87 Chicken Korma

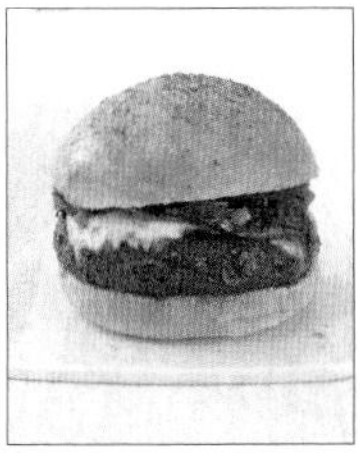
88 Chile Relleno Burgers

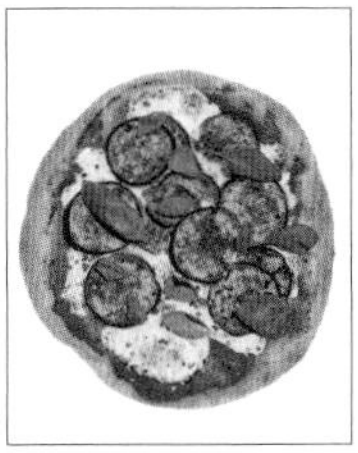
90 Mix & Match Pizza

Poultry

97 Poached Ginger Chicken

98 Drumsticks with Biscuits and Tomato Jam

101 Chicken with Apple, Onion and Cider Sauce

102 Chicken and Black Bean Tostadas

105 Sausage and Kraut

106 Chicken-and-Cheese Enchiladas

109 Chicken and Waffles

110 Glazed Chicken with Dried Fruit and Parsnips

113 Hoisin Chicken with Cucumber Salad

114 Sweet-and-Sour Chicken

117 Chicken with Creamy Mushrooms and Snap Peas

118 Chicken Schnitzel with Mustard Sauce

121 Inside-Out Chicken Cordon Bleu

122 Broiled Lemon-Garlic Chicken

125 Pepper-Jack Chicken with Succotash

126 Teriyaki Hens with Bok Choy

129 Oven-Fried Chicken

130 Garlic-Roasted Chicken

133 Spring Chicken Salad

134 Thai Chicken with Carrot-Ginger Salad

137 Chicken with Sun-Dried Tomato, Eggplant and Basil

138 Beer-Braised Chicken

141 Sausage-and-Pepper Skewers

142 Glazed Hens with Cucumber-Cantaloupe Salad

145 Chicken Tandoori

146 Skillet Rosemary Chicken

149 Grilled Chicken Caesar Salad

150 Smoked Turkey and Black-Eyed Pea Salad

153 Skillet Turkey with Roasted Vegetables

154 Mix & Match Stuffed Chicken

Meat

161 Skillet Pork and Peppers

162 Mojo Pork Chops with Plantains

165 Grilled Pork with Arugula and Grape Salad

166 Pork Tenderloin with Eggplant Relish

169 Moo Shu Pork

170 Pork and Fennel Ragoût

173 Pork with Squash and Apples

174 Chile-Rubbed Pork Chops

177 Rosemary-Mustard Pork with Peaches

178 Pork with Potato-Bean Salad

181 Cheese-Stuffed Pork Chops

182 Pork Tonnato

185 Japanese-Style Crispy Pork

186 Ham and Cheese Pie with Greens

189 Green Eggs and Ham

190 Ham and Cheese Pan Soufflé

193 Ricotta, Ham and Scallion Tart

194 Lamb Chops with Fennel and Tomatoes

197 Steak with Avocado Sauce and Tomato Salad

198 Spicy Chinese Beef

201 Tangerine Beef with Scallions

202 Mini Skillet Meatloaves

205 Beef Kefta with Melon Slaw

206 Flank Steak with Salsa Verde

209 Grilled Steak with Black-Eyed Peas

210 Slow-Cooker Corned Beef and Cabbage

211 Corned Beef Hash

213 Seared Steak with Chard Salad

214 Steak with Blue Cheese Butter and Celery Salad

216 Mix & Match Stir-Fries

Fish & Seafood

223 Pan-Fried Cod with Slaw

224 Moroccan Grilled Salmon

227 Smoked Trout and Potato Salad

228 Tilapia with Escarole and Lemon-Pepper Oil

231 Broiled Halibut with Ricotta-Pea Puree

232 Tilapia with Green Beans

235 Striped Bass with Mushrooms

236 Curried Salmon Cakes

239 Pesto Salmon and Smashed Potatoes

240 Baja Fish Tacos

242 Thai Red Curry Mahi Mahi Salad

243 Mahi Mahi Banh Mi (Vietnamese Sandwiches)

245 Rice and Peas with Trout

246 Popcorn Shrimp Salad

249 Home-Style Shrimp Curry

250 Cajun Shrimp and Rice

253 Scallops with Citrus and Quinoa

254 Clams and Mussels in Thai Curry Sauce

257 Spinach-Orzo Salad with Shrimp

258 Shrimp Boil

261 Shrimp Scampi with Garlic Toasts

262 Mix & Match Foil-Packet Fish

Pasta & Grains

269 Whole-Grain Pasta with Chickpeas and Escarole

270 Creamy Chicken and Pasta Salad

273 Croque Monsieur Mac and Cheese

274 Fontina Risotto with Chicken

275 Risotto Cakes with Mixed Greens

277 Garlic-and-Greens Spaghetti

278 Gnocchi Niçoise

281 BLT Pasta Salad

282 Spanish-Style Noodles with Chicken and Sausage

285 Udon with Tofu and Asian Greens

286 Vegetable Couscous with Moroccan Pesto

289 Skillet Lasagna

290 Spinach Ravioli with Tomato Sauce

293 Whole-Wheat Spaghetti with Leeks and Hazelnuts

294 Baked Penne with Fennel

297 Linguine with Tuna Puttanesca

298 Steamed Vegetables with Chickpeas and Rice

301 Spaghetti Carbonara

302 Swiss Chard Lasagna

305 Vegetable Fried Rice with Bacon

306 Roasted Pepper Pasta Salad

309 Lemon-Pepper Fettuccine

310 Pasta with Escarole

313 Orecchiette Salad with Roast Beef

314 Polenta with Roasted Tomatoes

317 Tortellini with Peas and Prosciutto

318 Pappardelle with Snap Peas

321 Pasta with Zucchini and Ham

322 Cold Curry-Peanut Noodles

324 Mix & Match Mac and Cheese

Side Dishes

 **330** Garlic Green Beans

 **330** Roasted Rutabaga

 **331** Glazed Radishes

 332 Israeli Couscous with Raisins

 **333** Mushroom Salad

 **333** Tomato Gratin

 **333** Tarragon Snap Peas

 **333** Cauliflower Tabouli

 334 Creamy Bibb Salad

 **334** Garlic-Sesame Spinach

 **335** Coriander Roasted Carrots

 **336** Roasted Peppers with Basil

 **337** Lemon Potatoes

 **337** Parmesan Broccoli

 **337** Cauliflower Gratin

 **337** Glazed Snow Peas

 **338** Baby Broccoli with Oyster Sauce

 **338** Watermelon-Cucumber Salad

 **339** Summer Squash Carpaccio

 **341** Curried Winter Squash

 **341** Carrot-Mustard Slaw

 **341** Cheesy Chile Rice

 **341** Spicy Sweet-Potato Fries

 **341** Roasted Asparagus

 **342** Fried Pickles

 **343** Bacon-Cheddar Mashed Potatoes

 343 Black Bean Salad

 **344** Glazed Turnips and Edamame

 **344** Corn Pudding

 **344** Braised Celery

344 Spicy Escarole with Garlic

345 Roasted Beet Salad

346 Tomato-Basil Lima Beans

347 Patatas Bravas

347 Curried Brown Rice Pilaf

347 Snow Pea and Avocado Slaw

347 Grilled Scallions

348 Buttered Egg Noodles

348 Eggplant with Peanut Dressing

349 Roasted Red Onions

350 Roasted Brussels Sprouts

351 Okra with Tomatoes

351 Green Bean and Celery Salad

351 Charm City Corn

351 Celery Root and Parsnip Puree

352 Herb Toasts

352 Carrots with Chickpeas and Pine Nuts

352 Brussels Sprout Hash

352 Mediterranean Bulgur

353 Garlicky Bok Choy

10-Minute Desserts

356 Chocolate-Glazed Pound Cake

357 Microwave Fudge

357 Affogato

357 Caramel Apples

357 Lemon Crêpes

358 Instant Chocolate Cake

358 Cinnamon-Anise Poached Pears

359 Cookies-and-Cream Parfaits

360 Chocolate Crème Brûlée

361 Pears with Chocolate Sauce

361 Apple Crisp

361 Chocolate-Nut Buttons

361 Peach Melba

362 Figs and Cream

362 Crispy-Crunchy Bars

363 Grapefruit Mousse

364 Ice Cream Wafflewiches

365 Candy Shakes

365 Chocolate Crostini

365 Caramel Pineapple Cake

365 Grapefruit Brûlée

366 Coconut Pineapple Sundae

366 Chocolate Fondue

366 Chocolate Cream Pie

368 Tiramisu Trifles

369 Mexican Chocolate S'mores

369 Ricotta with Balsamic Berries

369 Chilled Honeydew Soup

369 Caramelized Bananas

370 Mango Cloud

 **370** Cheesecake Pops

 **370** Rhubarb Crumble

 **370** Yogurt with Apricots

 **370** Shortcake Royale

 **372** Blue Cheese and Pears

 **373** Strawberry-Meringue Fools

 **373** Peaches and Cream

 **374** Rice Pudding with Plums

 **374** Berry Toast Tartlets

 **374** Sweet-and-Salty Shortbread

 **374** Grape Soda Floats

 **375** Cheesecake Parfaits

 **376** Cherries Jubilee

 **377** Waffle Cake

 **377** Chocolate–Peanut Butter Pie

 **378** Berry Ice Cream Sandwiches

 **378** Pears with Yogurt

 **378** Butter Pecan Brownie Sundae

 **378** Peanut Butter–Banana Mousse

 **379** Black-and-White Shakes

We get close to a thousand letters a month at *Food Network Magazine* asking us about everything: How to quarter a chicken, what to substitute for cake flour…a few readers have even asked if we could get Paula Deen to come to their house for a party. (Nice try!) But the question readers really want answered is: "What should I make for dinner?" The chefs in Food Network Kitchens pack every issue with new ideas for quick and easy weeknight meals, and now, after 606 hours of cooking and 225,000 calories of taste-testing, we've turned those great recipes into our first cookbook.

If you're a Food Network fan, you know that each chef brings different cooking styles and flavors to the mix. You can easily tell a Guy recipe from a Giada one, an Ina recipe from a Bobby one. Behind the scenes, the chefs in Food Network Kitchens are just as diverse. There's Katherine, a Middle Eastern–cooking expert; Claudia, an Italian-Colombian mother of three; Sarah, who's married to a Hungarian vegetarian; Bob, a Jersey boy who has traveled the world; Andrea, a Texan with Mexican and Jewish roots; Leah, the resident healthy cook; and Amy, the go-to girl for Italian and Eastern European dishes. This diversity means that *Food Network Magazine*'s weeknight dinners are never boring. Flip through this book and you'll see all kinds of creative ideas—plus a mix-and-match recipe in every chapter that leads to dozens, even hundreds, of twists on family favorites like mac and cheese, pizza and more.

And every recipe has a photograph right next to it so you can see how your finished dish will look. Readers always ask us if we use crazy tricks to get the food to look so great: Do we put shoe polish on chicken skin, for example, or glue extra sesame seeds onto our hamburger buns? Never! The meals in this book were made in a kitchen a lot like yours before we photographed them. No special equipment or secret tricks involved. The food looks so colorful and tasty because that's exactly how the dishes turn out.

Best of all, the recipes are foolproof. Food Network's incredible team of chefs tested each one at least four times to be sure of that. They're hoping you like every dish enough to make it again and again—that is, after you've tried the other 249!

Maile

Maile Carpenter
FOOD NETWORK MAGAZINE EDITOR IN CHIEF

Soups & Stews

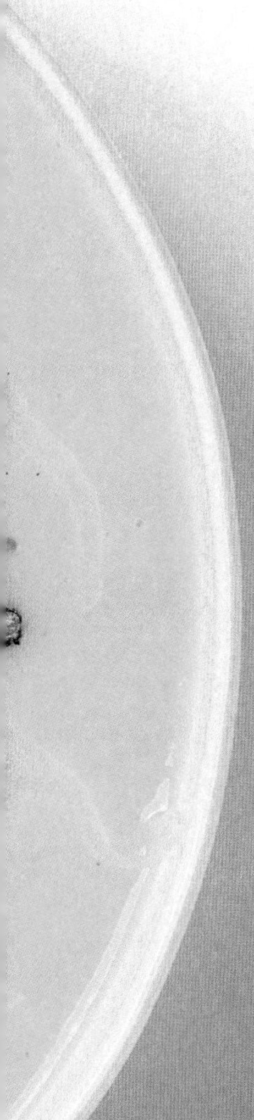

Apple-Cheddar-
Squash Soup,
page 15

Low-calorie dinner

VIETNAMESE NOODLE SOUP

ACTIVE: 30 min **I** TOTAL: 40 min **I** SERVES: 4

8   ounces rice noodles
12   ounces lean beef sirloin, fat trimmed
Kosher salt and freshly ground pepper
1   large onion, halved
1   4-inch piece ginger, unpeeled, halved
3   cups low-sodium beef broth
5   star anise pods
1   cinnamon stick
4   scallions
2   jalapeño peppers, preferably red and green
½   cup fresh cilantro
2 to 4 tablespoons fish sauce
1   cup fresh bean sprouts

1. Prepare the rice noodles as the label directs.
2. Meanwhile, place a large pot over high heat. Poke the meat all over with
a fork to tenderize it and season with salt and pepper. Sear the meat until
charred, 2 to 3 minutes per side, then transfer to a plate. Add the onion and
ginger to the pot; cook about 4 minutes. Add the broth, 3 cups water, the
star anise and cinnamon; reduce the heat and simmer about 20 minutes.
3. Meanwhile, thinly slice the scallions and jalapeños (remove the seeds for
less heat) and tear the cilantro. Thinly slice the meat. Drain the rice noodles.
4. Add the fish sauce to the broth and boil 5 minutes. Discard the ginger,
star anise and cinnamon stick. Remove and slice the onion. Divide the
noodles among 4 bowls; top with the broth, beef, scallions, cilantro,
bean sprouts, jalapeños and onion.

Per serving: Calories 334; Fat 4 g (Saturated 1 g); Cholesterol 34 mg;
Sodium 961 mg; Carbohydrate 51 g; Fiber 2 g; Protein 22 g

> This is a twist on pho, a classic
> Vietnamese noodle soup often
> sold as street food. We used
> strong herbs and spices to add
> flavor without adding fat.

PISTOU SOUP

ACTIVE: 30 min **I** TOTAL: 40 min **I** SERVES: 4

2   tablespoons extra-virgin olive oil
2   carrots, halved lengthwise and thinly sliced
1   medium onion, chopped
2 to 3 cloves garlic, chopped
2   tablespoons tomato paste
Kosher salt and freshly ground pepper
¼   pound green or yellow wax beans
1   small zucchini or yellow summer squash
1   15-ounce can white beans or chickpeas, drained and rinsed
½   cup broken spaghetti or other small pasta
¾   cup store-bought pesto
Grated parmesan cheese and crusty bread, for serving (optional)

1. Heat the olive oil in a large pot over medium-high heat. Add the carrots and onion and cook, stirring constantly, until the onion is lightly browned, about 5 minutes. Add the garlic, tomato paste and 1 tablespoon salt and cook 1 more minute. Add 7 cups water, cover and bring to a boil. Uncover, reduce the heat and simmer 5 minutes. Season with salt and pepper.
2. Meanwhile, trim the green beans and zucchini and cut into ½-inch pieces. Stir into the prepared broth along with the beans and spaghetti. Simmer until the pasta is al dente, about 10 minutes.
3. When ready to serve, whisk ⅓ cup pesto into the soup. Ladle into bowls and top with the remaining pesto and parmesan. Serve with bread, if desired.

Per serving: Calories 479; Fat 30 g (Saturated 7 g); Cholesterol 15 mg; Sodium 1,922 mg; Carbohydrate 39 g; Fiber 9 g; Protein 17 g

Use the leftover tomato paste in...

Sweet-and-Sour Chicken
page 114

Skillet Pork and Peppers
page 161

Gnocchi Niçoise
page 278

Pistou is the French version of pesto. We used store-bought pesto to save time, but you can also make your own (see Pesto Salmon, page 239).

SLOW-COOKER TEXAS CHILI

ACTIVE: 30 min **I** TOTAL: 30 min (plus 7-hr slow cooking) **I** SERVES: 6

2½ pounds beef chuck, cut into 2-inch cubes
2 tablespoons packed light brown sugar
Kosher salt
2 tablespoons vegetable oil
1 small onion, finely chopped
5 cloves garlic, smashed
2 4.5-ounce cans chopped green chiles, drained
1 tablespoon ground cumin
¾ cup chili powder
1 14-ounce can diced tomatoes with chiles
1 to 2 tablespoons green hot sauce
Sliced scallions, fresh cilantro and/or sour cream, for topping
Tortilla chips, for serving (optional)

1. Toss the beef with 1 tablespoon each brown sugar and salt in a large bowl.
Heat the vegetable oil in a large skillet over medium-high heat. Cook the beef
in batches until browned on all sides, 4 to 5 minutes (do not crowd the pan).
Transfer to a 5- to 6-quart slow cooker.
2. Reduce the heat to medium, add the onion to the skillet and cook until soft,
about 5 minutes. Stir in the garlic, chiles, cumin and chili powder and cook
3 minutes. Add 1½ cups water and the tomatoes and simmer, scraping up the
browned bits from the bottom, about 3 minutes. Transfer to the slow cooker,
cover and cook on low, 7 hours.
3. Add the remaining 1 tablespoon brown sugar and the hot sauce to the chili. Top
with scallions, cilantro and/or sour cream. Serve with chips, if desired.

Per serving: Calories 482; Fat 29 g (Saturated 11 g); Cholesterol 117 mg;
Sodium 1,227 mg; Carbohydrate 11 g; Fiber 0 g; Protein 36 g

> Don't be afraid of all the
> chili powder in this recipe—
> the chili flavor mellows out
> in the slow cooker.

CARROT-GINGER SOUP WITH TOFU

ACTIVE: 35 min **I** TOTAL: 40 min **I** SERVES: 4

½   cup vegetable oil
1   1-pound bag frozen chopped carrots, thawed
1   small onion, roughly chopped
1   2- to 3-inch piece ginger, peeled and grated
Kosher salt and freshly ground pepper
1   star anise pod or ½ teaspoon five-spice powder
2   cups carrot juice
1   pound extra-firm tofu
⅓   cup cornstarch
2   teaspoons curry powder
Torn fresh cilantro, for sprinkling (optional)

1. Heat 2 tablespoons vegetable oil in a large pot over medium heat. Add
the carrots, onion and ginger and cook, stirring, until the vegetables are just
soft, about 5 minutes. Season with salt and pepper. Add the star anise,
carrot juice and 3 cups water, then cover and boil until the vegetables are
tender, about 20 minutes.
2. Meanwhile, cut the tofu into 1-inch cubes. Mix the cornstarch and curry
powder on a shallow plate and season with salt. Pat the tofu dry and roll it in
the cornstarch mixture. Heat the remaining 6 tablespoons oil in a large skillet
over high heat. Add the tofu and fry, turning, until golden and crisp on all sides,
about 5 minutes. Drain on paper towels and season with salt.
3. Discard the star anise. Transfer the soup to a blender and puree in batches,
or puree directly in the pot with an immersion blender. Thin with water, if
needed, and season with salt and pepper. Ladle into bowls and top with the
fried tofu. Sprinkle with cilantro, if desired.

Per serving: Calories 433; Fat 29 g (Saturated 4 g); Cholesterol 0 mg;
Sodium 207 mg; Carbohydrate 33 g; Fiber 6 g; Protein 16 g

> Vegetable juices are great for
> adding flavor when you're cooking
> for vegetarians. Try carrot or
> tomato juice in place of chicken
> broth in curries, soups and stews.

Don't toss your cheese rinds! Store them in a bag in the freezer and simmer them in soups and stews to add rich, cheesy flavor.

BACON-AND-EGG SOUP

ACTIVE: 30 min **I** TOTAL: 40 min **I** SERVES: 4

½   pound slab or thick-cut bacon, cut into ¼-inch cubes
4   slices rustic Italian bread, cut into ½-inch cubes
2   tablespoons extra-virgin olive oil
Kosher salt and freshly ground pepper
2   cloves garlic, smashed
3   cups low-sodium chicken broth
1¼   cups grated parmesan cheese, plus 1 small piece rind
4   tablespoons torn fresh parsley
4   large eggs

1. Preheat the oven to 375°. Cook the bacon in a medium pot over medium heat until crisp, about 7 minutes. Transfer to a paper towel–lined plate with a slotted spoon, then discard all but 2 tablespoons drippings from the pot. While the bacon cooks, toss the bread cubes with the olive oil on a baking sheet and season with salt and pepper. Bake until golden and crisp, about 8 minutes.
2. Add the garlic to the bacon drippings and cook until slightly golden, 1 to 2 minutes. Add the broth, 1½ cups water, the parmesan rind and 2 tablespoons parsley; season with salt and pepper. Cover and bring to a boil, then reduce to a simmer and cook 10 minutes.
3. Adjust the heat so the broth is barely boiling. One at a time, crack each egg into a small bowl and gently slip into the broth. Poach until just set, about 2 minutes. Transfer the eggs with a slotted spoon to individual soup bowls. Stir 1 cup parmesan and the remaining 2 tablespoons parsley into the broth and season with salt and pepper. Ladle the broth into the bowls and top with the croutons, bacon and the remaining ¼ cup parmesan.

Per serving: Calories 555; Fat 40 g (Saturated 15 g); Cholesterol 275 mg; Sodium 1,374 mg; Carbohydrate 12 g; Fiber 1 g; Protein 29 g

Try it with these sides...

Creamy Bibb Salad
page 334

Herb Toasts
page 352

Carrots with Chickpeas and Pine Nuts page 352

HOT-AND-SOUR SEAFOOD SOUP

ACTIVE: 35 min **|** TOTAL: 35 min **|** SERVES: 4

1	tablespoon vegetable oil
1	bunch scallions, whites cut into ¼-inch pieces, greens cut into 2-inch pieces
1	tablespoon minced peeled ginger
1	tablespoon low-sodium soy sauce
½	teaspoon sugar

Kosher salt and freshly ground pepper

4	ounces shiitake mushrooms, stemmed and sliced
¼	cup cornstarch
2	plum tomatoes, cored and cut into large chunks
12	ounces firm white fish (such as pollock), cut into 1-inch pieces
6	ounces bay scallops
2	tablespoons balsamic vinegar

1. Heat the vegetable oil in a large pot over medium-high heat. Add the scallion whites and cook until slightly tender, 2 to 3 minutes. Stir in the ginger and cook about 1 minute. Add 7 cups water, the soy sauce, sugar, salt to taste, ¾ teaspoon pepper and the mushrooms. Cover and bring the broth to a simmer. Mix the cornstarch with ¼ cup cold water and gradually stir into the broth. Bring to a gentle boil, stirring; the broth will thicken slightly.
2. Add the scallion greens, tomatoes and white fish to the broth, and simmer until the fish is just opaque, about 3 minutes. Add the scallops and vinegar, and salt and pepper to taste (the scallops will cook instantly from the heat of the broth). Ladle the soup into bowls.

Per serving: Calories 200; Fat 5 g (Saturated 1 g); Cholesterol 46 mg; Sodium 274 mg; Carbohydrate 15 g; Fiber 2 g; Protein 25 g

Bay scallops are tiny (less than an inch in diameter) so they cook quickly. Add them to the soup right before serving.

APPLE-CHEDDAR-SQUASH SOUP

ACTIVE: 40 min **I** TOTAL: 40 min **I** SERVES: 4

5   tablespoons unsalted butter
1   medium onion, thinly sliced
2   medium apples, thinly sliced
1   large white potato, diced
1½ cups chopped peeled butternut squash, fresh or frozen
Kosher salt and freshly ground pepper
½   teaspoon dried sage
2   tablespoons all-purpose flour
⅓   cup apple cider
4   cups low-sodium chicken broth
1   cup milk
2   ounces thinly sliced prosciutto, torn into bite-size pieces
2   cups grated sharp cheddar cheese, plus more for topping
Chopped chives, for topping (optional)
Crusty bread, for serving (optional)

1. Melt 4 tablespoons butter in a large pot over medium-low heat and add the onion, apples, potato and squash. Season with salt and pepper and cook until the onion is soft, about 8 minutes. Stir in the sage and flour. Add the cider and cook over high heat, stirring, until thickened. Add the broth and milk, cover and bring to a boil; reduce to a simmer and cook, stirring, until the potato is soft, 8 to 10 minutes.
2. Meanwhile, heat the remaining 1 tablespoon butter in a large skillet over medium-high heat. Add the prosciutto and cook until crisp, turning occasionally, about 2 minutes. Drain on paper towels.
3. Add the cheese to the soup and stir over medium-low heat until melted. Puree in a blender in batches until smooth; season with salt and pepper. Top with the prosciutto, more cheese and chives, if using. Serve with bread, if desired.

Per serving: Calories 532; Fat 34 g (Saturated 19 g); Cholesterol 117 mg; Sodium 807 mg; Carbohydrate 35 g; Fiber 5 g; Protein 24 g

> If you have an immersion blender, use it to puree this soup directly in the pot.

CHINESE DUMPLING SOUP

ACTIVE: 10 min **I** TOTAL: 30 min **I** SERVES: 4

8	cups low-sodium chicken broth
1	2-inch piece ginger, peeled and julienned
1	tablespoon soy sauce, preferably dark
¼	cup Chinese rice wine, dry sherry or white vermouth
1	tablespoon balsamic vinegar
2	teaspoons toasted sesame oil
1	teaspoon sugar

Kosher salt
2	carrots, thinly sliced (about 1 cup)
1	pound frozen Chinese dumplings, pork or shrimp (about 24)
3	scallions, white and green parts, thinly sliced
4	cups baby spinach

Torn fresh cilantro, for topping (optional)

1. Bring the broth, ginger, soy sauce, wine, vinegar, sesame oil, sugar and a pinch of salt to a boil in a soup pot over high heat. Lower the heat and simmer about 10 minutes. Add the carrots and cook until just tender, about 5 minutes.
2. Add the dumplings and cook until just tender, about 3 minutes. Stir in the scallions and spinach and cook until wilted, about 1 minute. Top with cilantro, if desired.

Per serving: Calories 329; Fat 5 g (Saturated 75 g); Cholesterol 75 mg; Sodium 999 mg; Carbohydrate 26 g; Fiber 4 g; Protein 21 g

Try it with these sides...

Baby Broccoli with Oyster Sauce page 338

Eggplant with Peanut Dressing page 348

Garlicky Bok Choy page 353

Chinese rice wine, also called Shaoxing wine, adds a distinct nutty flavor to stir-fries, dumplings and other Chinese dishes.

SLOW-COOKER BLACK BEAN SOUP WITH TURKEY

ACTIVE: 20 min **I** TOTAL: 20 min (plus 6-hr slow cooking) **I** SERVES: 6

2	red onions, halved
2	tablespoons extra-virgin olive oil
3	medium carrots, cut into large chunks
4	cloves garlic, smashed
1	tablespoon all-purpose flour
1	pound dried black turtle beans, picked over, rinsed and drained
1	smoked turkey drumstick (1¾ to 2 pounds)
2	tablespoons pickling spice, tied in cheesecloth
¾	teaspoon red pepper flakes

Kosher salt and freshly ground pepper
½   cup chopped fresh cilantro
Sour cream and/or lime wedges, for serving (optional)

1. Set aside half an onion and chop the rest. Heat the olive oil in a large skillet over medium-high heat. Add the chopped onions, carrots and garlic; sprinkle with the flour and cook, stirring, until slightly browned, 5 minutes. Add 2 tablespoons water and scrape up any browned bits from the pan. Transfer the vegetables and cooking liquid to a slow cooker. Add the beans, turkey drumstick, pickling spice packet, red pepper flakes and 8 cups water. Cover and cook on low 6 hours.
2. Remove and discard the pickling spice packet. Remove the drumstick and shred the meat; keep warm. Remove about 2 cups beans from the cooker and blend until smooth (or partially blend with an immersion blender). Return the beans and turkey meat to the soup. Season with salt and pepper.
3. Mince the reserved ½ onion. Ladle the soup into bowls and top with the cilantro and minced onion. Serve with sour cream and lime wedges, if desired.

Per serving: Calories 487; Fat 12 g (Saturated 3 g); Cholesterol 64 mg; Sodium 936 mg; Carbohydrate 57 g; Fiber 20 g; Protein 8 g

> If your slow cooker has a removable pot for stovetop cooking, sauté the vegetables directly in that before adding the other ingredients.

BROCCOLI CHOWDER WITH CHEDDAR TOASTS

ACTIVE: 25 min I TOTAL: 35 min I SERVES: 4

2   strips bacon, thinly sliced
2   tablespoons unsalted butter
½   yellow onion, chopped (about 1 cup)
2   cloves garlic, smashed
½   teaspoon celery seeds
2   tablespoons all-purpose flour
2   cups low-sodium chicken broth
2   cups milk
4   small red-skinned potatoes (about 6 ounces), quartered
½   head broccoli (about 10 ounces), broken into florets, stem peeled and sliced
Kosher salt and freshly ground pepper
1   tablespoon dijon mustard
8   slices baguette
4   ounces cheddar cheese, cut into 8 thin slices

1. Cook the bacon in the butter in a medium saucepan over low heat until the fat renders slightly, about 2 minutes. Add the onion, garlic and celery seeds and cook until soft, about 4 minutes. Scatter the flour over the mixture and stir to coat. Gradually add the broth and the milk, whisking until smooth.
2. Add the potatoes and sliced broccoli stem; increase the heat to medium and simmer, covered, until slightly softened, about 5 minutes. Add the broccoli florets and season with ½ teaspoon salt. Continue cooking, uncovered, at a rapid simmer until the vegetables are tender, about 5 minutes; season with salt and pepper.
3. Meanwhile, position a rack in the upper part of the oven and preheat the broiler to high. Spread the mustard on each piece of baguette and top with a cheddar slice. Place on a baking sheet and broil until the cheese melts; serve with the soup.

Per serving: Calories 531; Fat 26 g (Saturated 14 g); Cholesterol 77 mg; Sodium 1,148 mg; Carbohydrate 50 g; Fiber 3 g; Protein 23 g

> Keep the broccoli stems! They're delicious in soups, slaws and stir-fries. Just peel the outer layer if it's too tough.

Done in
30
minutes

CHILE-CHICKEN POSOLE

ACTIVE: 30 min I TOTAL: 30 min I SERVES: 4

1   pound skinless, boneless chicken breasts, diced
1   teaspoon dried thyme
Kosher salt and freshly ground pepper
2   tablespoons vegetable oil
1   large white onion, diced
1   jalapeño pepper, chopped (remove seeds for less heat)
2   cloves garlic, minced
3   6-ounce cans whole green chiles, drained
1   cup fresh cilantro
4   cups low-fat, low-sodium chicken broth
2   15-ounce cans hominy, drained
Sliced avocado and radishes and/or baked corn chips, for topping (optional)

1. Season the chicken with ½ teaspoon thyme and salt and pepper to taste on both sides; set aside.
2. Heat the vegetable oil in a large saucepan over medium heat. Add the onion, jalapeño and garlic and cook until soft, about 4 minutes. Transfer to a blender, then add the chiles, cilantro and the remaining ½ teaspoon thyme and puree until smooth. Return to the saucepan and cook over medium heat, stirring, until the sauce thickens and turns deep green, about 5 minutes.
3. Add the broth, hominy and chicken to the saucepan. Cover and simmer until the chicken is tender, about 10 minutes. Top with avocado, radishes and/or corn chips, if desired.

Per serving: Calories 385; Fat 10 g (Saturated 2 g); Cholesterol 91 mg; Sodium 1,591 mg; Carbohydrate 43 g; Fiber 8 g; Protein 36 g

Hominy is hulled corn with the germ removed. When you buy it in cans, it is ready to eat—no boiling required.

SAUSAGE-AND-VEGETABLE STEW

ACTIVE: 20 min ▎ TOTAL: 40 min ▎ SERVES: 4

3	tablespoons extra-virgin olive oil
1	large red onion, diced
4	cloves garlic, smashed
1	tablespoon Hungarian paprika, plus more for sprinkling

Kosher salt

3	tablespoons all-purpose flour
6	ounces kielbasa, cut into small chunks
3	medium carrots, peeled and cut into large chunks
2	parsnips, peeled and cut into large chunks
14	ounces small red-skinned or new potatoes (6 to 8), quartered
1	tablespoon cider vinegar

Freshly ground pepper

½	cup fresh parsley, roughly chopped
¾	cup sour cream

Crusty bread, for serving

1. Heat the olive oil in a Dutch oven or heavy pot over medium heat. Add the onion and garlic; cook, stirring occasionally, until soft and glistening, about 6 minutes. Add the paprika and 1 teaspoon salt; cook until the oil turns deep red, about 1 minute. Add the flour and cook until just toasted, 30 more seconds. Immediately whisk in 4 cups water. Add the kielbasa, carrots, parsnips, potatoes and 1½ teaspoons salt.
2. Bring the soup to a boil, then reduce to a simmer; cover and cook until the vegetables are tender and the broth has thickened, about 20 minutes. Add the vinegar and season with pepper.
3. Combine about half of the parsley with the sour cream in a small bowl and season with salt and pepper. Ladle the stew into bowls; top with the remaining parsley, a dollop of herbed sour cream and a sprinkle of paprika. Serve with bread.

Per serving: Calories 455; Fat 26 g (Saturated 9 g); Cholesterol 60 mg; Sodium 1,774 mg; Carbohydrate 43 g; Fiber 7 g; Protein 12 g

Hungarian paprika is sweeter and milder than the Spanish kind; it tastes great in this soup.

One-pot
meal

Turn your leftovers into this...

You can use bone-in chicken thighs instead of turkey.

SLOW-COOKER MOROCCAN TURKEY STEW

ACTIVE: 20 min **I** TOTAL: 20 min (plus 6-hr slow cooking) **I** SERVES: 4 (with leftovers for Moroccan Burritos, opposite)

1 teaspoon ground allspice
Kosher salt
4 skinless, bone-in turkey thighs (about 4 pounds)
½ butternut squash, peeled and cut into 2-inch chunks
2 15-ounce cans chickpeas, drained and rinsed
1 28-ounce can whole peeled tomatoes with juices, broken up
1 cup dried apricots
½ cup golden raisins
8 medium carrots, cut into 1½-inch pieces
3 medium red onions, halved and cut into wedges
2 whole dried red chiles
½ lemon
2 cups fresh cilantro (leaves and some stems)
1 cup fresh parsley
1 clove garlic, smashed
½ teaspoon ground cumin
½ cup extra-virgin olive oil

1. Combine the allspice and 3 teaspoons salt in a small bowl. Season the turkey thighs with half the salt mixture and place in a 5-quart slow cooker.
2. Toss the squash, chickpeas, tomatoes, apricots, raisins, carrots, onions and chiles with the remaining spiced salt. Pour the vegetables over the turkey (the cooker will be full; arrange the mixture so the lid fits). Cover and cook on high for 6 hours or on low for 7 to 8 hours.
3. Spoon the vegetables and broth into bowls. Remove and discard the turkey bones and place the meat on top of the vegetables.
4. Juice the lemon; pulse with the cilantro, parsley, garlic, cumin and 1 teaspoon salt in a food processor. Add the oil and process until smooth. Serve the stew in bowls; drizzle with the cilantro sauce.

Per serving: Calories 723; Fat 27 g (Saturated 4 g); Cholesterol 143 mg; Sodium 1,794 mg; Carbohydrate 74 g; Fiber 14 g; Protein 46 g

Done in 15 minutes

MOROCCAN BURRITOS WITH TAHINI HERB SAUCE

ACTIVE: 15 min | TOTAL: 15 min | MAKES: 4 burritos

FOR THE SAUCE
½ cup fresh parsley
⅓ cup fresh lemon juice
¼ cup tahini (sesame paste, available in the international foods aisle)
2 teaspoons honey
1 clove garlic, smashed
Kosher salt and freshly ground pepper

FOR THE BURRITOS
4 10-inch flour tortillas
2 cups cooked rice or couscous, heated
1⅓ cups shredded pepper or monterey jack cheese
3 cups leftover Slow-Cooker Moroccan Turkey Stew, heated (opposite)

1. Make the herb sauce: Puree the parsley, lemon juice, tahini, honey and garlic with 1 teaspoon salt, ½ teaspoon pepper and ¼ cup water in a blender.
2. Make the burritos: Wrap the tortillas in a damp kitchen towel and heat in the microwave until pliable, about 1 minute. (Alternatively, warm individual tortillas in a large dry skillet.)
3. Place ½ cup rice in the middle of each tortilla and scatter about ⅓ cup cheese on top. Spoon a quarter of the stew over the cheese. Fold in the two sides of each tortilla and roll into a tight burrito. Serve with the herb sauce.

Per serving: Calories 759; Fat 22 g (Saturated 5 g); Cholesterol 82 mg; Sodium 1,631 mg; Carbohydrate 105 g; Fiber 10 g; Protein 38 g

CURRIED CHICKEN AND RICE SOUP

ACTIVE: 20 min **I** TOTAL: 35 min **I** SERVES: 4

1   bone-in chicken breast (about 1½ pounds), halved
2   medium carrots, sliced diagonally into 2-inch pieces
1   bay leaf
Kosher salt
6   cups low-sodium chicken broth
2   tablespoons unsalted butter
1   large onion, very thinly sliced
1   teaspoon sugar
1½   teaspoons Madras curry powder
⅓   cup jasmine rice
3   tablespoons finely chopped fresh mint
3   tablespoons chopped fresh dill
1   lemon, cut into wedges

1. Combine the chicken, carrots, bay leaf and a pinch of salt in a medium saucepan. Add 3 cups broth and bring to a boil; immediately reduce the heat to low, cover and cook until the chicken is just firm, about 20 minutes.
2. Meanwhile, heat the butter in another saucepan over medium-low heat. Add the onion, sugar and 1 teaspoon salt; cook until the onion is soft, about 5 minutes. Add the curry powder and cook 1 minute. Add the rice and the remaining 3 cups broth. Increase the heat to medium, cover and simmer until the rice falls apart, 15 to 20 minutes.
3. Remove the chicken from its broth; discard the skin and shred the meat into pieces. Return the shredded chicken to the same broth.
4. Puree the rice mixture with an immersion blender until smooth (or use a regular blender, then return to the pan). Pour in the shredded chicken and broth, stirring gently to combine; bring to a simmer. Toss in the chopped herbs and serve the soup with lemon wedges.

Per serving: Calories 390; Fat 11 g (Saturated 5 g); Cholesterol 130 mg; Sodium 740 mg; Carbohydrate 18 g; Fiber 2 g; Protein 55 g

> Leftover rice works fine in this dish if you have some on hand. Just simmer it for about 5 minutes before pureeing.

SLOW-COOKER BARBECUE BEANS AND SAUSAGE

ACTIVE: 15 min I TOTAL: 30 min (plus 6-hr slow cooking) I SERVES: 6

3	cups low-sodium chicken broth
⅓	cup tomato paste
⅓	cup packed light brown sugar
3	tablespoons molasses
3	tablespoons honey mustard
2	tablespoons barbecue seasoning blend
4	cloves garlic, chopped
1	pound dried navy beans, rinsed and picked over
2	cloves
1	small onion, halved
1½	pounds chicken-apple sausages, each halved lengthwise
2	tablespoons cider vinegar
1	tablespoon Worcestershire sauce

Pickled peppers, sliced scallions and/or sour cream, for topping (optional)

1. Whisk the broth, 3 cups water, tomato paste, brown sugar, molasses, mustard, barbecue seasoning and garlic in a slow cooker. Add the beans. Push a clove into each onion half; tuck the onion and sausages into the beans in the slow cooker. Cover and cook on high until the beans are tender, about 6 hours.
2. Discard the onion halves. Stir in the vinegar and Worcestershire sauce, then let the mixture sit, uncovered, about 15 minutes. (The longer the beans sit, the more flavorful they will be.) Top with pickled peppers, scallions and/or sour cream, if desired.

Per serving: Calories 549; Fat 11 g (Saturated 3 g); Cholesterol 102 mg; Sodium 1,796 mg; Carbohydrate 75 g; Fiber 20 g; Protein 38 g

> Buy dried beans: They're much cheaper than canned ones, and when you're using a slow cooker, you don't need to soak them first.

THAI CORN CHOWDER

ACTIVE: 30 min **I** TOTAL: 40 min **I** SERVES: 4

4	ears corn
2	cups diced red-skinned potatoes (about 12 ounces)
¾	cup chopped scallions
2	tablespoons grated peeled ginger
4	cloves garlic, smashed
8	black peppercorns
1	stalk lemongrass, cut into thirds (optional)
4	tablespoons unsalted butter
Kosher salt	
1	red jalapeño pepper, seeded and minced
1	13.5-ounce can coconut milk
8	fresh basil leaves
8	fresh mint leaves
4	radishes, thinly sliced
¼	cup roughly chopped fresh cilantro
Juice of ½ lime, plus lime wedges for serving	
1	tomato, seeded and diced

1. Cut off the corn kernels; set aside. Combine the cobs, 1 cup potatoes, ½ cup scallions, 1 tablespoon ginger, the garlic, peppercorns and 5 cups water in a pot. Smash the lemongrass, if using, and add to the pot. Bring to a boil, then simmer for 25 to 30 minutes.

2. About 10 minutes before the broth is finished, melt the butter over medium-high heat in a separate pot. Add the remaining 1 cup potatoes, season with salt and cook until slightly soft, 5 minutes. Add the remaining 1 tablespoon ginger and the jalapeño; cook 1 minute. Add the corn kernels; cook until the vegetables are just tender, 3 to 4 minutes.

3. Strain the broth, pressing out as much liquid as possible; discard the solids. Add 2 cups of the strained broth to the potatoes and corn; bring to a boil, cover and simmer for 10 minutes. Add the coconut milk, basil and mint; season with salt. Stir until simmering. Remove from the heat and add the radishes, cilantro and lime juice. Top with diced tomato and the remaining ¼ cup scallions and serve with lime wedges.

Per serving: Calories 407; Fat 32 g (Saturated 25 g); Cholesterol 30 mg; Sodium 31 mg; Carbohydrate 28 g; Fiber 4 g; Protein 6 g

Use the leftover mint in...

Spinach-Orzo Salad with Shrimp
page 257

Steamed Vegetables with Chickpeas and Rice
page 298

Orecchiette Salad with Roast Beef
page 313

Lemongrass is usually sold in bunches of 4 or 5 stalks near the fresh herbs. It adds a subtle lemony flavor to this soup.

CARROT-MUSHROOM-BARLEY STEW

ACTIVE: 40 min **I** TOTAL: 40 min **I** SERVES: 4

2   cups carrot juice
10 ounces shiitake mushrooms, stems removed and reserved, caps sliced
2   tablespoons extra-virgin olive oil
4   tablespoons unsalted butter
1   cup instant barley
1   medium onion, chopped
1   stalk celery with leaves, finely diced
¼   teaspoon dried rosemary, crumbled
Kosher salt and freshly ground pepper
4   medium carrots, cut into ½-inch pieces
4   cups kale or mustard greens, stems removed and leaves torn
1   tablespoon grated peeled ginger

1. Bring the carrot juice, 3 cups water and the mushroom stems to a boil in a saucepan over medium heat. Meanwhile, heat the olive oil and 2 tablespoons butter in a pot over medium-high heat. Add the mushroom caps and barley and cook until the barley is toasted, about 5 minutes.
2. Add the onion, celery and rosemary to the pot and season with salt and pepper. Cook, stirring occasionally, until the onion is translucent, about 2 minutes. Add the carrots and cook 2 more minutes.
3. Increase the heat to high and add half of the carrot juice mixture, leaving the mushroom stems in the pan. Bring to a boil and cook, stirring occasionally, until the liquid is almost absorbed, about 6 minutes.
4. Add the remaining carrot juice mixture, the kale and ginger and cook, stirring, until the barley and vegetables are tender, about 5 minutes. Stir in the remaining 2 tablespoons butter, then ladle the stew into bowls.

Per serving: Calories 333; Fat 14 g (Saturated 5 g); Cholesterol 15 mg; Sodium 375 mg; Carbohydrate 50 g; Fiber 8 g; Protein 8 g

Use your leftover instant barley in place of rice or couscous as a side dish sometime: It cooks in just 10 minutes.

GAZPACHO WITH LIME CHICKEN

ACTIVE: 30 min **I** TOTAL: 30 min **I** SERVES: 4

1   large shallot, minced
Juice of 2 limes, plus wedges for serving
⅓   cup extra-virgin olive oil, plus more for drizzling
Kosher salt and freshly ground pepper
1¼   pounds chicken cutlets
½   cup large-cut croutons
3   large tomatoes, diced
1   small cucumber, peeled, seeded and diced
1   bell pepper (any color), stemmed, seeded and diced
¼   cup roughly chopped fresh cilantro

1. Preheat a grill to high. Soak the minced shallot in cold water, about
10 minutes. Meanwhile, mix 1 tablespoon lime juice, 2 tablespoons olive oil,
and salt and pepper to taste in a shallow dish; add the chicken and turn to
coat. Grill the chicken until golden and cooked through, about 3 minutes per
side. Let cool, then slice.
2. Crush half of the croutons; set aside. Soak the remaining croutons in ¼ cup
water for 5 minutes, then squeeze out the water and put in a blender. Drain
the shallot and add to the blender along with half each of the diced tomatoes,
cucumber and bell pepper. With the motor running, drizzle in the remaining
3 tablespoons plus 1 teaspoon olive oil. Add 2 cups ice and blend until smooth. Stir
in half of the cilantro and the remaining lime juice; season with salt and pepper.
3. Divide the soup among bowls. Top with the chicken, the remaining
tomatoes, cucumber, bell pepper and cilantro and the crushed croutons.
Drizzle with olive oil and serve with lime wedges.

Per serving: Calories 383; Fat 23 g (Saturated 4 g); Cholesterol 78 mg;
Sodium 105 mg; Carbohydrate 14 g; Fiber 3 g; Protein 31 g

To make your own chicken
cutlets, slice two 10-ounce
skinless, boneless breasts in
half horizontally.

Done in
30
minutes

SLOW-COOKER PORK STEW

ACTIVE: 20 min **|** TOTAL: 20 min (plus 8-hr slow cooking) **|** SERVES: 4 to 6

1   pound fingerling potatoes
3   carrots, cut into 2-inch chunks
2   stalks celery, cut into 2-inch chunks
3   cloves garlic, smashed
1   2-inch piece ginger, peeled and grated
⅓   cup all-purpose flour
Kosher salt and freshly ground pepper
3   bay leaves
1   bone-in pork shoulder or pork sirloin roast (2 to 2½ pounds)
1   teaspoon dried thyme
½   teaspoon ground allspice
1   14-ounce can diced tomatoes

1. Combine the potatoes, carrots, celery, garlic and ginger in a slow cooker.
Toss in half of the flour and season with salt and pepper. Scatter the bay leaves
over the vegetables.
2. Season the pork generously with salt and pepper, sprinkle with the thyme
and allspice and toss with the remaining flour to coat. Place the pork over the
vegetables in the slow cooker. Add 2 cups water and the tomatoes, cover and
cook on low 8 hours.
3. Discard the bay leaves. Remove the pork roast and slice or pull the meat off
the bone into large pieces. Serve in bowls with the vegetables and broth.

Per serving: Calories 634; Fat 29 g (Saturated 10 g); Cholesterol 210 mg;
Sodium 601 mg; Carbohydrate 30 g; Fiber 5 g; Protein 61 g

> Use fingerling potatoes if
> you can find them: They
> become creamy and
> buttery in the slow cooker.

Mix & Match

CHICKEN SOUP

Mexican Chicken Soup
with Green Chiles,
Poblanos and Zucchini

1 PICK A STYLE

Heat 1 tablespoon olive oil in a large pot over medium-high heat; add the base ingredients for your soup and cook until softened, 4 to 6 minutes.

MEXICAN
- 1 chopped onion
- 3 minced garlic cloves
- 14.5-ounce can diced tomatoes

ITALIAN
- 1 chopped onion
- 2 minced garlic cloves
- 1 chopped celery stalk
- 1 chopped carrot

ASIAN
- 1 sliced onion
- 2 minced garlic cloves

2 FLAVOR YOUR BROTH

Add your choice of ingredients; cook 1 minute. Add 8 cups chicken broth, and salt and pepper. Bring to a boil.

MEXICAN
(choose one)
- 1½ tablespoons chopped chipotle peppers in adobo sauce
- two 4-ounce cans chopped green chiles

ITALIAN
(choose one or more)
- 2 teaspoons chopped fresh oregano
- ½ teaspoon red pepper flakes
- 1 piece parmesan rind
- 2 sprigs thyme

ASIAN
(choose one or more; plus 1 tablespoon each fish sauce and lime juice)
- 1 tablespoon green curry paste
- ½ cup peanut butter
- 14-ounce can coconut milk

3 ADD VEGETABLES

Stir in one or both vegetables and cook, partially covered, 4 to 6 minutes.

MEXICAN
- 2 cups diced sweet potatoes
- 2 chopped poblano peppers

ITALIAN
- 2 cups diced yellow potatoes
- 14.5-ounce can diced tomatoes

ASIAN
- 2 cups sliced mushrooms
- 2 cups sliced red bell pepper

4 ADD MORE VEGETABLES

Stir in one or both ingredients and simmer, partially covered, until tender.

MEXICAN
- 2 cups chopped zucchini
- 2 cups corn or two 15-ounce cans hominy (drained and rinsed)

ITALIAN
- 3 cups chopped kale
- two 15-ounce cans white beans or 1 cup small pasta

ASIAN
- 2 cups chopped tomatoes
- 1 cup chopped baby corn

5 ADD PROTEIN

Add the shredded meat from ½ rotisserie chicken, season with salt and pepper and simmer 2 to 3 minutes.

6 CHOOSE YOUR TOPPINGS

Sprinkle with one or more ingredients for your style of soup.

MEXICAN
- chopped avocado
- chopped cilantro
- sliced radishes
- sour cream
- fried tortilla strips

ITALIAN
- grated parmesan cheese
- pesto
- croutons
- chopped basil or parsley
- grated lemon zest

ASIAN
- chopped mint
- chopped cilantro
- chopped scallions
- peanuts
- bean sprouts

Melissa says...

66 The kitchen is the focal point of our home; the kids and I (and my husband!) cook together almost every day. I have four young daughters, and I always try to include them in meal preparation when time allows, whether it's taking them to the market to pick out a special ingredient or finding a kid-friendly prep step for them to do along with me. And while this sometimes means a bit more of a mess, it's certainly worth it to me to have that extra family time together and for the girls to learn something new every day."

—MELISSA D'ARABIAN IS THE HOST OF *TEN DOLLAR DINNERS.*

KITCHEN SECRET

Melissa was a huge Bobby Flay fan before she became a star herself (and she still is!). She waited in line for hours to get her copy of his *Grill It!* cookbook signed for her four daughters. She keeps the book handy in her kitchen.

Bacon-Tomato
Cheese Toasts,
page 52

Sandwiches & Pizza

Done in
15
minutes

BISTRO EGG SANDWICHES

ACTIVE: 15 min **|** TOTAL: 15 min **|** MAKES: 4 sandwiches

6   tablespoons unsalted butter, at room temperature
1 to 2 teaspoons dijon mustard
1 to 2 teaspoons anchovy paste
1   baguette, cut into 4 pieces, each halved lengthwise
4   large eggs
Kosher salt and freshly ground pepper
¼   pound country pâté or ham, cut into 4 slices
2   ounces gruyère or comté cheese, thinly sliced
1   cup frisée or other greens
Finely sliced fresh chives, for topping

1. Preheat the broiler to high. Mix 4 tablespoons butter with the mustard and anchovy paste in a small bowl until smooth. Spread the anchovy butter on the cut sides of the bread; place buttered-side up on a baking sheet and broil until toasted, 1 to 2 minutes. Set aside.
2. Melt the remaining 2 tablespoons butter in a large skillet over medium-high heat. Crack in the eggs; season with salt and pepper and let cook until the yolks just begin to firm up and the edges are slightly crisp, about 3 minutes. Assemble the sandwiches: place 2 bread halves on each of 4 plates; top with a slice of pâté, an egg, some cheese, greens and chives.

Per serving: Calories 555; Fat 36 g (Saturated 19 g); Cholesterol 290 mg; Sodium 1,095 mg; Carbohydrate 36 g; Fiber 2 g; Protein 20 g

A tube of anchovy paste lasts for months in the fridge. Use a little to punch up pasta sauces and salad dressings.

TURKEY REUBENS

ACTIVE: 25 min **I** TOTAL: 25 min **I** SERVES: 4

2½ tablespoons unsalted butter, softened
3   scallions, white parts and 2 inches of green, finely chopped
1   8-ounce can sauerkraut, drained and rinsed
1   small apple, peeled and grated
Kosher salt and freshly ground pepper
¼   cup mayonnaise
2 to 3 tablespoons chili sauce
2   teaspoons capers, chopped, plus 1 teaspoon liquid from the jar
8   slices dill pickle, plus 1 teaspoon pickling liquid from the jar
8   slices seeded rye bread
1   pound deli-sliced turkey
1½ to 2 cups grated Swiss cheese (about 6 ounces)

1. Heat 1 tablespoon butter in a medium saucepan over medium-high heat.
Add the scallion whites and cook until light brown, about 3 minutes. Add
the sauerkraut and apple, and season with salt and pepper. Cook until the
sauerkraut is lightly browned and dry, about 10 minutes. Add half of the
scallion greens and cook for 1 minute.
2. Preheat the broiler. Mix the mayonnaise, chili sauce, the remaining scallion
greens, the capers and their liquid, and the dill pickling liquid.
3. Spread about ½ teaspoon butter on one side of each bread slice. Place
4 slices, buttered-side down, on a foil-lined baking sheet. Spread each with
some of the mayonnaise mixture, then layer the turkey, dill pickles and
sauerkraut mixture on top. Sprinkle with the cheese and broil until the
cheese melts, about 2 minutes.
4. Spread more of the mayonnaise mixture on the unbuttered sides of the
other 4 bread slices; place buttered-side up on the sandwiches. Return to the
broiler until golden, turning once, about 2 minutes.

Per serving: Calories 625; Fat 33 g (Saturated 12 g); Cholesterol 102 mg;
Sodium 2,381 mg; Carbohydrate 46 g; Fiber 6 g; Protein 39 g

Sauerkraut has a strong vinegar flavor; be sure to rinse it well before using.

Done in
30
minutes

WHITE CLAM PIZZA

ACTIVE: 20 min | TOTAL: 30 min | SERVES: 4

3   large cloves garlic, chopped
¼   cup extra-virgin olive oil, plus more for drizzling
1   pound refrigerated pizza dough
All-purpose flour, for kneading
Cornmeal, for dusting
Kosher salt
½   cup thinly sliced mozzarella cheese (4 ounces)
2   6.5-ounce cans chopped clams, juice drained and reserved
¼   teaspoon dried oregano
2   tablespoons grated parmesan cheese
2   cups baby arugula
Juice of 1 lemon
Red pepper flakes, for topping (optional)

1. Preheat the oven to 500°. Place a pizza stone or inverted rimmed baking sheet on the bottom rack.

2. Mix the garlic and ¼ cup olive oil in a small bowl. Knead the dough about 6 times on a lightly floured surface. Roll and stretch into a 12-inch round. Place the dough on a pizza peel or another inverted baking sheet, dusted with cornmeal.

3. Brush half of the garlic oil over the dough; season with salt. Scatter the mozzarella and clams over the crust; drizzle with 2 tablespoons of the reserved clam juice and the remaining garlic oil. Sprinkle with the oregano, parmesan, and salt to taste. Slip the pizza onto the preheated pizza stone or baking sheet (the cornmeal will help it slide off). Bake until the crust is light brown, 13 to 15 minutes.

4. Just before the pizza is done, drizzle the arugula with olive oil and lemon juice. Slice the pizza; top each piece with arugula and season with red pepper flakes, if desired.

Per serving: Calories 698; Fat 33 g (Saturated 9 g); Cholesterol 82 mg; Sodium 821 mg; Carbohydrate 63 g; Fiber 2 g; Protein 39 g

> If you don't own a pizza stone, you can buy unglazed quarry tiles from a hardware store and bake your pies right on them instead. You don't even need to take them out of the oven afterward; just leave them there for next time. You can still bake on the other racks.

BACON-TOMATO CHEESE TOASTS

ACTIVE: 20 min **I** TOTAL: 40 min **I** SERVES: 4

2	ripe tomatoes

Kosher salt

8	strips bacon
4	slices Texas toast or other thick sandwich bread
¾	cup grated cheddar cheese
¾	cup grated part-skim mozzarella cheese
¾	cup mayonnaise
5	scallions, finely chopped
¼	cup chopped fresh parsley
½	small zucchini, very thinly sliced

Freshly ground pepper

1. Preheat the oven to 400˚. Core the tomatoes and thinly slice. Place in a colander in the sink and sprinkle with ½ teaspoon salt; let drain for at least 15 minutes.

2. Meanwhile, cook the bacon in a large skillet over medium heat until crisp, about 10 minutes; transfer to a paper towel–lined plate. Pour off and reserve the drippings, leaving 1 tablespoon in the skillet; toast the bread on one side in the drippings until golden (do this in batches, adding more drippings as needed). Place the bread, toasted-side down, on a baking sheet.

3. Combine the cheeses with the mayonnaise, scallions and parsley in a bowl. Spread the cheese mixture on the toasts, reserving about ⅓ cup. Crumble the bacon on top. Shake any excess liquid from the tomatoes; distribute the zucchini and tomatoes among the toasts. Dot with the reserved cheese mixture and season with pepper. Bake until golden brown, 15 to 20 minutes. Serve warm.

Per serving: Calories 680; Fat 55 g (Saturated 15 g); Cholesterol 65 mg; Sodium 1,181 mg; Carbohydrate 28 g; Fiber 2 g; Protein 19 g

Salt works like magic to draw water out of the tomatoes so they won't make your sandwiches soggy.

FRIED CATFISH ROLLS

ACTIVE: 25 min **|** TOTAL: 25 min **|** SERVES: 4

Vegetable oil, for frying
1 to 2 jalapeño or serrano peppers, diced (remove seeds for less heat)
2   scallions, roughly chopped
½   cup mayonnaise
1 to 2 tablespoons pickling liquid, plus sliced pickles for topping
Kosher salt and freshly ground pepper
½   cup instant flour (such as Wondra)
1   pound catfish fillets, cut into ½-inch chunks
1   12-count package miniature potato buns (do not separate)
2   tablespoons unsalted butter, melted
1   large ripe tomato, thinly sliced
1   stalk celery, thinly sliced

1. Heat about 2 inches of oil in a heavy-bottomed pot over medium heat until a deep-fry thermometer registers 350°.
2. Combine the jalapeño, scallions, mayonnaise and pickling liquid in a blender and puree until almost smooth. Season with salt and pepper.
3. Place the flour in a bowl and season with salt and pepper. Dredge the catfish in the flour; shake off any excess in a strainer. Working in batches, fry the fish until lightly golden and just cooked through, about 1 minute. Remove from the oil with a slotted spoon and drain on a paper towel–lined plate; let cool. Preheat the broiler.
4. While the fish cools, divide the buns into four 3-roll rows (they'll look like hot dog buns). Split open down the center; brush the tops and insides with the melted butter, and broil until golden, 1 to 2 minutes.
5. Toss the fried catfish with the spiced mayonnaise and divide among the buns. Top with tomato, pickles and celery.

Per serving: Calories 781; Fat 53 g (Saturated 11 g); Cholesterol 78 mg; Sodium 675 mg; Carbohydrate 51 g; Fiber 3 g; Protein 26 g

Instant flour makes a great coating. You can dredge just about anything in it and get a light, crisp crust.

MANCHEGO-STUFFED PORK BURGERS

ACTIVE: 30 min **I** TOTAL: 30 min **I** SERVES: 4

2 tablespoons vegetable oil, plus more for brushing
¼ cup pimiento-stuffed Spanish olives
4 cloves garlic
1 tablespoon dried oregano
1 tablespoon chili powder
2 teaspoons smoked paprika
1 teaspoon ground coriander
1 teaspoon ground cumin
½ teaspoon ground allspice
3 tablespoons mayonnaise
1¼ pounds coarsely ground pork
Kosher salt and freshly ground pepper
¼ pound manchego cheese, broken into bite-size pieces
4 Portuguese rolls, split
Pimientos, tomato, red onion and/or lettuce, for topping

1. Preheat a grill to medium-high. Place the 2 tablespoons vegetable oil, the olives, garlic, oregano, chili powder, paprika, coriander, cumin and allspice in a food processor; pulse until smooth. Scrape the mixture into a large bowl and stir in 2 tablespoons mayonnaise.

2. Mix the pork into the olive mixture and season with salt and pepper. Shape into 4 patties, about ½ inch thick. Make a deep pocket in each; stuff with some manchego, then close the patty around the cheese.

3. Brush the burgers with oil and season with salt and pepper. Brush the grill with oil; grill the burgers until marked on the bottom, 5 minutes. Flip and continue grilling until just cooked through, 5 more minutes.

4. Brush the cut sides of the rolls with the remaining 1 tablespoon mayonnaise and grill until lightly toasted. Serve the burgers on the rolls with your choice of toppings.

Per serving: Calories 751; Fat 51 g (Saturated 18 g); Cholesterol 117 mg; Sodium 1,024 mg; Carbohydrate 33 g; Fiber 4 g; Protein 39 g

Try it with these sides...

Spicy Sweet-Potato Fries
page 341

Snow Pea and Avocado Slaw page 347

Charm City Corn
page 351

Resist the urge to flatten the burgers with a spatula as they cook: You don't want to lose all the juices!

Low-calorie dinner

CHICKEN SALAD PITA WITH BABA GHANOUSH

ACTIVE: 20 min I TOTAL: 30 min I SERVES: 4

1   tablespoon red wine vinegar
3   teaspoons dried mint, crumbled
¾   teaspoon red pepper flakes
2   cloves garlic, finely minced
Kosher salt
4   tablespoons extra-virgin olive oil, plus more for drizzling
4   chicken scallopine (4 to 5 ounces each)
1   cup grape or cherry tomatoes, halved
1   unpeeled Kirby cucumber, chopped
Freshly ground pepper
4   pocketless pitas
½   cup baba ghanoush
2   cups chopped romaine lettuce

1. Whisk the vinegar, mint, red pepper flakes, 1 clove garlic and ¼ teaspoon salt in a shallow dish. Gradually whisk in 3 tablespoons olive oil. Add the chicken and marinate about 15 minutes.
2. Meanwhile, mix the tomatoes, cucumber and the remaining 1 clove garlic in a bowl. Drizzle with olive oil and season with salt and pepper.
3. Preheat a grill pan over medium-high heat. Grill the chicken until cooked through, 2 to 3 minutes per side. Transfer to a cutting board and slice into ½-inch-thick strips. Toss with the vegetables.
4. Brush the pitas with the remaining 1 tablespoon olive oil and season with salt. Grill, turning once, until marked. Place a pita on each plate and spread with baba ghanoush. Top with lettuce and chicken salad, and drizzle with any juices from the bowl.

Per serving: Calories 342; Fat 15 g (Saturated 2 g); Cholesterol 74 mg; Sodium 587 mg; Carbohydrate 24 g; Fiber 4 g; Protein 29 g

Baba ghanoush is a spread made from roasted eggplant. Look for it in the refrigerated section near the hummus.

MEXICAN MEATBALL SUBS

ACTIVE: 30 min **I** TOTAL: 40 min **I** SERVES: 4

1	pound meatloaf mix (ground beef, pork and veal)
¼	cup finely crushed tortilla chips
1	large egg, beaten
¼	cup chopped fresh cilantro, plus 3 sprigs
¼	cup finely chopped scallions, plus more for topping (optional)
3	cloves garlic; 1 minced, 2 smashed
3	teaspoons ancho chili powder
2	teaspoons ground cumin

Kosher salt

1	tablespoon extra-virgin olive oil
2	cups canned fire-roasted diced tomatoes
4	crusty sub rolls, halved and split open

Diced avocado and crumbled queso fresco, for topping (optional)

1. Preheat the oven to 350˚. Mix the meat, tortilla chips, egg, chopped cilantro, ¼ cup scallions, minced garlic, 1 teaspoon chili power, 1 teaspoon cumin, and salt to taste in a bowl. Roll into 16 small meatballs.

2. Heat the olive oil in a nonstick skillet over medium heat. Add the meatballs and lightly brown, turning as needed, about 5 minutes. Add the smashed garlic and the remaining 2 teaspoons chili powder and 1 teaspoon cumin; cook for 1 to 2 minutes. Add the tomatoes, cilantro sprigs and 1½ cups water and season with salt. Bring to a simmer, then cover, reduce the heat to low, and cook until the sauce thickens and the meatballs are tender, about 15 minutes.

3. About 5 minutes before the meatballs are done, toast the rolls in the oven. Place 2 roll halves in each of 4 shallow bowls and top with 4 meatballs. Drizzle with sauce, then pour the remaining sauce into the bowls. Top with avocado, cheese and/or scallions, if desired.

Per serving: Calories 499; Fat 22 g (Saturated 7 g); Cholesterol 127 mg; Sodium 794 mg; Carbohydrate 43 g; Fiber 5 g; Protein 31 g

This sub, called *torta ahogada* or "drowned sandwich" in Spanish, is a Mexican classic.

PARISIAN TUNA SANDWICHES

ACTIVE: 20 min **I** TOTAL: 35 min **I** SERVES: 4

3   large eggs
3   tablespoons red wine vinegar
Kosher salt and freshly ground pepper
¼   cup extra-virgin olive oil, plus more for drizzling
4   Italian rolls or other soft rolls, halved
1   medium bunch arugula or 2 cups spring salad mix
1   large tomato, thinly sliced
¼   small red onion, thinly sliced
1   cup jarred artichoke hearts, well drained and sliced
2   6-ounce cans oil-packed tuna
4 to 8 anchovy fillets, drained (optional)
¼   cup niçoise or kalamata olives, pitted and chopped
4   medium radishes, thinly sliced

1. Place the eggs in a saucepan; cover with water. Bring to a boil and cook for 8 to 10 minutes. Drain and cool in a bowl of cold water.

2. Meanwhile, combine the vinegar, ½ teaspoon salt, and pepper to taste in a medium bowl. Whisk in the olive oil. Put the rolls cut-side up on a work surface and lightly drizzle with a quarter of the dressing. Place the arugula on the roll bottoms. Top with the sliced tomato, onion and artichokes. Season with salt and drizzle with another quarter of the dressing.

3. Drain the tuna, but leave lightly coated with oil. Toss the tuna in the remaining dressing, then divide among the sandwiches. Peel and thinly slice the hard-boiled eggs and layer the slices over the tuna. Top with the anchovy fillets, if desired, then the olives and radishes. Cover with the roll tops, pressing gently but firmly. Wrap the sandwiches in plastic wrap and place a skillet on top to weigh them down; set aside for at least 15 minutes so the bread absorbs the flavors.

Per serving: Calories 520; Fat 29 g (Saturated 5 g); Cholesterol 187 mg; Sodium 611 mg; Carbohydrate 30 g; Fiber 2 g; Protein 34 g

> If you usually buy cans of tuna packed in water, try the kind in olive oil: It's much more flavorful.

SESAME BEEF SANDWICHES

ACTIVE: 30 min **I** TOTAL: 30 min **I** SERVES: 4

1   pound refrigerated pizza dough (fresh, not frozen)
3   tablespoons vegetable oil, plus more for greasing
2   tablespoons sesame seeds
Kosher salt
2   cups shredded coleslaw mix
1   tablespoon rice wine vinegar
¼ to ½ teaspoon chili oil
6   ounces deli-sliced roast beef
1   tablespoon toasted sesame oil
3   scallions, thinly sliced
½   teaspoon grated peeled ginger
½   cup fresh cilantro

1. Microwave the pizza dough on 50 percent power to soften, 1 to 2 minutes, then let rest 5 minutes. Grease a large plate with vegetable oil; shape the dough into a 9-inch round and place on the plate. Sprinkle the top of the dough with 1 tablespoon sesame seeds and ¼ teaspoon salt.
2. Toss the coleslaw mix, vinegar, chili oil, and salt to taste in a bowl. In another bowl, toss the roast beef, sesame oil, scallions and ginger.
3. Heat 3 tablespoons vegetable oil in a large nonstick skillet over medium-high heat. Add the dough seed-side down and sprinkle with the remaining 1 tablespoon sesame seeds. Cover and fry, shaking the pan occasionally, until the dough is golden, about 3 minutes per side, turning with tongs. Transfer to paper towels, season with salt and cool.
4. Wipe out the skillet and place over high heat. Add the roast beef mixture and stir-fry until crisp, 1 to 2 minutes. Slice the flatbread in half horizontally. Layer the beef, coleslaw mixture and cilantro on the bottom half. Cover with the top and cut into 4 wedges.

Per serving: Calories 561; Fat 27 g (Saturated 5 g); Cholesterol 27 mg; Sodium 906 mg; Carbohydrate 62 g; Fiber 4 g; Protein 22 g

You can use store-bought refrigerated pizza dough, but better yet, buy some unbaked dough from a pizza joint. Small local restaurants are usually willing to sell it—just ask!

TURKEY PICADILLO SANDWICHES

ACTIVE: 30 min **I** TOTAL: 40 min **I** SERVES: 4

3   tablespoons extra-virgin olive oil, plus more for drizzling
1   medium onion, diced
8   cloves garlic, chopped
3   bay leaves
1   tablespoon ground cumin
1   teaspoon chili powder
½   teaspoon ground allspice
1¼   pounds ground turkey
Kosher salt and freshly ground pepper
1   6-ounce can tomato paste
⅓   cup golden raisins
½   cup chopped pimiento-stuffed olives, plus 2 tablespoons olive juice
4   soft sesame buns or Portuguese rolls, split
Sliced avocado, for topping (optional)

1. Preheat the oven to 350˚. Heat 3 tablespoons olive oil in a large skillet over medium-high heat. Add the onion and garlic and cook until slightly soft, about 2 minutes. Add the bay leaves, cumin, chili powder and allspice; toast 1 to 2 minutes. Add the turkey, 1 teaspoon salt, and pepper to taste. Cook about 5 minutes, breaking up the meat.

2. Add the tomato paste and stir until brick red, 3 to 4 minutes. Add 2 cups water, the raisins, olives and olive juice. Bring to a simmer, cover and cook over medium heat until thickened, about 15 minutes. Uncover and cook, stirring, 3 more minutes. Season with salt and pepper.

3. Drizzle the cut sides of the rolls with olive oil, place on a baking sheet and warm in the oven, about 5 minutes. Fill the rolls with the turkey mixture. Top with avocado, if desired.

Per serving: Calories 484; Fat 16 g (Saturated 2 g); Cholesterol 56 mg; Sodium 944 mg; Carbohydrate 47 g; Fiber 6 g; Protein 43 g

Picadillo is a traditional Latin American dish made with ground beef. We lightened it up by using turkey.

CHICKEN AND BEAN BURRITOS

ACTIVE: 20 min **|** TOTAL: 40 min **|** SERVES: 4

½ cup brown rice
2 cloves garlic; 1 smashed, 1 minced
Kosher salt and freshly ground pepper
½ pound (about 2 cups) frozen diced butternut squash, thawed
1 cup shredded rotisserie chicken, skin removed
1 15-ounce can black beans
1 cup grape tomatoes
½ cup fresh cilantro
¼ cup pickled jalapeño peppers, plus 2 tablespoons pickling liquid
4 8-inch whole-wheat tortillas, warmed
½ cup shredded reduced-fat cheddar cheese
1 avocado, sliced
Plain low-fat yogurt or sour cream, for serving (optional)

1. Heat a medium skillet over high heat. Add the rice and smashed garlic and cook, stirring, until fragrant, 2 to 3 minutes. Add 1 cup water, season with salt and pepper and bring to a boil. Add the squash and reduce the heat to low; cover and simmer, undisturbed, about 25 minutes. Sprinkle the chicken over the rice mixture, cover and remove from the heat.

2. Meanwhile, make the bean salsa: Drain and rinse the beans, quarter the tomatoes and chop the cilantro and jalapeños. Toss with the pickling liquid and minced garlic in a bowl. Season with salt and pepper.

3. Stir the chicken-rice mixture and spoon it down the center of each tortilla, then top with half of the bean salsa and sprinkle with the cheese. Fold in the sides and roll up. Slice in half and serve with avocado, the remaining bean salsa and yogurt, if desired.

Per serving: Calories 497; Fat 15 g (Saturated 3 g); Cholesterol 25 mg; Sodium 620 mg; Carbohydrate 70 g; Fiber 11 g; Protein 24 g

This dish is a great way to use up leftover chicken.

TOFU PARMESAN SUBS

ACTIVE: 35 min **I** TOTAL: 35 min **I** SERVES: 4

1   14-ounce can crushed tomatoes
1   clove garlic, smashed
8   fresh basil leaves, torn
Kosher salt and freshly ground pepper
½   cup breadcrumbs
⅓   cup grated parmesan cheese
½   teaspoon dried Italian seasoning
1   large egg
1   12-ounce package firm tofu, drained and sliced into 8 pieces
2½ tablespoons extra-virgin olive oil, plus more for drizzling
1   loaf whole-wheat Italian bread, cut into 4 pieces and split in half
¼   cup shredded part-skim mozzarella cheese
½   pound baby spinach (about 8 cups)

1. Preheat the broiler. Combine the tomatoes, garlic, basil and 1 cup water in a saucepan over medium-high heat. Season with salt and pepper and simmer until slightly thickened, about 15 minutes.
2. Toss the breadcrumbs, 2 tablespoons parmesan and the Italian seasoning on a plate; season with salt and pepper. Beat the egg in a shallow bowl. Dip the tofu in the egg, then in the crumbs, turning to coat.
3. Heat 2 tablespoons olive oil in a nonstick skillet over medium heat. Add the tofu and cook until crisp, 3 to 4 minutes per side. Place the bread cut-side up on a broiler pan; spread the bottom halves with sauce, then top with the tofu, more sauce, the mozzarella and remaining parmesan. Broil until the cheese melts and the bread is toasted, about 2 minutes.
4. Meanwhile, heat the remaining ½ tablespoon olive oil in the empty skillet over medium-high heat. Add the spinach, season with salt and pepper and let wilt, about 1 minute. Place on top of the cheese and cover with the bread tops.

Per serving: Calories 491; Fat 22 g (Saturated 5 g); Cholesterol 60 mg; Sodium 1,202 mg; Carbohydrate 50 g; Fiber 7 g; Protein 24 g

Use the leftover basil in...

Chicken with Sun-Dried Tomato, Eggplant and Basil page 137

Spinach Ravioli with Tomato Sauce page 290

Tomato-Basil Lima Beans page 346

PATTY MELTS

ACTIVE: 40 min **I** TOTAL: 40 min **I** SERVES: 4

3   tablespoons extra-virgin olive oil
2   medium onions, thinly sliced
10   ounces button mushrooms, sliced
Kosher salt and freshly ground pepper
2   teaspoons balsamic vinegar
2   tablespoons plus 2 teaspoons Worcestershire sauce
10   ounces 93% lean ground turkey
6   ounces lean ground beef sirloin
8   slices multigrain bread
8   thin slices monterey jack or Swiss cheese (2 to 3 ounces)

1. Heat 1 teaspoon olive oil in a large nonstick skillet over medium-high heat. Add the onions and cook, stirring, until soft, 2 to 3 minutes. Push to one side of the skillet; add the mushrooms and cook until browned, about 2 minutes. Season with salt and pepper, then mix the mushrooms and onions together and cook until the onions are golden, about 10 more minutes. Add the vinegar and 2 tablespoons Worcestershire sauce. Transfer the mixture to a bowl and keep warm.
2. Meanwhile, mix the turkey, beef and the remaining 2 teaspoons Worcestershire sauce in a bowl. Shape into 4 equal-size oval patties.
3. Wipe out the skillet, add 1 tablespoon olive oil and place over medium-high heat. Season the patties with salt and pepper and cook until browned on the bottom, about 4 minutes. Flip and cook through, 1 to 2 more minutes.
4. Divide the onions and mushrooms among 4 bread slices; top with a slice of cheese, a patty, another slice of cheese and another bread slice. Wipe out the skillet; add 1 tablespoon olive oil and place over medium heat. Cook the sandwiches in two batches until the bread is toasted and the cheese melts, 1 to 2 minutes per side, adding the remaining 2 teaspoons oil as needed.

Per serving: Calories 534; Fat 26 g (Saturated 7 g); Cholesterol 83 mg; Sodium 848 mg; Carbohydrate 40 g; Fiber 10 g; Protein 37 g

Try it with these sides...

Roasted Peppers with Basil page 336

Carrot-Mustard Slaw page 341

Roasted Asparagus page 341

Cut fat (but keep great beefy flavor) by using a combination of ground turkey and beef.

Done in
20
minutes

AVOCADO BLTS

ACTIVE: 20 min **I** TOTAL: 20 min **I** SERVES: 4

½   pound bacon slices
4   plum tomatoes, halved lengthwise
Kosher salt
1   whole-wheat baguette, cut into 4 pieces and split open
4   tablespoons extra-virgin olive oil
1   clove garlic
Freshly ground pepper
2   avocados, halved, pitted and thinly sliced
1   cup frisée or other salad greens

1. Cook the bacon in a large skillet over medium heat until crisp,
8 to 10 minutes. Transfer to a paper towel–lined plate. Season the cut
sides of the tomatoes with salt.
2. Heat a grill pan over high heat. Brush the cut sides of the baguette with
the olive oil and grill, cut-side down, until toasted, about 2 minutes. Rub
the grilled sides with the garlic. Rub just the bottom halves of bread with the
tomatoes until most of the juice is absorbed, then top with the tomato skins
and season with salt and pepper.
3. Layer the avocado slices on top of the tomatoes, then add the bacon and
frisée. Close with the bread tops.

Per serving: Calories 540; Fat 39 g (Saturated 7 g); Cholesterol 21 mg;
Sodium 742 mg; Carbohydrate 37 g; Fiber 11 g; Protein 15 g

> You can make delicious
> garlic bread by rubbing
> toasted bread with peeled
> garlic cloves. You'll get all
> the garlic flavor without
> any of the bitterness.

POPPY SEED–CHICKEN PITAS

ACTIVE: 25 min **I** TOTAL: 40 min **I** SERVES: 4

3   skin-on, bone-in chicken breasts (about 2 pounds)
Kosher salt
1   large orange
½   cup mayonnaise
⅓   cup sour cream or low-fat Greek yogurt
1   tablespoon dijon mustard
1   stalk celery, chopped
½   cup chopped pecans, almonds or walnuts, toasted
¼   cup chopped fresh chives
1½   tablespoons poppy seeds
Freshly ground pepper
½   cup dried apricots, chopped (optional)
Torn lettuce leaves, for serving
4   whole-wheat pitas, halved

1. Cover the chicken with cold water in a saucepan and add 1 teaspoon salt.
Remove strips of zest from half of the orange with a vegetable peeler; add the
zest to the water. Cover and bring to a boil over high heat, then reduce the heat
to medium-low and simmer, uncovered, until the chicken is cooked through,
about 18 minutes. Remove the chicken and let cool.
2. Grate the remaining orange zest into a large bowl; juice the orange into the
bowl. Stir in the mayonnaise, sour cream, mustard, celery, nuts, chives, poppy
seeds, ½ teaspoon salt, and pepper to taste. Add the apricots, if desired.
3. Shred the chicken, discarding the bones and skin, and toss with the dressing.
Stuff a few lettuce leaves and some of the chicken salad into each pita.

Per serving: Calories 749; Fat 41 g (Saturated 7 g); Cholesterol 109 mg;
Sodium 957 mg; Carbohydrate 51 g; Fiber 8 g; Protein 43 g

To save time, make
this dish with shredded
rotisserie chicken.

JERK TURKEY BURGERS
WITH MANGO SLAW

ACTIVE: 35 min **I** TOTAL: 35 min **I** SERVES: 4

1   pound ground turkey
1   tablespoon jerk seasoning, plus more for sprinkling
1   small green apple, peeled and grated
½   cup finely chopped scallions
¼   cup panko (Japanese breadcrumbs)
Kosher salt and freshly ground pepper
¼   cup mayonnaise, plus more for brushing
¼   cup mango chutney, roughly chopped
3   cups shredded green cabbage
1   carrot, shredded
Canola oil, for the grill
4   hamburger buns or challah rolls, split

1. Preheat a grill or grill pan to medium high. Mix the turkey, jerk seasoning,
apple, ¼ cup scallions and the panko in a bowl; season with salt and pepper.
Form into four 1-inch-thick patties and make a small indentation in the middle
of each with your thumb to prevent it from puffing up on the grill. Refrigerate.
2. Whisk the mayonnaise and chutney in a large bowl. Add the cabbage, carrot
and the remaining ¼ cup scallions, season with salt and pepper and toss to coat.
3. Brush the grill with canola oil. Grill the turkey patties until browned and
cooked through, 4 to 5 minutes per side.
4. Brush the cut sides of the buns with mayonnaise and sprinkle with jerk
seasoning; toast on the grill, about 30 seconds. Serve the burgers and slaw
on the buns.

Per serving: Calories 504; Fat 20 g (Saturated 3 g); Cholesterol 51 mg;
Sodium 894 mg; Carbohydrate 51 g; Fiber 4 g; Protein 36 g

> Mango chutney makes the slaw
> sweet and spicy. If you don't
> have any, mix the juice of 1 lime,
> 1 tablespoon curry powder and
> 2 teaspoons honey.

MEATY QUESADILLAS

ACTIVE: 30 min **I** TOTAL: 30 min **I** SERVES: 4

2   tablespoons extra-virgin olive oil, plus more for brushing
3   cloves garlic, minced
1   teaspoon ancho chile powder
1   pound lean ground beef or lamb
1   tablespoon finely chopped fresh oregano
Kosher salt and freshly ground pepper
4   scallions, thinly sliced
4   10-inch flour tortillas
3½ cups shredded muenster or monterey jack cheese
Fresh salsa and/or sour cream, for serving

1. Heat the olive oil in a large skillet over medium heat. Add the garlic and chile powder and cook 1 to 2 minutes. Add the beef, oregano, 1 teaspoon salt, and pepper to taste. Cook, breaking up the meat with a spoon, until it is no longer pink, about 2 minutes. Add the scallions and cook 5 to 6 more minutes.
2. Heat a large griddle or skillet over medium heat. Brush 1 side of each tortilla with olive oil. Place 2 tortillas on the griddle (or 1 if using a skillet), oiled-side down, and scatter about one-quarter of the cheese on each. Cook until the bottoms are golden brown and the cheese is melted. Put about a quarter of the beef mixture on half of each tortilla and fold into a half-moon. Continue to cook until the quesadillas are crisp, turning once. Repeat to make 4 quesadillas. Cut into wedges and top with salsa and/or sour cream.

Per serving: Calories 813; Fat 48 g (Saturated 23 g); Cholesterol 155 mg; Sodium 1,889 mg; Carbohydrate 43 g; Fiber 3 g; Protein 52 g

Use the leftover oregano in...

Mojo Pork Chops with Plantains
page 162

Lamb Chops with Fennel and Tomatoes
page 194

Tilapia with Escarole and Lemon-Pepper Oil
page 228

Done in
30
minutes

SLOW-COOKER BRISKET SANDWICHES

ACTIVE: 30 min **I** TOTAL: 30 min (plus 8-hr slow cooking) **I** SERVES: 4 (with leftovers)

2 tablespoons vegetable oil
1 5-to-6-pound first-cut or flat-cut brisket, cut into 3 pieces
Kosher salt and freshly ground pepper
4 cloves garlic, smashed and peeled
1 12-ounce bottle stout beer
4 stalks celery, cut into large pieces
⅔ cup packed dark brown sugar
½ cup tomato paste
½ cup red wine vinegar
⅓ cup dijon mustard
⅓ cup soy sauce
2 bay leaves
1 teaspoon paprika
2 brioche or other rolls, split open and toasted
Coleslaw, for serving

1. Heat the vegetable oil in a large skillet over medium-high heat. Season the brisket with salt and pepper, then brown on all sides, about 10 minutes, adding the garlic in the last 2 minutes. Transfer the meat and garlic to a 5-to-6-quart slow cooker. Pour the beer into the skillet and simmer 30 seconds, scraping up the browned bits from the pan; add the beer mixture to the slow cooker.
2. Nestle the celery around the meat and add the brown sugar, tomato paste, vinegar, mustard, soy sauce, bay leaves and paprika. Stir, then cover and cook on low 8 hours or on high 6 hours. Transfer the meat to a cutting board and let rest 10 minutes, then thinly slice.
3. Serve on brioche halves with coleslaw; drizzle with the cooking liquid.

Per serving: Calories 474; Fat 16 g (Saturated 7 g); Cholesterol 128 mg; Sodium 265 mg; Carbohydrate 18 g; Fiber 0 g; Protein 61 g

You'll have plenty of leftover brisket: Use it in tacos, quesadillas, chili or even on a pizza.

GRILLED PITA PIZZAS

ACTIVE: 30 min **I** TOTAL: 30 min **I** SERVES: 4

3   medium tomatoes
1   tablespoon extra-virgin olive oil, plus more for brushing and drizzling
Kosher salt and freshly ground pepper
3   cups baby arugula
½   cup pitted kalamata olives, roughly chopped
1   tablespoon fresh rosemary, roughly chopped
1   large red onion, cut into 1-inch-thick rounds
4   6-to-8-inch pocketless pitas
½   cup ricotta cheese
¼   pound part-skim mozzarella cheese, diced
Pinch of red pepper flakes

1. Core the tomatoes and halve them crosswise, then squeeze the juices and seeds into a large bowl. Whisk in 1 tablespoon olive oil and season with salt and pepper. Add the arugula but don't toss; set aside. Dice the tomatoes and toss in a separate bowl with the olives and rosemary.
2. Preheat a grill to medium high. Brush the onion rounds with olive oil and season with salt. Grill until soft, 3 to 4 minutes per side. Transfer to a plate and separate the rings. Reduce the grill heat to medium.
3. Brush both sides of the pitas with olive oil and grill until marked, 2 to 3 minutes per side. Top with some of the tomato-olive mixture, ricotta, mozzarella and onion. Cover and grill until the cheese melts, 2 to 3 minutes.
4. Toss the arugula with the dressing and pile on top of the pitas. Season with salt and the red pepper flakes and drizzle with olive oil.

Per serving: Calories 564; Fat 35 g (Saturated 9 g); Cholesterol 31 mg; Sodium 798 mg; Carbohydrate 46 g; Fiber 3 g; Protein 18 g

You can make the pizzas on a cast-iron grill pan, too. Transfer to a 400° oven to melt the cheese.

CHICKEN KORMA

ACTIVE: 35 min **I** TOTAL: 35 min **I** SERVES: 4

1   large red onion; ½ chopped, ½ sliced
1   1-inch piece ginger, peeled and thinly sliced
2   cloves garlic, smashed
½   teaspoon ground coriander
1   teaspoon ground cumin
Kosher salt
¼   cup vegetable oil, plus more for brushing
¾   pound ground chicken
¼   cup plain low-fat yogurt, plus more for topping
¼   cup frozen peas, thawed
¼   cup chopped fresh cilantro, plus more for topping
4   pocketless pitas
Chopped cashews and/or hot sauce, for topping (optional)

1. Puree the chopped onion in a food processor with the ginger, garlic, coriander, cumin, ½ teaspoon salt and ½ cup water.
2. Heat the vegetable oil in a skillet over medium-high heat. Add the sliced onion and cook until golden, 4 to 5 minutes. Add the spice paste and cook, stirring, until slightly dry, 8 to 10 minutes. Add the chicken and cook until opaque, breaking up the meat. Mix the yogurt with ¼ cup water, add to the pan and simmer over medium-low heat until the meat is cooked through, 2 to 3 more minutes. Add the peas and cilantro and season with salt.
3. Meanwhile, heat another skillet over high heat. Brush the pitas with oil, season with salt and toast in the skillet, about 1 minute per side. Divide the chicken mixture among the pitas. Top with yogurt, cilantro, cashews and/or hot sauce, if desired.

Per serving: Calories 463; Fat 25 g (Saturated 4 g); Cholesterol 57 mg; Sodium 748 mg; Carbohydrate 41 g; Fiber 3 g; Protein 21 g

You can serve the chicken on top of rice, too.

CHILE RELLENO BURGERS

ACTIVE: 25 min **|** TOTAL: 35 min **|** SERVES: 4

2   large poblano peppers, halved lengthwise and seeded
2   plum tomatoes or 1 large tomato, cored and halved
1   small onion, quartered
3   cloves garlic, unpeeled
Kosher salt
4   hamburger buns, split open
1   large egg white, lightly beaten
½   teaspoon dried oregano
½   teaspoon ground cumin
½   teaspoon chili powder
1½   pounds ground beef chuck
6   slices muenster cheese

1. Preheat the broiler. Put the poblanos cut-side down on a foil-lined broiler pan. Add the tomatoes, onion and garlic and broil until charred, 7 to 8 minutes. Cool slightly, then peel the garlic. Chop the garlic, onion and tomatoes; toss in a bowl with salt to taste. Peel the poblanos and cut each in half.

2. Preheat the oven to 350°. Brush the bun tops with the egg white. Mix the oregano, cumin and chili powder, sprinkle on the bun tops and put the tops and bottoms on a baking sheet. Bake 5 minutes.

3. Heat a large cast-iron skillet over medium-high heat. Shape the beef into four ¾-inch-thick patties; make an indentation in the centers. Sprinkle the skillet with salt, then cook the burgers until browned on the bottom, about 4 minutes. Flip, then top each burger with some of the tomato mixture and cheese. Cover and cook 3 to 5 minutes. Serve on the spiced buns with the poblanos and the remaining tomato mixture.

Per serving: Calories 571; Fat 32 g (Saturated 14 g); Cholesterol 124 mg; Sodium 999 mg; Carbohydrate 30 g; Fiber 3 g; Protein 40 g

> Dress up your burger bun:
> Brush the top with egg whites,
> then sprinkle with dried herbs,
> spices or seeds and bake.

Mix & Match

PIZZA

Margherita Pizza with
Eggplant and Basil

PREHEAT THE OVEN

Put a pizza stone or inverted baking sheet on the lowest oven rack;
preheat the oven to 500° for 45 minutes.

PRECOOK THE CRUST

Roll 1 pound pizza dough into a 12-to-14-inch round on a floured pizza peel or board. Slide onto the
stone or baking sheet and bake until just firm, about 3 minutes. Slide back onto the peel or board.

PICK A PIZZA

MARGHERITA
Spread 1½ cups tomato sauce over the crust. Top with 1 cup sliced mozzarella. (To make your own sauce, heat 2 tablespoons olive oil in saucepan over medium heat. Add 2 sliced garlic cloves and cook 1 minute. Add a 28-ounce can San Marzano tomatoes, crushing them with your hands, plus 6 basil leaves and salt and pepper. Bring to a boil, then simmer over low heat for 30 minutes, stirring occasionally.)

HERB
Mix ¼ cup olive oil, 1 tablespoon chopped mixed fresh herbs (rosemary, oregano, sage and/or thyme), and salt and pepper. Brush over the crust. Sprinkle with ¾ cup shredded mozzarella and ¼ cup grated parmesan, if desired.

WHITE
Mix ¾ cup ricotta, ¼ cup grated parmesan, 1 grated garlic clove and 1 tablespoon each olive oil and chopped rosemary and/or oregano; spread over the crust.

CHOOSE YOUR TOPPING COMBO

Sprinkle one of these combos on top of the prepared pizza base:

- cooked diced pancetta and thinly sliced Brussels sprouts
- crumbled uncooked spicy sausage and chopped blanched broccoli rabe
- sliced cooked meatballs
- thinly sliced eggplant, drizzled with olive oil and sprinkled with red pepper flakes
- artichoke hearts and baby spinach

- raw ground lamb and thinly sliced leeks
- shredded chicken, sliced bell pepper and sliced onion tossed with fajita seasoning and topped with shredded pepper jack
- sliced radicchio and thinly sliced prosciutto
- small cauliflower florets and cooked diced pancetta

- roasted red peppers, diced yellow squash and baby spinach
- anchovies and pitted kalamata olives
- thinly sliced fennel, thinly sliced prosciutto, pine nuts and sea salt
- robiola or mascarpone cheese, halved grapes and sea salt (use on white or herb pizzas)

BAKE

Slide the pizza back onto the stone or baking sheet and bake until the crust is golden and the cheese is melted, about 8 minutes. Season with salt. Top with fresh basil or salad greens, if desired.

Guy says...

" The kitchen is the epicenter of the Fieri casa. Family dinners...kids doin' homework and playing cards on the 14-foot dinner table...recipe testing for *Guy's Big Bite*...the kitchen is where it all happens!"

—GUY FIERI IS THE HOST OF *DINERS, DRIVE-INS AND DIVES* AND *GUY'S BIG BITE*, AND THE AUTHOR OF *DINERS, DRIVE-INS AND DIVES: AN ALL-AMERICAN ROAD TRIP...WITH RECIPES!*, *MORE DINERS, DRIVE-INS AND DIVES: A DROP-TOP CULINARY CRUISE THROUGH AMERICA'S FINEST AND FUNKIEST JOINTS* AND *GUY FIERI FOOD*.

KITCHEN SECRET

Guy built a 900-square-foot addition onto his Northern California house just for his dream kitchen. He says the project drove his wife, Lori, crazy but he made amends by installing "his" and "her" refrigerators.

Skillet Rosemary Chicken, page 146

Poultry

Low-
calorie
dinner

POACHED GINGER CHICKEN

ACTIVE: 25 min **I** TOTAL: 35 min **I** SERVES: 4

4   boneless, skinless chicken breasts (1¾ to 2 pounds)
Kosher salt
1   2-inch piece ginger, peeled
1   large shallot
4   tablespoons peanut oil
1   tablespoon toasted sesame oil
½   teaspoon sugar
1   seedless cucumber, halved lengthwise, seeded and thinly sliced
1   bunch radishes, thinly sliced, or 1 small daikon radish, peeled and cut into matchsticks
1   teaspoon Asian chili sauce (such as sambal oelek)
1   bunch watercress, trimmed
Juice of 1 lime

1. Put the chicken in a medium pot with just enough water to cover; add 1 tablespoon salt. Bring to a gentle simmer over medium heat and cook until the chicken is firm to the touch, about 15 minutes. Meanwhile, prepare a bowl of salted ice water. Drain the chicken and plunge into the ice water for about 30 seconds to stop the cooking. Drain again.
2. Grate the ginger and shallot into a small bowl. Stir in 3 tablespoons peanut oil, the sesame oil and ¼ teaspoon each sugar and salt.
3. Toss the cucumber and radishes with the chili sauce, ¾ teaspoon salt, the remaining 1 tablespoon peanut oil and the remaining ¼ teaspoon sugar in a large bowl. Add the watercress and toss.
4. Divide the salad among plates. Slice the chicken and add to the plates, then top with the ginger mixture. Drizzle with the lime juice.

Per serving: Calories 432; Fat 23 g (Saturated 4 g); Cholesterol 118 mg; Sodium 614 mg; Carbohydrate 9 g; Fiber 2 g; Protein 47 g

> Poaching is a fast and healthy way to cook chicken. Just make sure the water isn't boiling; it should barely simmer, with just a few tiny bubbles breaking the surface.

DRUMSTICKS WITH BISCUITS AND TOMATO JAM

ACTIVE: 25 min **I** TOTAL: 40 min **I** SERVES: 4

2   pints grape tomatoes
3 to 4 tablespoons sugar
2   sprigs thyme, plus 2 teaspoons chopped leaves
Kosher salt and freshly ground pepper
Juice of 1 lemon
⅓   cup honey mustard
2   tablespoons Worcestershire sauce
1   cup all-purpose flour
8   skin-on chicken drumsticks (about 2½ pounds)
5   tablespoons unsalted butter
Biscuits, for serving

1. Preheat the oven to 400˚. Put the tomatoes, sugar, thyme sprigs, 1 cup water, ½ teaspoon salt, and pepper to taste in a small saucepan. Bring to a boil over high heat, then reduce the heat and simmer, stirring occasionally, until thick, about 30 minutes.
2. Meanwhile, mix half of the lemon juice, the chopped thyme, mustard and Worcestershire sauce in a large bowl. Season the flour with salt and pepper in another bowl.
3. Heat a large cast-iron skillet over medium-high heat. Season the drumsticks with salt and pepper. Dip in the mustard mixture, then dredge in the seasoned flour. Melt the butter in the skillet and fry the drumsticks, turning, until golden on all sides, about 6 minutes. Transfer the skillet to the oven; bake until the chicken is golden and a thermometer inserted into the center registers 155˚, about 15 minutes.
4. Add the remaining lemon juice to the tomato jam and season with salt and pepper. Serve the drumsticks with the jam and biscuits.

Per serving: Calories 535; Fat 33 g (Saturated 13 g); Cholesterol 149 mg; Sodium 859 mg; Carbohydrate 28 g; Fiber 3 g; Protein 36 g

You can make the tomato jam in the microwave: Combine the ingredients in a large microwave-safe bowl, then cut a hole in the middle of a paper plate and place on top. Microwave 20 minutes, stirring every 5 minutes.

Done in
30
minutes

CHICKEN WITH APPLE, ONION AND CIDER SAUCE

ACTIVE 30 min **I** TOTAL: 30 min **I** SERVES: 4

4   boneless, skinless chicken breasts (about 2 pounds)
Kosher salt and freshly ground pepper
All-purpose flour, for dredging
2 to 3 tablespoons vegetable oil
1   large red onion, cut into large pieces
1   sweet cooking apple (such as Golden Delicious or Cortland), cored and
     cut into large pieces
3   tablespoons apple cider vinegar
1½   cups low-sodium chicken broth
2   tablespoons cold unsalted butter
Chopped fresh parsley, for sprinkling

1. Preheat the oven to 350˚. Heat a large skillet over medium-high heat.
Season the chicken breasts with salt and pepper and dredge in the flour,
shaking off the excess. Add 2 tablespoons oil to the pan. Place the chicken in
the skillet, smooth-side down, and cook until golden, about 5 minutes per side.
Transfer to a baking dish and bake until cooked through, about 8 minutes.
2. Meanwhile, add the onion and apple to the skillet, along with 1 tablespoon
oil if the pan is dry, and increase the heat to high. Cook, tossing, until the onion
has wilted slightly and the apple is golden brown, about 2 minutes. Add the
vinegar and use a wooden spoon to scrape up the browned bits from the pan.
Let the mixture boil until the vinegar becomes syrupy, about 1 minute. Add
the chicken broth and return to a boil. Cook until the broth reduces by half.
Remove from the heat, season with salt and pepper and whisk in the butter.
3. Remove the chicken from the oven; add any collected juices to the sauce.
Divide the chicken among 4 plates and spoon the apple, onion and pan sauce
over each piece. Sprinkle with parsley.

Per serving: Calories 437; Fat 16 g (Saturated 5 g); Cholesterol 156 mg;
Sodium 198 mg; Carbohydrate 16 g; Fiber 1 g; Protein 55 g

> Don't wash out the skillet. Pour
> in some liquid to unstick all the
> tasty caramelized bits and turn
> them into a sauce. We used
> vinegar to "deglaze" in this
> recipe, but you can use water,
> broth or even beer.

CHICKEN AND BLACK BEAN TOSTADAS

ACTIVE: 30 min **I** TOTAL: 30 min **I** SERVES: 4

¼ cup canola oil, plus more for frying
4 corn tortillas, preferably white
Kosher salt
1 15.5-ounce can black beans, drained and rinsed
1 teaspoon ground cumin
¼ cup low-sodium chicken broth
Freshly ground pepper
1 clove garlic, minced
1 tablespoon adobo sauce (from a can of chipotle peppers in adobo)
¼ cup fresh lime juice
2 teaspoons brown sugar
2 cups finely shredded green or red cabbage
1 bunch radishes (about 6), julienned
½ bunch fresh cilantro, roughly chopped
½ cup sour cream
½ rotisserie chicken, skinned and shredded into large pieces

1. Heat ½ inch oil in a small heavy skillet over medium heat until shimmering. Fry tortillas one at a time until golden and crisp, 2 minutes per side. Drain on paper towels and sprinkle with salt.
2. Cool the oil slightly and discard all but 2 tablespoons. Add the beans and cumin and cook, stirring, 1 minute. Add the broth and cook, smashing the beans, until saucy and hot. Season with salt and pepper.
3. Whisk the garlic, adobo sauce, 2 tablespoons lime juice, the sugar and ½ teaspoon salt in a large bowl. Slowly whisk in ¼ cup oil to make a dressing; add the cabbage, radishes and cilantro and toss. Mix the sour cream and the remaining 2 tablespoons lime juice in another bowl; season with salt and pepper.
4. Top each tortilla with beans, chicken, cabbage salad and sour cream.

Per serving: Calories 355; Fat 19 g (Saturated 5 g); Cholesterol 72 mg; Sodium 1,285 mg; Carbohydrate 24 g; Fiber 6 g; Protein 22 g

> Transfer leftover chipotle peppers in adobo sauce to an airtight container, press a piece of plastic wrap on the surface and cover. They'll keep in the fridge for about a month.

SAUSAGE AND KRAUT

ACTIVE: 30 min **I** TOTAL: 40 min **I** SERVES: 4

1   1-pound bag sauerkraut, rinsed
8   small fingerling or red-skinned potatoes, halved if large
1   tablespoon vegetable oil
12 ounces turkey kielbasa or chicken sausage, cut into 2-inch pieces
1   6-ounce boneless smoked pork chop, trimmed and sliced
1   large onion, chopped
2   cloves garlic, smashed
1   teaspoon coriander seeds, crushed
1   teaspoon juniper berries (available in the spice aisle), crushed
Kosher salt and freshly ground pepper
1   apple, grated
1   cup dry white wine
2   tablespoons chopped fresh parsley
Whole-grain mustard, for serving

1. Soak the sauerkraut in a bowl of warm water. Cover the potatoes with water in a small saucepan and simmer over medium heat until tender, about 10 minutes. Drain and keep warm.

2. Meanwhile, heat the vegetable oil in a large pot over medium-high heat. Prick the sausage with a fork and add to the pot along with the pork; cook until browned on one side, about 4 minutes. Turn the meats and add the onion, garlic, coriander, juniper berries, and salt and pepper to taste. Cook until the onion is golden brown, about 6 minutes. Add the apple and cook 2 more minutes.

3. Drain the sauerkraut, then add to the pot along with the wine and 1 cup water. Cover and simmer 10 minutes, then uncover and cook until thickened, about 5 more minutes. Transfer the sauerkraut, meats and potatoes to a platter. Top with the parsley and serve with mustard.

Per serving: Calories 417; Fat 14 g (Saturated 3 g); Cholesterol 90 mg; Sodium 1,382 mg; Carbohydrate 33 g; Fiber 7 g; Protein 29 g

> Juniper berries are sold dried in jars, like peppercorns. Just crush them to release their gin-like flavor.

CHICKEN-AND-CHEESE ENCHILADAS

ACTIVE: 35 min **I** TOTAL: 40 min **I** SERVES: 4

1   small red onion, halved
1½ pounds tomatillos, husked and rinsed
1 to 2 serrano chile peppers, stemmed and seeded
½   cup low-sodium chicken broth
Kosher salt
Pinch of sugar
8   corn tortillas
3   cups shredded rotisserie chicken
2½ cups shredded mozzarella and/or monterey jack cheese
⅓   cup fresh cilantro
2   tablespoons extra-virgin olive oil, plus more for greasing
¾   cup crumbled queso fresco or feta cheese

1. Preheat the broiler. Slice half of the onion into thin rings and set aside. Place the other onion half, tomatillos and serranos on a foil-lined baking sheet and broil until the vegetables are soft and slightly brown, 7 to 10 minutes, turning as needed. Transfer the vegetables and any liquid to a blender, add the broth and puree. Season with ½ teaspoon salt and the sugar.
2. Meanwhile, stack the tortillas, wrap in a damp paper towel and microwave just until warm and soft, 1 minute; keep covered. Toss the chicken with 2 cups shredded cheese in a bowl. Spoon a portion of the chicken mixture down the middle of each tortilla. Add a few cilantro leaves and roll up. Place the enchiladas side by side in a lightly oiled 9-by-13-inch baking dish and brush with the 2 tablespoons olive oil. Broil until crisp and golden, 3 minutes.
3. Pour the tomatillo sauce over the enchiladas and top with the remaining ½ cup shredded cheese. Return to the oven and broil until the cheese is bubbly and golden brown, 3 to 5 minutes. Top with the onion rings, queso fresco and any remaining cilantro.

Per serving: Calories 626; Fat 32 g (Saturated 13 g); Cholesterol 98 mg; Sodium 1,056 mg; Carbohydrate 46 g; Fiber 6 g; Protein 47 g

Tomatillos can be sticky; be sure to rinse them well after removing the husks.

Done in
20
minutes

CHICKEN AND WAFFLES

ACTIVE: 20 min **I** TOTAL: 20 min **I** SERVES: 4

Vegetable oil, for shallow frying
¼   cup hot sauce
1   large egg, lightly beaten
8   chicken tenders (about 1 pound)
¾   cup instant flour (such as Wondra)
1   teaspoon poultry seasoning
Kosher salt and freshly ground pepper
3   tablespoons unsalted butter
2   scallions, sliced, plus more for sprinkling
1½   cups low-sodium chicken broth
4   buttermilk or Belgian-style frozen waffles
Maple syrup, for serving

1. Heat about 1 inch of oil in a large cast-iron or heavy-bottomed skillet over high heat. Whisk the hot sauce and egg in a medium bowl; toss the chicken in the mixture to coat.
2. Combine the flour, poultry seasoning, and salt and pepper to taste in a medium bowl. Set aside 3 tablespoons seasoned flour in a separate bowl; dredge the chicken in the remaining seasoned flour until coated, shaking off any excess.
3. Place the chicken in the hot oil and fry until golden and cooked through, 2 to 3 minutes per side, turning once. Transfer to a rack to cool slightly; discard the oil.
4. Melt the butter in the same skillet and whisk in the reserved seasoned flour until smooth. Whisk in the scallions, then slowly pour in the broth. Bring to a simmer, whisking until the gravy is smooth. Meanwhile, toast the waffles.
5. Place a waffle on each plate and drizzle with maple syrup. Top with chicken and gravy and sprinkle with scallions.

Per serving: Calories 865; Fat 68 g (Saturated 15 g); Cholesterol 150 mg; Sodium 677 mg; Carbohydrate 32 g; Fiber 1 g; Protein 34 g

> Don't fear all the hot sauce in this dish; it just adds a subtle kick.

GLAZED CHICKEN WITH DRIED FRUIT AND PARSNIPS

ACTIVE: 15 min **I** TOTAL: 40 min **I** SERVES: 4

2	tablespoons extra-virgin olive oil
6	medium shallots
4	medium-large parsnips, peeled and cut into 1-inch chunks
⅓	cup apricot preserves
2	tablespoons whole-grain mustard
1	teaspoon ground ginger
½	teaspoon ground cumin
8	medium skin-on, bone-in chicken thighs

Kosher salt and freshly ground pepper
½ cup pitted prunes, roughly chopped
½ cup dried apricots, roughly chopped
1 tablespoon apple cider vinegar

1. Position a rack in the center of the oven and preheat to 425°. Heat the olive oil in a large ovenproof skillet over high heat. Add the shallots and parsnips and cook until golden, shaking the pan, 2 minutes.
2. Whisk the apricot preserves, mustard, ginger and cumin in a bowl. Season the chicken with salt and pepper; toss with the apricot glaze.
3. Scatter the dried fruit in the skillet. Place the chicken, skin-side up, on top. Add ¼ cup water and bring to a boil. Cover and cook until heated through, 6 minutes. Uncover and transfer the skillet to the oven. Cook until the chicken and vegetables are tender and golden, 20 to 25 minutes.
4. Push the chicken to the side of the skillet, then stir the vinegar into the pan juices (add up to 2 tablespoons water if the sauce is too thick). Serve from the skillet.

Per serving: Calories 757; Fat 36 g (Saturated 9 g); Cholesterol 158 mg; Sodium 464 mg; Carbohydrate 71 g; Fiber 6 g; Protein 38 g

─ Use the leftover dried apricots in... ─

Slow-Cooker Moroccan Turkey Stew page 26

Poppy Seed–Chicken Pitas page 76

Mediterranean Bulgur page 352

One-pan meal

Low-calorie dinner

HOISIN CHICKEN WITH CUCUMBER SALAD

ACTIVE: 25 min **I** TOTAL: 35 min **I** SERVES: 4

FOR THE CHICKEN
¾   cup hoisin sauce
3   scallions, coarsely chopped
5   cloves garlic
1   2-inch piece fresh ginger, sliced
1   jalapeño pepper, stemmed and halved (remove seeds for less heat)
Zest and juice of 2 limes, plus lime wedges for serving
2   tablespoons rice vinegar
Kosher salt and freshly ground pepper
2   pounds skin-on chicken thighs and drumsticks (separate pieces)

FOR THE SALAD
½   cup rice vinegar
2   tablespoons sugar
Kosher salt
1   seedless cucumber, thinly sliced
½   red onion, thinly sliced

1. Prepare the chicken: Preheat a grill to medium on one side. Combine the hoisin sauce, scallions, garlic, ginger, jalapeño, lime zest and juice, vinegar, and salt and pepper to taste in a mini food processor or blender; process until almost smooth. Season the chicken with salt; toss with the hoisin mixture in a large bowl.
2. Make the salad: Bring the vinegar, sugar and 1½ teaspoons salt to a boil in a small saucepan, stirring. Remove from the heat; stir in ¼ cup ice cubes until melted. Toss the cucumber and red onion in a serving bowl with the vinegar mixture; place in the refrigerator.
3. Grill the chicken over direct heat until the skin is crisp, 5 minutes per side, basting with extra marinade. Transfer to the cooler side of the grill; cover and grill until cooked through, 10 to 15 more minutes. Serve with the cucumber salad and lime wedges.

Per serving: Calories 375; Fat 16 g (Saturated 4 g); Cholesterol 107 mg; Sodium 1,906 mg; Carbohydrate 30 g; Fiber 1 g; Protein 32 g

> We used indirect heat to cook the chicken all the way through without burning the skin. If you're using a charcoal grill, bank the coals to one side; on a gas grill, light the burners on just one side.

SWEET-AND-SOUR CHICKEN

ACTIVE: 30 min **I** TOTAL: 40 min **I** SERVES: 4

1   3½-to-4-pound chicken, cut into 8 pieces
Kosher salt and freshly ground pepper
All-purpose flour, for dusting
2   tablespoons extra-virgin olive oil
1   pound shallots, halved
1   tablespoon tomato paste
1   tablespoon fresh thyme
½   cup apple cider vinegar
½   cup unfiltered apple cider
⅓   cup golden raisins
2   tablespoons cold unsalted butter, cut into cubes

1. Position a rack in the upper third of the oven and preheat to 450°.
2. Pat the chicken dry and season with salt and pepper. Dust the skin side with flour. Place a large ovenproof skillet over medium-high heat, add the olive oil and heat until shimmering. Add the chicken, skin-side down, and cook until the skin is golden, about 5 minutes. Turn the pieces and pour off the excess fat. Tuck the shallots under and around the chicken and cook until just golden, about 2 more minutes.
3. Push the chicken aside, then stir in the tomato paste and thyme and cook until the paste darkens, about 30 seconds. Add the vinegar, apple cider and raisins, bring to a boil and simmer 1 minute. Transfer the skillet to the oven and roast the chicken until just cooked through, 10 to 12 minutes.
4. Transfer the chicken, skin-side up, to a heatproof serving dish and return to the oven (turn the oven off). Bring the sauce left in the pan to a boil and reduce by half, 3 to 4 minutes. Lower the heat and whisk in the butter. Spoon the sauce over the chicken.

Per serving: Calories 722; Fat 38 g (Saturated 12 g); Cholesterol 181 mg; Sodium 203 mg; Carbohydrate 38 g; Fiber 2 g; Protein 55 g

Cold unsalted butter is the key to a great sauce. Just whisk it into the pan drippings.

Done in
25
minutes

CHICKEN WITH CREAMY MUSHROOMS AND SNAP PEAS

ACTIVE: 25 min **I** TOTAL: 25 min **I** SERVES: 4

4   chicken cutlets (about 1¼ pounds), patted dry
Kosher salt and freshly ground pepper
2   tablespoons vegetable oil
All-purpose flour, for dredging
1   tablespoon unsalted butter
2   scallions, thinly sliced
8   ounces mushrooms (button, cremini, shiitake or a
       combination), quartered
1¼ cups low-sodium chicken broth
¾   cup heavy cream
2   cups sugar snap peas, stemmed and halved lengthwise

1. Preheat the oven to 200°. Heat a large skillet over medium-high heat. Season the chicken with salt and pepper. Add 1 tablespoon oil to the skillet. Dredge 2 chicken cutlets in flour, shake off any excess and place in the skillet. Cook until golden, about 1½ minutes per side; transfer to a baking dish. Repeat with the remaining 1 tablespoon oil and the other 2 chicken cutlets. Cover the dish loosely with foil; place in the oven while you prepare the vegetables.
2. Add the butter to the hot skillet, then add the scallions and mushrooms; cook, stirring occasionally, until the mushrooms brown, about 4 minutes. Pour in the broth and bring to a boil, scraping up any browned bits with a wooden spoon. Cook until the liquid is reduced by half, about 3 minutes. Add the cream and boil until the sauce thickens slightly, 3 to 4 more minutes. Stir in the snap peas and heat through; season with salt and pepper. Serve the chicken topped with the creamy vegetables.

Per serving: Calories 445; Fat 29 g (Saturated 13 g); Cholesterol 152 mg; Sodium 140 mg; Carbohydrate 8 g; Fiber 2 g; Protein 38 g

You can substitute thawed frozen peas for the sugar snap peas.

CHICKEN SCHNITZEL WITH MUSTARD SAUCE

ACTIVE: 35 min **I** TOTAL: 35 min **I** SERVES: 4

½ cup plain low-fat Greek yogurt
¼ cup whole-grain mustard
5 slices white bread, torn
¾ teaspoon dried marjoram
Kosher salt and freshly ground pepper
½ cup all-purpose flour
½ teaspoon paprika
Pinch of freshly grated nutmeg
2 large eggs
4 chicken cutlets, about ⅛ inch thick (about 1½ pounds total)
Vegetable oil, for frying
Applesauce, for serving (optional)

1. Whisk the yogurt and mustard in a bowl until smooth; set aside.
2. Pulse the bread in a food processor until finely ground. Transfer to a shallow dish and add the marjoram, and salt and pepper to taste. In another shallow dish, season the flour with the paprika and nutmeg. Beat the eggs in a third dish. Season the chicken with salt and pepper.
3. Dredge each cutlet in the flour, shaking off the excess. Dip in the eggs and then in the breadcrumbs, pressing to coat both sides. Place on parchment paper until ready to fry.
4. Heat ⅛ inch of vegetable oil in a large skillet over medium-high heat until hot. Add 2 cutlets, swirling the skillet so the oil washes over them, and cook until golden brown, about 3 minutes per side. Transfer to a paper towel–lined plate and season with salt. Repeat with the remaining chicken, adjusting the heat as needed. Serve with the mustard sauce and applesauce, if desired.

Per serving: Calories 629; Fat 35 g (Saturated 5 g); Cholesterol 192 mg; Sodium 953 mg; Carbohydrate 34 g; Fiber 2 g; Protein 45 g

Try it with these sides...

Cauliflower Gratin
page 337

Buttered Egg Noodles
page 348

Roasted Red Onions
page 349

When you're breading, designate one hand for dry ingredients and the other for wet ones. Use your "dry" hand to dredge the chicken in the flour. Pick it up with your "wet" hand, swish it around in the egg and place it in the crumbs. Then remove the chicken from the crumbs with your "dry" hand.

Done in
25
minutes

INSIDE-OUT CHICKEN CORDON BLEU

ACTIVE: 20 min **I** TOTAL: 25 min **I** SERVES: 4

3   tablespoons fig jam
½   teaspoon chopped fresh thyme
Kosher salt and freshly ground pepper
4   6-ounce skinless, boneless chicken breasts
1   cup shredded gruyère cheese (about 3 ounces)
8   thin slices Black Forest ham
5   tablespoons extra-virgin olive oil
1   shallot, minced
½   teaspoon dijon mustard
2   tablespoons white wine vinegar
2   cups baby greens

1. Mix the jam, thyme, and salt and pepper to taste in a bowl. Lay out a long piece of plastic wrap on a cutting board. Place the chicken on the plastic and brush half of the jam mixture evenly on top of each breast. Mound a quarter of the cheese on each piece of chicken, then wrap 2 slices of ham around each breast to cover the cheese. Place another piece of plastic over the chicken and gently pound with a mallet or heavy skillet until about ¼ inch thick.
2. Heat 2 tablespoons olive oil in a medium nonstick skillet over medium-high heat. Add the chicken and cook until golden and crisp, 3 to 4 minutes. Turn and cook on the other side until cooked through but still moist, 3 to 4 more minutes.
3. Meanwhile, whisk the shallot, mustard, vinegar and the remaining jam mixture in a medium bowl. Slowly whisk in the remaining 3 tablespoons olive oil to make a smooth dressing.
4. Place each piece of chicken on a plate and drizzle with dressing. Toss the greens with the remaining dressing; serve with the chicken.

Per serving: Calories 500; Fat 26 g (Saturated 7 g); Cholesterol 124 mg; Sodium 486 mg; Carbohydrate 22 g; Fiber 1 g; Protein 46 g

Traditional chicken cordon bleu is made by layering ham and cheese between two thin chicken breasts, then breading and frying them. This inside-out version is much simpler!

BROILED LEMON-GARLIC CHICKEN

ACTIVE: 15 min **I** TOTAL: 40 min **I** SERVES: 4

2　lemons
2　tablespoons unsalted butter, at room temperature
2 to 3 cloves garlic, finely chopped
Kosher salt and freshly ground pepper
2　half chickens (3 to 3¼ pounds total)

1. Position an oven rack about 8 to 10 inches from the broiler and preheat. Grate the lemon zest and combine in a small bowl with the butter, garlic, ½ teaspoon salt, and pepper to taste. Mash with a fork to make a smooth paste.
2. With your fingers, gently loosen the skin on the chicken breasts, legs and thighs. Spread the flavored butter under the skin as evenly as possible. Halve the lemons and squeeze 2 halves over the chicken; season with salt and pepper.
3. Place the chicken skin-side up on a broiler pan (or a rack on a baking sheet). Position the halves about 2 inches apart, with the thick parts of the legs facing the center. Arrange the remaining 2 lemon halves cut-side down next to the chicken.
4. Broil the chicken until the skin is light brown and crisp, about 8 minutes. If the chicken browns too quickly, lower the oven rack. Flip the chicken and the lemons and continue to broil until almost cooked through (a thermometer inserted into the thickest part will register 160°), about 15 minutes. Remove the lemons, if browned; turn the chicken again and broil until the skin is brown and crisp and the thermometer registers 165°, about 2 more minutes. Serve the chicken with the broiled lemons for squeezing on top.

Per serving: Calories 453; Fat 29 g (Saturated 10 g); Cholesterol 149 mg; Sodium 491 mg; Carbohydrate 3 g; Fiber 1 g; Protein 42 g

Try it with these sides...

Parmesan Broccoli
page 337

Celery Root and Parsnip Puree page 351

Brussels Sprout Hash
page 352

5
ingredient
dinner

PEPPER-JACK CHICKEN WITH SUCCOTASH

ACTIVE: 30 min **I** TOTAL: 40 min **I** SERVES: 4

4   ounces pepper-jack cheese, shredded
4   cups baby arugula, roughly chopped
2   large skinless, boneless chicken breasts (12 ounces each)
1   tablespoon olive oil, plus more for brushing
Kosher salt
1½ to 2 tablespoons Cajun spice blend
1   cup frozen lima beans, thawed
1   medium yellow summer squash, diced
1   cup grape tomatoes, halved
Juice of 1 lime

1. Preheat the oven to 375°. Combine the cheese and 2 cups arugula in a bowl. Cut a deep 2-inch-wide pocket in the thickest part of each chicken breast with a paring knife. Stuff with the arugula mixture. Brush with olive oil and season with salt and the Cajun spice blend.
2. Heat a large cast-iron skillet over high heat until hot, about 5 minutes. Cook the chicken until blackened on the bottom, 3 to 4 minutes. Turn and cook until blackened on the other side, about 2 more minutes. Transfer the skillet to the oven and cook until a thermometer inserted into the thickest part registers 155°, 10 to 15 minutes. Transfer the chicken to a cutting board.
3. Wipe out the skillet and add 1 tablespoon olive oil. Add the lima beans and squash, season with salt and cook until the squash is just tender, 2 to 3 minutes. Add the tomatoes and cook 2 more minutes. Remove from the heat and stir in the remaining 2 cups arugula and the lime juice. Slice the chicken and serve with the succotash.

Per serving: Calories 398; Fat 16 g (Saturated 6 g); Cholesterol 120 mg; Sodium 1,249 mg; Carbohydrate 16 g; Fiber 5 g; Protein 46 g

You can make this dish on the grill, too: Just grill for 8 to 10 minutes per side.

TERIYAKI HENS WITH BOK CHOY

ACTIVE: 30 min **I** TOTAL: 40 min **I** SERVES: 4

2	Cornish game hens (about 1½ pounds each), cut in half with kitchen shears
	Kosher salt and freshly ground pepper
¾	cup low-sodium soy sauce
¼	cup hoisin sauce
¼	cup rice vinegar
1	2-inch piece ginger, peeled and sliced
2	small red chile peppers, halved (remove seeds for less heat)
1	bunch scallions
1	grapefruit, halved
1	medium head bok choy, thinly sliced
1	tablespoon toasted sesame oil
2	teaspoons sesame seeds, toasted

1. Preheat the oven to 425°. Season the hens with salt and pepper and place skin-side up in a roasting pan. Roast until the skin is slightly crisp, about 25 minutes.

2. Meanwhile, combine the soy sauce, hoisin sauce, vinegar, ginger, 1 chile pepper and ¼ cup water in a pot. Cut half of the scallions into large pieces, and zest and juice half of the grapefruit; add to the pot. Simmer, stirring occasionally, until thick and syrupy, about 20 minutes. Brush the hens with a few tablespoons of the sauce and continue roasting until golden, about 8 more minutes.

3. Peel and segment the remaining grapefruit half and place in a bowl. Thinly slice the remaining scallions and mince the remaining chile pepper; add to the bowl along with the bok choy, sesame oil, and salt and pepper to taste. Place half a hen on each plate. Stir any pan drippings into the remaining sauce and drizzle over the top. Serve with the bok choy salad and sprinkle with the sesame seeds.

Per serving: Calories 514; Fat 28 g (Saturated 7 g); Cholesterol 168 mg; Sodium 2,662 mg; Carbohydrate 32 g; Fiber 4 g; Protein 36 g

> Cornish game hens look fancy, but they're just small chickens, and you can get them at most grocery stores. We cut them in half so they cooked in less than 40 minutes.

OVEN-FRIED CHICKEN

ACTIVE: 15 min **I** TOTAL: 40 min **I** SERVES: 4

Cooking spray
1⅓ cups crispy rice cereal
2¼ cups bagel chips or Melba toasts
5   teaspoons extra-virgin olive oil
¾   teaspoon hot paprika
Kosher salt and freshly ground pepper
1½ cups low-fat plain Greek yogurt
1   teaspoon dijon mustard
4   skinless, bone-in chicken thighs or halved bone-in breasts
     (about 6 ounces each)
2   bunches scallions
Harissa, chili sauce or ketchup, for the sauce

1. Preheat the oven to 475°. Set a rack on a foil-lined baking sheet and generously coat the rack with cooking spray.
2. Finely grind the cereal and bagel chips in a food processor and transfer to a large resealable plastic bag. Add 3 teaspoons olive oil, the paprika, 2 teaspoons salt, and pepper to taste and toss.
3. Whisk ½ cup yogurt and the mustard in a shallow bowl. Add the chicken and turn to coat, then transfer to the bag; seal and shake to coat. Place the chicken on the rack and mist with cooking spray.
4. Toss the scallions with the remaining 2 teaspoons olive oil and place alongside the chicken. Bake until the chicken is crisp and a thermometer inserted into the thickest part registers 160°, about 30 minutes.
5. Make the dipping sauce: Mix the remaining 1 cup yogurt and harissa to taste in a bowl. Serve the chicken and scallions with the sauce.

Per serving: Calories 369; Fat 13 g (Saturated 3 g); Cholesterol 86 mg; Sodium 1,274 mg; Carbohydrate 33 g; Fiber 3 g; Protein 30 g

> Harissa is a hot red pepper sauce used in African cooking. Look for it with the international foods or condiments.

GARLIC-ROASTED CHICKEN

ACTIVE: 15 min **I** TOTAL: 30 min **I** SERVES: 4

2   tablespoons extra-virgin olive oil
4   skin-on, boneless chicken breasts (about 1½ pounds)
Kosher salt and freshly ground pepper
2   heads garlic
4   sprigs rosemary
4   slices sourdough bread, grilled or toasted
2   tablespoons white wine vinegar

1. Preheat the oven to 425˚. Heat the olive oil in a large ovenproof skillet over medium-high heat. Season the chicken with salt and pepper and cook, skin-side down, until browned, about 5 minutes.
2. Separate the heads of garlic into cloves but do not peel. Flip the chicken, add the garlic and rosemary to the skillet and transfer to the oven. Roast until the chicken is cooked through but still moist, 15 to 20 more minutes.
3. Place the bread on a platter and top each slice with a chicken breast. Add the vinegar to the skillet and scrape up any browned bits with a wooden spoon. Add 3 tablespoons water and simmer until the sauce thickens slightly, about 2 minutes. Pour the sauce and garlic over the chicken and bread.

Per serving: Calories 404; Fat 23 g (Saturated 6 g); Cholesterol 109 mg; Sodium 234 mg; Carbohydrate 10 g; Fiber 2 g; Protein 37 g

Try it with these sides...

Garlic-Sesame Spinach
page 334

Roasted Beet Salad
page 345

Green Bean and Celery Salad page 351

Squeeze the roasted garlic out of its skin and spread it on crusty bread.

Done in
20
minutes

SPRING CHICKEN SALAD

ACTIVE: 20 min **I** TOTAL: 20 min **I** SERVES: 4

½   pound small red-skinned potatoes, halved
Kosher salt
2   tablespoons chopped fresh chives
2   tablespoons chopped fresh tarragon
2   tablespoons white wine vinegar
¼   cup low-fat plain Greek yogurt
Freshly ground pepper
¼   cup extra-virgin olive oil
4   romaine hearts, torn
1   rotisserie chicken, skin removed and meat shredded (about 2 cups)
1   Kirby cucumber, peeled, halved lengthwise, seeded and sliced
4   radishes, cut into wedges
1   yellow bell pepper, thinly sliced

1. Place the potatoes in a small pot and cover with water. Season with salt, cover and boil until fork-tender, about 6 minutes. Drain and cool.
2. Meanwhile, pulse the chives, tarragon, vinegar, yogurt, ½ teaspoon salt, and pepper to taste in a food processor. Slowly drizzle in the olive oil and pulse to make a thick dressing.
3. Toss the romaine, potatoes, chicken, cucumber, radishes and bell pepper with the dressing in a large bowl. Season with salt and pepper.

Per serving: Calories 393; Fat 22 g (Saturated 4 g); Cholesterol 101 mg; Sodium 836 mg; Carbohydrate 19 g; Fiber 3 g; Protein 31 g

Use the leftover chives in...

Grilled Steak with Black-Eyed Peas page 209

Shrimp Scampi with Garlic Toasts page 261

BLT Pasta Salad page 281

THAI CHICKEN WITH CARROT-GINGER SALAD

ACTIVE: 25 min   TOTAL: 40 min   SERVES: 4

2   tablespoons unsalted butter, softened
3   garlic cloves; 2 chopped, 1 crushed
4   teaspoons Thai green curry paste (available in the international aisle)
4   teaspoons finely chopped peeled ginger
Grated zest and juice of 3 limes
4   skin-on, bone-in chicken breasts (2 to 2½ pounds)
Kosher salt
1   tablespoon vegetable oil
1   pound carrots
2   tablespoons chopped fresh cilantro

1. Preheat the oven to 450°. Place a rack in a roasting pan. Mix the butter, chopped garlic, curry paste, 3 teaspoons ginger, the zest of 2 limes and the juice of 1 lime in a bowl.

2. Season the chicken with salt. Loosen the skin and rub the curry butter underneath. Place skin-side up on the rack and pour about ½ cup water into the pan. Roast until the chicken is cooked through and the skin is crisp, 20 to 25 minutes.

3. Meanwhile, mix the crushed garlic with the remaining 1 teaspoon ginger, the zest of 1 lime and the juice of 2 limes. Whisk in the vegetable oil. Shave the carrots into ribbons with a vegetable peeler and toss with the dressing. Add the cilantro and ½ teaspoon salt and toss. Serve the chicken with the carrot-ginger salad.

Per serving: Calories 407; Fat 20 g (Saturated 7 g); Cholesterol 126 mg; Sodium 235 mg; Carbohydrate 16 g; Fiber 4 g; Protein 41 g

> You don't need any fancy tools to make this carrot salad—just a vegetable peeler.

Done in
15
minutes

CHICKEN WITH SUN-DRIED TOMATO, EGGPLANT AND BASIL

ACTIVE: 15 min **I** TOTAL: 15 min **I** SERVES: 4

4 tablespoons extra-virgin olive oil
1 baby eggplant, halved
Kosher salt
1 tablespoon pine nuts
4 thin chicken cutlets (about 1 pound total)
Freshly ground pepper
All-purpose flour, for dredging
3 cloves garlic, sliced
¼ cup sun-dried tomatoes packed in oil, drained, rinsed and chopped
¼ cup fresh basil leaves, torn
½ cup low-sodium chicken broth
¼ cup ricotta cheese
Rustic bread, for serving

1. Drizzle 1 tablespoon olive oil over the eggplant in a microwave-safe bowl and sprinkle with salt. Cover with a microwave-safe plate; microwave 5 minutes.
2. Meanwhile, toast the pine nuts in a skillet over high heat, about 1 minute; transfer to a bowl and add the remaining 3 tablespoons olive oil to the skillet. Season the chicken cutlets with salt and pepper and dredge in the flour, shaking off the excess. Add to the skillet and cook until brown on one side, 2 to 3 minutes. Flip the chicken, add the garlic and cook 2 more minutes. Remove the eggplant from the microwave, cool slightly and slice into chunks. Reduce the skillet heat to medium-low; add the sun-dried tomatoes, eggplant, basil, nuts and chicken broth to the skillet and bring to a simmer.
3. Transfer the chicken to plates; top each with ricotta and the eggplant mixture. Serve with the bread.

Per serving: Calories 336; Fat 20 g (Saturated 4 g); Cholesterol 77 mg; Sodium 122 mg; Carbohydrate 8 g; Fiber 2 g; Protein 30 g

Use the leftover pine nuts in...

Pasta with Escarole
page 310

Roasted Asparagus
page 341

Carrots with Chickpeas and Pine Nuts page 352

BEER-BRAISED CHICKEN

ACTIVE: 25 min I TOTAL: 40 min I SERVES: 4

¼	pound slab or thick-cut bacon, cut into ½-inch pieces
8	skinless, boneless chicken thighs (about 2½ pounds)

Kosher salt and freshly ground pepper
All-purpose flour, for dredging

1	tablespoon extra-virgin olive oil
1	12-ounce bottle beer (preferably brown ale)
1	cup frozen pearl onions, thawed
½	pound small red-skinned new potatoes, halved
2	tablespoons whole-grain mustard
2	tablespoons packed dark brown sugar
4	sprigs thyme
3	tablespoons chopped fresh parsley

1. Heat a large pot over medium-high heat. Add the bacon and cook until browned, about 5 minutes. Remove with a slotted spoon and transfer to a paper towel–lined plate.
2. Season the chicken with salt and pepper and dredge in flour, shaking off the excess. Add the olive oil to the drippings in the pot. Add the chicken in batches and cook over medium-high heat until golden on the bottom, 6 to 7 minutes, then flip and sear the other side, about 1 minute.
3. Add the beer, onions, potatoes, mustard, sugar, thyme and 1 cup water to the pot and stir, making sure the chicken is fully submerged. Simmer until the chicken is cooked through, about 15 minutes. Discard the thyme and stir in the bacon and parsley.

Per serving: Calories 543; Fat 28 g (Saturated 8 g); Cholesterol 118 mg; Sodium 450 mg; Carbohydrate 33 g; Fiber 2 g; Protein 34 g

Many chefs prefer thick slabs of bacon over thin slices. The quality of slab bacon is often better, and it's easier to dice. Plus, you can buy just as much as you need.

Low-calorie dinner

SAUSAGE-AND-PEPPER SKEWERS

ACTIVE: 30 min **I** TOTAL: 40 min **I** SERVES: 4

1   cup couscous
2   bell peppers (red and yellow), cut into chunks
1   12-ounce package chicken sausage (preferably garlic-flavored), cut into 1-inch pieces
1   large red onion, cut into chunks
1   cup cherry tomatoes
3   tablespoons extra-virgin olive oil
Kosher salt and freshly ground pepper
¼   cup fresh parsley
¼   cup fresh cilantro
4   scallions, roughly chopped
1   tablespoon white wine vinegar

1. Soak eight 8-inch wooden skewers in water at least 15 minutes. Preheat a grill or grill pan to medium high. Prepare the couscous as the label directs.
2. Meanwhile, toss the bell peppers, sausage, onion and tomatoes in a bowl with 1 tablespoon olive oil; season with salt and pepper. Thread onto the skewers, alternating the sausage and vegetables. Grill, turning, until the vegetables are slightly softened and the sausage begins to brown, 6 to 7 minutes.
3. Meanwhile, puree the parsley, cilantro and scallions in a blender with the remaining 2 tablespoons olive oil, the vinegar and 2 tablespoons water. Season with salt and pepper. Brush the skewers with some of the pesto and continue to cook, turning, until the tomatoes are tender and the sausage is charred, 6 to 7 more minutes.
4. Toss the couscous with half of the remaining pesto and season with salt and pepper. Serve with the skewers and the remaining pesto, for dipping.

Per serving: Calories 396; Fat 13 g (Saturated 2 g); Cholesterol 56 mg; Sodium 356 mg; Carbohydrate 45 g; Fiber 5 g; Protein 24 g

> Soak wooden skewers in water before you use them on a grill to keep them from scorching.

GLAZED HENS WITH CUCUMBER-CANTALOUPE SALAD

ACTIVE: 25 min ▐ TOTAL: 40 min ▐ SERVES: 4

2   Cornish game hens (about 1½ pounds each)
Kosher salt and freshly ground pepper
2 to 3 teaspoons Asian chili sauce (such as sambal oelek)
3   tablespoons fresh lime juice
3   tablespoons packed dark brown sugar
3   tablespoons extra-virgin olive oil
½   small cantaloupe
1   shallot
1   English cucumber

1. Preheat the oven to 500°. Season the hens all over with salt and pepper, place on a rack in a roasting pan and roast 15 minutes.
2. Meanwhile, whisk the chili sauce, lime juice, brown sugar, olive oil and 2 teaspoons salt in a measuring cup to dissolve the sugar. Set half of the mixture aside in a bowl for the salad. Baste the hens with some of the remaining dressing, then rotate the pan and continue to cook until the hens are golden and a thermometer inserted into the thickest part of the thigh registers 160°, about 20 more minutes.
3. Meanwhile, peel and thinly slice the cantaloupe and shallot. Peel the cucumber, then halve lengthwise, seed and thinly slice. Toss the cantaloupe, shallot and cucumber with the reserved dressing.
4. Divide the salad among plates. Use kitchen shears to cut each hen in half and place one half on each plate. Drizzle the pan juices over the hens and salad.

Per serving: Calories 508; Fat 34 g (Saturated 8 g); Cholesterol 168 mg; Sodium 159 mg; Carbohydrate 20 g; Fiber 1 g; Protein 30 g

To save time, buy 2 cups peeled and chopped cantaloupe for the salad.

Low-
calorie
dinner

CHICKEN TANDOORI

ACTIVE: 20 min I TOTAL: 40 min I SERVES: 4

8   skinless, boneless chicken thighs (about 2½ pounds)
Juice of 1 lemon
Kosher salt
½   cup plus 2 tablespoons plain yogurt
1   tablespoon vegetable oil
½   small red onion, roughly chopped
3   cloves garlic, smashed
1   2-inch piece ginger, peeled and roughly chopped
4   teaspoons tomato paste
2   teaspoons ground coriander
1½   teaspoons ground cumin
1¾   teaspoons hot paprika
2   tablespoons chopped fresh cilantro
Cooked rice, for serving (optional)

1. Preheat the broiler. Make shallow cuts in the chicken thighs with a
sharp knife. Toss the chicken with the lemon juice and 1½ teaspoons salt
in a large bowl.
2. Pulse 2 tablespoons yogurt, the vegetable oil, onion, garlic, ginger,
tomato paste, coriander, cumin, 1½ teaspoons paprika and ½ teaspoon salt
in a food processor to make a paste. Toss the chicken in the mixture and let
marinate 15 minutes.
3. Place the chicken on a foil-lined broiler pan. Broil, turning once, until
slightly charred and a thermometer inserted into the center registers 165°,
5 to 6 minutes per side.
4. Meanwhile, combine the remaining ½ cup yogurt and ¼ teaspoon paprika,
the cilantro and a pinch of salt in a bowl. Top the chicken with the yogurt sauce
and serve with rice, if desired.

Per serving (without rice): Calories 237; Fat 9 g (Saturated 2 g); Cholesterol 115 mg;
Sodium 1,266 mg; Carbohydrate 8 g; Fiber 2 g; Protein 30 g

> We made shallow cuts in
> the chicken so the marinade
> would reach the inside.

SKILLET ROSEMARY CHICKEN

ACTIVE: 20 min **I** TOTAL: 40 min **I** SERVES: 4

¾ pound small red-skinned potatoes, halved, or quartered if large
Kosher salt
2 sprigs rosemary, plus 1 tablespoon leaves
1 clove garlic, smashed
Pinch of red pepper flakes
Juice of 2 lemons (squeezed halves reserved)
2 tablespoons extra-virgin olive oil
4 skin-on, bone-in chicken breasts (6 to 8 ounces each)
10 ounces cremini mushrooms, halved

1. Preheat the oven to 450°. Cover the potatoes with cold water in a saucepan and salt the water. Bring to a boil over medium-high heat and cook until tender, about 8 minutes; drain and set aside.
2. Pile the rosemary leaves, garlic, 2 teaspoons salt and the red pepper flakes on a cutting board, then mince and mash into a paste using a large knife. Transfer the paste to a bowl. Stir in the juice of 1 lemon and the olive oil. Add the chicken and turn to coat.
3. Heat a large cast-iron skillet over medium-high heat. Add the chicken, skin-side down, cover and cook until the skin browns, about 5 minutes. Turn the chicken; add the mushrooms and potatoes to the skillet and drizzle with the juice of the remaining lemon. Add the rosemary sprigs and the squeezed lemon halves to the skillet; transfer to the oven and roast, uncovered, until the chicken is cooked through and the skin is crisp, 20 to 25 minutes.

Per serving: Calories 413; Fat 23 g (Saturated 5 g); Cholesterol 87 mg; Sodium 1,055 mg; Carbohydrate 19 g; Fiber 2 g; Protein 32 g

Mash your garlic into a paste as we did in this recipe to distribute it evenly. No one likes biting down on a chunk of raw garlic!

Done in
30
minutes

GRILLED CHICKEN CAESAR SALAD

ACTIVE: 30 min I TOTAL: 30 min I SERVES: 4

3   cloves garlic
½   cup extra-virgin olive oil, plus more for brushing
2 to 4 anchovy fillets, chopped
Juice of 1 lemon
Kosher salt and freshly ground pepper
1   pound skin-on, boneless chicken breasts
4   ½-inch-thick slices focaccia or whole-wheat Italian bread
4   romaine lettuce hearts, halved lengthwise
¾   cup freshly grated parmesan cheese, plus more for sprinkling

1. Preheat a grill or grill pan to medium-high. Make the Caesar dressing: Chop 2 garlic cloves and puree with ½ cup olive oil, the anchovies and lemon juice in a blender until smooth; season with salt and pepper.
2. Pound the chicken with a mallet or heavy skillet until about ⅛ inch thick. Season with salt and pepper and toss with 1 tablespoon of the dressing. Grill the chicken until golden and crisp, 3 to 4 minutes per side.
3. Brush the bread with olive oil on both sides and grill, turning, until toasted, about 2 minutes. Rub with the remaining garlic clove. Brush the romaine with 1 to 2 tablespoons of the dressing and grill until marked, 1 to 2 minutes per side. Chop the lettuce and transfer to a bowl.
4. Cut the bread and chicken into bite-size pieces and add to the bowl. Toss with the remaining dressing, the parmesan, and pepper to taste. Sprinkle with more parmesan.

Per serving: Calories 610; Fat 44 g (Saturated 9 g); Cholesterol 85 mg; Sodium 565 mg; Carbohydrate 18 g; Fiber 5 g; Protein 36 g

> Grill something unexpected—like lettuce! Grilling makes the greens heartier and brings another dimension of flavor to the salad.

SMOKED TURKEY AND BLACK-EYED PEA SALAD

ACTIVE: 30 min | TOTAL: 30 min | SERVES: 4

2	cloves garlic, minced
4	sprigs thyme
4	tablespoons extra-virgin olive oil
1	10-ounce box frozen black-eyed peas, thawed
⅓	cup sliced bread-and-butter pickles, plus 4 tablespoons pickling liquid from the jar
8	ounces smoked turkey leg or breast, skin removed and meat shredded
4	scallions, thinly sliced

Kosher salt

Cayenne pepper

1	tablespoon Creole or whole-grain mustard
1	cup grape tomatoes, halved
10	cups torn arugula, escarole and/or romaine
2	stalks celery, chopped (with leaves)

1. Combine the garlic, thyme and 1 tablespoon olive oil in a nonstick skillet over medium heat and cook until fragrant, about 2 minutes. Add the black-eyed peas and 2 tablespoons pickling liquid and cook until tender, about 10 minutes. Add the turkey and heat through, about 3 more minutes. Remove from the heat and add the scallions, and salt and cayenne to taste. Discard the thyme.
2. Meanwhile, whisk the mustard and the remaining 2 tablespoons pickling liquid in a large bowl. Add salt and cayenne to taste, then gradually whisk in the remaining 3 tablespoons olive oil. Add the tomatoes and toss. Add the arugula, celery and pickles and toss again. Divide among bowls and top with the black-eyed peas and turkey.

Per serving: Calories 318; Fat 18 g (Saturated 3 g); Cholesterol 43 mg; Sodium 1,047 mg; Carbohydrate 18 g; Fiber 5 g; Protein 23 g

> Don't pour out the pickle juice: A few spoonfuls taste great in place of vinegar in this salad dressing.

Low-calorie dinner

SKILLET TURKEY WITH ROASTED VEGETABLES

ACTIVE: 20 min **I** TOTAL: 40 min **I** SERVES: 4

1	skin-on boneless turkey breast (1½ to 1¾ pounds)
3	tablespoons extra-virgin olive oil
¾	teaspoon dried marjoram
2	cloves garlic, finely chopped

Kosher salt and freshly ground pepper

2	bunches spring onions or small regular onions, trimmed and halved
4	stalks celery, cut into 3-inch pieces
2	bunches small carrots, trimmed
1	10-to-12-ounce package mixed mushrooms, stemmed
2	tablespoons chopped fresh parsley

1. Preheat the oven to 475°. Heat a large cast-iron skillet over high heat. Rub the turkey skin with 1 tablespoon olive oil; rub over and under the skin with the marjoram, garlic, salt and pepper.

2. Sear the turkey, skin-side down, without moving, until golden, 4 to 5 minutes. Flip the turkey, then add the onions, cut-side down, and cook until slightly browned, 4 to 5 more minutes. Scatter the celery and carrots over the onions, drizzle with 1 tablespoon olive oil and season with salt and pepper. Add the mushrooms, drizzle with the remaining 1 tablespoon oil and season with salt and pepper.

3. Transfer the skillet to the oven and roast until a thermometer inserted into the thickest part of the turkey registers 160° and the vegetables are tender, 20 to 25 minutes. Let the turkey rest 5 minutes before slicing. Serve with the vegetables and sprinkle with the parsley.

Per serving: Calories 371; Fat 15 g (Saturated 3 g); Cholesterol 119 mg; Sodium 671 mg; Carbohydrate 14 g; Fiber 4 g; Protein 44 g

> Try spring onions and fresh baby carrots in this recipe when they're in season.

Mix & Match

STUFFED CHICKEN

Spinach–Goat Cheese Stuffed Chicken with Herbed Mayonnaise

MAKE A FILLING

SPINACH-GOAT CHEESE
Mix ½ cup softened goat cheese, 2 cups chopped fresh spinach and 1 minced garlic clove; season with salt and pepper.

MANCHEGO-CHORIZO
Mix ¾ cup shredded manchego, ½ cup diced dried chorizo and ¼ cup chopped scallions.

FETA-OLIVE
Mix ¾ cup crumbled feta, ⅓ cup chopped kalamata olives and ¼ cup chopped parsley.

TOMATO-MOZZARELLA
Mix ¾ cup shredded mozzarella, ½ cup diced tomatoes and ¼ cup chopped fresh basil.

ARTICHOKE-HERB
Mix 1 cup chopped canned artichoke hearts, ¼ cup chopped mixed fresh herbs, the juice of ½ lemon and 1 chopped garlic clove.

STUFF THE CHICKEN

Preheat the oven to 375°. Insert a paring knife into the thickest part of four 6-to-8-ounce skinless, boneless chicken breasts to make a 3-inch-deep pocket. Stuff the filling into the pockets. Brush the chicken with olive oil, season with salt and rub with Italian or Mediterranean seasoning (or a mix of dried oregano, basil, rosemary and thyme).

COOK THE CHICKEN

Heat a large nonstick ovenproof skillet over high heat, about 5 minutes. Add the chicken and cook until golden on the bottom, 3 to 4 minutes, then flip and cook 2 more minutes. Transfer to the oven and cook until a thermometer inserted into the thickest part of a breast registers 155°, about 12 minutes. Let rest 15 minutes.

MAKE A SAUCE

Prepare a sauce while the chicken rests, then serve alongside.

CHIMICHURRI
Pulse 2 cloves garlic, 1 shallot, 1 cup fresh parsley, 2 tablespoons fresh oregano, ½ teaspoon red pepper flakes and salt to taste in a food processor. Blend in ½ cup olive oil, ¼ cup red wine vinegar and a few tablespoons water.

MUSTARD-TARRAGON
Mix ½ cup sour cream, ¼ cup whole-grain mustard and 2 tablespoons chopped fresh tarragon.

TOMATO-BASIL
Grate 2 tomatoes; toss with 1 grated garlic clove, 3 tablespoons olive oil and ½ cup chopped fresh basil. Season with salt and pepper.

HERBED MAYONNAISE
Puree 1 cup mixed fresh herbs (such as chives, tarragon, basil and/ or parsley) with ¼ cup mayonnaise, the juice of ½ lemon, and salt and pepper to taste in a food processor.

The Neelys say...

" Probably the biggest misconception people have is that we don't cook because of all that cooking on TV. But we cook at home all the time. We made two dinners one night recently, because my girls couldn't decide what they wanted! We refrigerated one and ate the other." —PAT NEELY

" I have always felt that the kitchen was the main focus of the house. If you notice when entertaining, everyone migrates to the kitchen because food and the aromas have a way of opening the soul and allowing conversations to just flow. Even to this day when I have serious talks with Pat or the girls, we have them in the kitchen. We call the kitchen 'the neutral zone.'" —GINA NEELY

THE NEELYS ARE THE HOSTS OF *DOWN HOME WITH THE NEELYS* AND THE AUTHORS OF *DOWN HOME WITH THE NEELYS: A SOUTHERN FAMILY COOKBOOK.*

KITCHEN SECRET
Gina collects pigs in every imaginable form (she has a whole room in the house for them!), but producers will only allow her to keep a few of them out in the kitchen when she's shooting *Down Home with the Neelys*. "My pigs are there to remind everyone who's the boss," she says.

Meat

Steak with
Blue Cheese Butter
and Celery Salad,
page 214

Low-
calorie
dinner

SKILLET PORK AND PEPPERS

ACTIVE: 25 min **I** TOTAL: 30 min **I** SERVES: 4

1   large pork tenderloin (about 1½ pounds), trimmed
Kosher salt
3   tablespoons extra-virgin olive oil
1   small onion, thickly sliced
2   red and/or yellow bell peppers, sliced into wide strips
6   cloves garlic, smashed
16   fresh sage leaves
2   tablespoons tomato paste
¼   cup sliced pickled peperoncini, plus 2 teaspoons pickling liquid
     from the jar
⅓   cup dry white wine
⅔   cup low-sodium chicken broth
¼   cup grated parmesan cheese

1. Preheat the broiler. Slice the pork on an angle into 1-inch-thick pieces;
season with salt. Heat a large ovenproof skillet over medium-high heat;
add 1 tablespoon olive oil. Add the onion and bell peppers; season with
½ teaspoon salt and cook until the vegetables are crisp-tender and slightly
browned, 4 to 6 minutes. Transfer to a plate.
2. Add the remaining 2 tablespoons oil to the skillet. Add the pork and sear
over high heat until browned, 2 to 4 minutes per side. Transfer the pork to
the plate with the onion and peppers.
3. Reduce the heat to medium and add the garlic, sage and tomato paste to the
skillet. Cook, stirring, until the tomato paste turns brick-red, about 1 minute.
Add the peperoncini slices and their liquid, then pour in the wine and bring to a
boil. Add the broth and return to a simmer. Arrange the pork in a single layer in
the skillet; add the onion and peppers and sprinkle with cheese. Transfer to the
oven and broil until the pork is cooked through, 4 to 7 minutes.

Per serving: Calories 380; Fat 18 g (Saturated 4 g); Cholesterol 115 mg;
Sodium 586 mg; Carbohydrate 10 g; Fiber 2 g; Protein 40 g

> Pork tenderloin is just
> as lean as skinless,
> boneless chicken breast.

MOJO PORK CHOPS WITH PLANTAINS

ACTIVE: 30 min | TOTAL: 40 min | SERVES: 4

1	orange
1	grapefruit
½	cup extra-virgin olive oil, plus more for drizzling
3	tablespoons white wine vinegar
2	tablespoons chopped fresh oregano
2	teaspoons cumin seeds, crushed

Kosher salt and freshly ground pepper

2	pounds thin bone-in pork chops
1	clove garlic, chopped
½	cup chopped fresh parsley
3	ripe plantains (or 1 pound potatoes), peeled and quartered

1. Cut a 2-inch strip of zest from both the orange and grapefruit; place in a glass bowl. Squeeze 3 tablespoons juice from each fruit into the bowl (set the fruit aside). Whisk in 3 tablespoons olive oil, 2 tablespoons vinegar, 1 tablespoon oregano, the cumin seeds, and salt and pepper to taste. Poke the pork chops with a fork, then add them to the marinade, turning to coat. Set aside for 20 minutes.

2. Meanwhile, make the mojo sauce: Squeeze 1 tablespoon each orange and grapefruit juice into another bowl; whisk in the remaining 1 tablespoon vinegar, 5 tablespoons olive oil, 1 tablespoon oregano, garlic and parsley. Season with ½ teaspoon salt, and pepper to taste.

3. Boil the plantains in a saucepan of salted water, covered, until tender, about 15 minutes. Drain, reserving about ½ cup cooking liquid. Smash the plantains with a potato masher, drizzling with olive oil and some of the cooking liquid. Season with salt and pepper; keep warm.

4. Heat 2 medium skillets over medium-high heat. Remove the pork from the marinade; pat dry. Brush the chops lightly with some of the mojo sauce; sear until golden and slightly crisp on one side, about 5 minutes. Turn and cook about 3 more minutes. Divide the pork and plantains among plates and drizzle with more mojo sauce.

Per serving: Calories 619; Fat 39 g (Saturated 9 g); Cholesterol 81 mg; Sodium 87 mg; Carbohydrate 44 g; Fiber 3 g; Protein 27 g

> When you're buying plantains for this recipe, look for ones that are already ripe; they're a brownish-yellow color.

Done in
20
minutes

GRILLED PORK WITH ARUGULA AND GRAPE SALAD

ACTIVE: 15 min **I** TOTAL: 20 min **I** SERVES: 4

1	medium shallot, finely chopped
2	tablespoons balsamic vinegar
2	teaspoons chopped fresh thyme
	Kosher salt and freshly ground pepper
¼	cup extra-virgin olive oil
4	5-ounce boneless pork chops
¾	cup red seedless grapes, halved
4	heaping cups baby arugula
½	cup crumbled gorgonzola or other blue cheese

1. Combine the shallot, vinegar, 1 teaspoon thyme, 1 teaspoon salt and ¼ teaspoon pepper in a medium bowl. Gradually whisk in the oil, starting with a few drops and adding the rest in a steady stream.

2. Put the pork chops in a shallow dish and season all over with salt. Add the remaining 1 teaspoon thyme and 3 tablespoons of the dressing. Coat the pork and set aside to marinate for 5 minutes.

3. Heat a grill pan over medium-high heat. Grill the pork until cooked through but still moist, 4 to 5 minutes per side.

4. Add the grapes and arugula to the remaining dressing and toss to coat. Transfer the pork chops to a serving platter or individual plates; top with the salad and sprinkle with the gorgonzola.

Per serving: Calories 414; Fat 31 g (Saturated 10 g); Cholesterol 88 mg; Sodium 751 mg; Carbohydrate 7 g; Fiber 1 g; Protein 27 g

Use the leftover thyme in...

Drumsticks with Biscuits and Tomato Jam
page 98

Striped Bass with Mushrooms
page 235

Fontina Risotto with Chicken
page 274

PORK TENDERLOIN WITH EGGPLANT RELISH

ACTIVE: 35 min | TOTAL: 35 min | SERVES: 4

3   mild frying peppers, such as Hungarian or banana, halved and seeded
1   small jalapeño pepper, halved (remove seeds for less heat)
2   medium Japanese eggplants (about 14 ounces total)
1   bunch scallions
6   cloves garlic, unpeeled
2   pork tenderloins (about 1½ pounds total), trimmed and cut into 4 pieces
1   teaspoon ground cumin
Kosher salt and freshly ground pepper
1   tablespoon extra-virgin olive oil
2   tablespoons fresh lemon juice
½   teaspoon paprika, plus more for sprinkling
2   tablespoons chopped fresh parsley

1. Preheat the broiler and line a broiler pan with foil. Broil the frying peppers, jalapeño, eggplants, scallions and garlic on the foil until charred, about 3 minutes per side. Cover with a damp towel to cool, then peel the peppers and eggplants. Squeeze the garlic from its skin. Roughly chop the vegetables and garlic and toss in a bowl.
2. Season the pork with the cumin and salt and pepper. Heat the olive oil in a skillet over medium-high heat. Add the pork; cook, turning, until golden, about 6 minutes. Reduce the heat to medium and cook, turning, until a thermometer inserted into the center registers 150°, about 8 more minutes. Set the pork aside.
3. Add the lemon juice to the skillet, then add the eggplant mixture and paprika; warm through. Season with salt and pepper and add the parsley. Slice the pork; serve with the eggplant relish and sprinkle with paprika.

Per serving: Calories 297; Fat 10 g (Saturated 3 g); Cholesterol 95 mg; Sodium 317 mg; Carbohydrate 16 g; Fiber 6 g; Protein 37 g

Japanese eggplant is more slender than regular eggplant, so it gets soft after just a few minutes of broiling.

Low-calorie dinner

MOO SHU PORK

ACTIVE: 30 min **|** TOTAL: 40 min **|** SERVES: 4

3   tablespoons hoisin sauce, plus more for serving
3   tablespoons rice vinegar
2   cloves garlic, minced
Kosher salt and freshly ground pepper
1   ¾-pound pork tenderloin, trimmed and cut into thin strips
2   tablespoons vegetable oil
8   ounces shiitake mushrooms, stemmed and sliced
1   14-ounce bag coleslaw mix
1   bunch scallions, thinly sliced
12 Bibb lettuce leaves

1. Whisk the hoisin sauce, vinegar, garlic and ½ teaspoon each salt and pepper in a large bowl. Add the pork and marinate 10 minutes.
2. Heat 1 tablespoon vegetable oil in a large skillet over high heat. Remove the pork from the marinade using tongs (reserve the marinade), add to the skillet and stir-fry until browned, about 4 minutes. Transfer the pork to a plate. Add 3 to 4 tablespoons water to the skillet, then pour the pan juices over the pork on the plate.
3. Add the remaining 1 tablespoon vegetable oil to the skillet; when hot, add the mushrooms and stir-fry until slightly golden, about 2 minutes. Add the coleslaw mix and cook until wilted, about 3 minutes. Add the pork, the reserved marinade and half of the scallions; stir-fry 2 more minutes. Season with salt and sprinkle with the remaining scallions. Serve the stir-fry in the lettuce leaves with more hoisin sauce.

Per serving: Calories 237; Fat 10 g (Saturated 2 g); Cholesterol 55 mg; Sodium 716 mg; Carbohydrate 18 g; Fiber 4 g; Protein 22 g

> You can serve the stir-fry in tortillas, too.

PORK AND FENNEL RAGOÛT

ACTIVE: 25 min | TOTAL: 40 min | SERVES: 4

1 teaspoon fennel seeds
Kosher salt and freshly ground pepper
Zest and juice of 1 lemon
3 1-inch-thick boneless pork loin chops (1 pound total),
   trimmed and sliced into ¼-inch-wide strips
3 tablespoons all-purpose flour
5 tablespoons chopped fresh parsley
3 tablespoons extra-virgin olive oil
1 cup sliced shallots
1 small fennel bulb, trimmed and chopped
2 tablespoons tomato paste
10 ounces cremini mushrooms, sliced
1½ cups red or white wine

1. Grind the fennel seeds with 1 teaspoon salt and ½ teaspoon pepper in a spice grinder or chop with a knife. Transfer to a medium bowl; mix with the lemon juice and pork. Add the flour and toss to coat. In another bowl, mix the lemon zest with 2 tablespoons parsley.
2. Heat a deep skillet or pot over high heat and add the olive oil. Brown the pork in batches, about 1 minute per side; transfer to a plate. Add the shallots, fennel, the remaining 3 tablespoons parsley, and salt to taste to the skillet. Reduce the heat and cook until the vegetables are wilted, about 2 minutes. Add the tomato paste and cook, stirring, about 3 minutes.
3. Add the mushrooms, wine and ½ cup water; scrape up any browned bits with a wooden spoon. Cover and simmer over low heat until the fennel is tender, about 12 minutes. Add the pork and heat through, 2 to 3 minutes. Season with salt and pepper and top with the lemon zest–parsley mixture.

Per serving: Calories 435; Fat 18 g (Saturated 4 g); Cholesterol 62 mg; Sodium 882 mg; Carbohydrate 24 g; Fiber 4 g; Protein 30 g

Try it with these sides...

Roasted Asparagus
page 341

Spicy Escarole with Garlic
page 344

Brussels Sprout Hash
page 352

To clean your spice grinder, grind a scoop of uncooked rice until powdery, then dump it out and wipe the grinder clean with a paper towel.

PORK WITH SQUASH AND APPLES

ACTIVE: 25 min **I** TOTAL: 40 min **I** SERVES: 4

1   teaspoon freshly grated nutmeg
1½   teaspoons minced garlic (about 2 large cloves)
2   tablespoons chopped fresh sage
2   1-pound pork tenderloins, trimmed
Kosher salt and freshly ground pepper
1   small butternut squash, peeled and cut into 1-inch pieces
2   cooking apples, peeled and cut into ½-inch pieces
1   medium red onion, cut into ½-inch pieces
1   tablespoon honey mustard
1   sprig rosemary
5   tablespoons unsalted butter, cut into pieces

1. Preheat the oven to 425°. Mix the nutmeg, 1 teaspoon garlic and the sage in a bowl. Rub over the pork and season with salt and pepper.
2. Toss the squash, apples, onion, the remaining ½ teaspoon garlic, the honey mustard, and salt and pepper to taste in a bowl. Spread out on a long sheet of foil. Add the rosemary and 3 tablespoons butter, then bring the ends of the foil together and crimp to seal into a packet. Place the packet on a baking sheet and roast on the upper rack until tender, 30 to 35 minutes. Poke holes in the packet to release steam.
3. Meanwhile, heat a large ovenproof skillet over medium-high heat. Add the remaining 2 tablespoons butter, then brown the pork on all sides, about 8 minutes. Add 2 tablespoons water and scrape up any browned bits from the pan, then transfer the skillet to the lower oven rack and roast until a thermometer registers 150°, about 15 minutes. Transfer the meat to a cutting board and let rest 5 minutes.
4. Return the skillet to medium heat. Add ½ cup water, scrape up any browned bits and simmer about 2 minutes. Slice the pork and drizzle with the pan juices. Serve with the squash and apples.

Per serving: Calories 487; Fat 22 g (Saturated 12 g); Cholesterol 164 mg; Sodium 367 mg; Carbohydrate 25 g; Fiber 5 g; Protein 47 g

> To break down butternut squash, cut off both ends and scoop the seeds out of the wide end with a spoon. Wearing an apron, hold the squash against your chest and remove the skin with a peeler, working toward you; then chop the squash.

CHILI-RUBBED PORK CHOPS

ACTIVE: 30 min **I** TOTAL: 30 min **I** SERVES: 4

2 large onions
⅓ cup New Mexico chile powder
Kosher salt
½ teaspoon dried oregano
½ teaspoon ground cumin
¼ teaspoon ground cloves
2 cloves garlic, smashed
Vegetable oil, for brushing
8 thin-cut boneless pork chops (about 2 pounds total), trimmed
Spanish rice, for serving (optional)

1. Roughly chop ½ onion and place in a blender with the chile powder, 1½ teaspoons salt, the oregano, cumin, cloves and garlic. Puree, adding about ⅓ cup water to make a thick paste.
2. Slice the remaining 1½ onions into thin rings and place in a bowl with the chili puree and pork; toss to coat.
3. Lightly brush a large cast-iron skillet or grill pan with vegetable oil and place over high heat until almost smoking. Place 4 pork chops in the skillet and surround with half of the onions. Cook until the pork starts to blacken on the outside and is cooked through, about 4 minutes per side. Repeat with the remaining pork chops and onions. Serve with rice, if desired.

Per serving (without rice): Calories 400; Fat 17 g (Saturated 5 g); Cholesterol 133 mg; Sodium 925 mg; Carbohydrate 14 g; Fiber 5 g; Protein 49 g

New Mexico chile powder is made of pure ground chile peppers and has a great earthy flavor. (Standard chili powder is a blend of chiles and spices.) Look for other pure chile powders, like ancho or chipotle, in the spice aisle.

Done in
30
minutes

Low-calorie dinner

ROSEMARY-MUSTARD PORK WITH PEACHES

ACTIVE: 35 min | TOTAL: 35 min | SERVES: 4

2   1-pound pork tenderloins, trimmed
Kosher salt and freshly ground pepper
Vegetable oil, for the grill
3   firm-ripe peaches, halved, pitted and cut into wedges
½   cup dry white wine
⅓   cup packed light brown sugar
1   lemon
2   teaspoons whole-grain mustard
¼   teaspoon chopped fresh rosemary, plus 1 or 2 small sprigs

1. Preheat a grill to high. Pat the pork dry and season with salt and pepper. Lightly oil the grill, then grill the pork, turning, until marked, about 10 minutes.
2. Meanwhile, combine the peaches, wine, brown sugar, and ½ cup water in a saucepan. Remove strips of zest from the lemon with a vegetable peeler and add to the pan; squeeze in the lemon juice. Cover and cook over medium-high heat until the peaches are just tender, 5 to 7 minutes. Transfer to a bowl with a slotted spoon.
3. Add the mustard, ½ teaspoon salt and ¼ teaspoon pepper to the juices in the pan. Transfer ⅓ cup of the liquid to a small bowl and stir in the chopped rosemary; brush onto the pork and continue grilling until a thermometer inserted into the thickest part registers 145°, 10 to 15 more minutes. Transfer to a cutting board to rest.
4. Meanwhile, simmer the remaining liquid in the saucepan until syrupy, about 3 minutes. Remove from the heat and season with salt. Return the peaches to the pan along with the rosemary sprigs. Slice the pork and serve with the peaches.

Per serving: Calories 376; Fat 8 g (Saturated 3 g); Cholesterol 147 mg; Sodium 181 mg; Carbohydrate 26 g; Fiber 1 g; Protein 49 g

---

Use the leftover rosemary in...

Skillet Rosemary Chicken
page 146

Pork with Squash and Apples page 173

Spaghetti Carbonara
page 301

PORK WITH POTATO-BEAN SALAD

ACTIVE: 30 min **I** TOTAL: 30 min **I** SERVES: 4

1   pound Yukon gold potatoes, peeled and cut into 2-inch chunks
Kosher salt
½   pound green beans, trimmed and halved
4   tablespoons whole-grain mustard
3   tablespoons extra-virgin olive oil
1½   teaspoons celery salt
2   small pork tenderloins (about 1¾ pounds total)
¼   cup mayonnaise
3   tablespoons sour cream
1   tablespoon chopped fresh tarragon or parsley
Juice of 1 lemon, plus 1 teaspoon grated zest
Freshly ground pepper
¼   red onion, thinly sliced

1. Preheat the broiler. Cover the potatoes with cold water in a saucepan and salt the water. Bring to a boil over medium-high heat and cook until tender, about 10 minutes. Transfer to a colander with a skimmer or slotted spoon. Add the green beans to the boiling water and cook until crisp-tender, about 3 minutes. Transfer to the colander with the potatoes, run under cold water and pat dry.
2. Meanwhile, mix 3 tablespoons mustard, the olive oil and celery salt in a bowl and rub over the pork. Broil on a foil-lined broiler pan until golden brown, 7 to 8 minutes; flip and broil until cooked through, 2 to 3 more minutes. Let rest 5 minutes before slicing.
3. Mix the mayonnaise, sour cream, the remaining 1 tablespoon mustard, the tarragon, lemon juice and zest, ½ teaspoon salt, and pepper to taste in a bowl. Add the potatoes, green beans and onion; season with salt and pepper, and toss. Slice the pork and serve with the potato salad.

Per serving: Calories 588; Fat 30 g (Saturated 7 g); Cholesterol 141 mg; Sodium 939 mg; Carbohydrate 29 g; Fiber 3 g; Protein 49 g

> Use a wire skimmer to remove the potatoes so you can save the boiling water for the beans. A skimmer is a great tool for draining ravioli too; you can buy one for around $5.

Done in **30** minutes

CHEESE-STUFFED PORK CHOPS

ACTIVE: 40 min **I** TOTAL: 40 min **I** SERVES: 4

Kosher salt
¼   cup sugar
4   bone-in, thick-cut pork chops (6 to 8 ounces each)
½   medium head escarole
2   cloves garlic
4   tablespoons extra-virgin olive oil, plus more for brushing
Freshly ground pepper
4   slices provolone cheese (about 2 ounces)
4   fresh sage leaves, chopped
1   19-ounce can cannellini beans, drained and rinsed

1. Dissolve ¼ cup salt and the sugar in 3 cups warm water in a large bowl. Insert a paring knife into the curved side of each pork chop to make a deep pocket, about 2 inches wide. Soak the chops in the brine, about 5 minutes.
2. Meanwhile, finely chop the escarole and garlic. Toss with 2 tablespoons olive oil and salt and pepper to taste.
3. Remove the chops from the brine and pat dry. Fold each cheese slice and tuck into the pocket of a pork chop, then stuff with the escarole mixture. Brush the pork with olive oil, sprinkle with the sage and season with salt and pepper.
4. Heat the remaining 2 tablespoons olive oil in a large skillet over medium-high heat. Sear the pork in batches, turning once, until golden brown, 3 to 4 minutes. Transfer to a plate. Add the beans and ⅓ cup water to the skillet, scraping up any browned bits; season with salt and pepper. Return the pork to the skillet, cover and cook over medium heat until no longer pink, 5 to 7 more minutes. Serve the pork with the beans.

Per serving: Calories 463; Fat 28 g (Saturated 7 g); Cholesterol 63 mg; Sodium 693 mg; Carbohydrate 21 g; Fiber 6 g; Protein 31 g

> Brining the pork chops, even for just 5 minutes, helps make them moist and flavorful.

PORK TONNATO

ACTIVE: 30 min **I** TOTAL: 40 min **I** SERVES: 4

2   tablespoons extra-virgin olive oil
2   small pork tenderloins (about 2 pounds total)
Kosher salt and freshly ground pepper
2   medium shallots, roughly chopped
1   medium carrot, roughly chopped
4   fresh sage leaves
1   cup dry white wine or water
1   5-to-6-ounce can light tuna packed in olive oil, drained,
     reserving 2 tablespoons of the oil
2   tablespoons capers, plus more for sprinkling
⅓   cup mayonnaise
Juice of 1 lemon
4   ounces baby arugula or mixed field greens (about 4 cups)

1. Heat 1 tablespoon olive oil in a large skillet over high heat. Season the pork with salt and pepper, then brown on all sides, about 5 minutes. Transfer to a plate. Reduce the heat to medium-low; add the remaining 1 tablespoon olive oil, the shallots and carrot to the skillet, and cook until the vegetables are just tender, about 5 minutes.
2. Add the sage and wine and bring to a simmer. Return the pork to the skillet along with the tuna and capers. Cover and cook until a thermometer inserted into the pork registers 150°, 10 to 15 minutes. Transfer the pork to a cutting board and let rest about 5 minutes.
3. Meanwhile, discard the sage and transfer the remaining contents of the skillet to a blender. Add the reserved tuna oil, the mayonnaise, lemon juice, and salt and pepper to taste; puree until smooth.
4. Slice the pork and divide among plates. Top with the sauce and greens, season with salt and pepper, and sprinkle with more capers.

Per serving: Calories 485; Fat 30 g (Saturated 5 g); Cholesterol 103 mg; Sodium 744 mg; Carbohydrate 12 g; Fiber 2 g; Protein 36 g

Use the leftover capers in...

Turkey Reubens
page 48

Flank Steak with Salsa Verde page 206

Linguine with Tuna Puttanesca page 297

JAPANESE-STYLE CRISPY PORK

ACTIVE: 40 min **I** TOTAL: 40 min **I** SERVES: 4

1   pound thin-cut boneless pork chops or cutlets, trimmed
Kosher salt
2   tablespoons Chinese rice wine, sake or sherry
1½   teaspoons finely grated peeled ginger
2   medium cucumbers
½ to 1 teaspoon sugar
2   teaspoons rice wine vinegar
1½   teaspoons red pepper flakes
3   large eggs
2   cups panko (Japanese breadcrumbs)
¾   cup cornstarch
Peanut oil, for frying
¼   cup tonkatsu sauce (a sweet-spicy Japanese dipping sauce,
      sold near the soy sauce; see below to make your own)

1. Season the pork with salt. Mix the rice wine and 1 teaspoon ginger and spread on the pork. Stack the pork and set aside.
2. Peel, quarter and seed the cucumbers; cut into 4-inch spears. Toss with the sugar and vinegar. Toast the pepper flakes with 1 tablespoon salt in a skillet over medium heat, about 4 minutes; set aside.
3. Beat the eggs with ½ cup water in a shallow bowl. Put the panko and cornstarch in 2 separate shallow bowls. Dredge each piece of pork in cornstarch, dip in egg, then coat with the panko. Heat ¼ inch of peanut oil in a large skillet over high heat. Fry the pork in batches until golden, 3 to 4 minutes per side. Drain on a paper towel–lined plate.
4. Sprinkle the cucumbers with some of the spiced salt. Mix the tonkatsu sauce and the remaining ½ teaspoon ginger in a bowl. Serve the pork with the cucumbers and sauce.

Per serving: Calories 419; Fat 19 g (Saturated 5 g); Cholesterol 170 mg; Sodium 1,388 mg; Carbohydrate 29 g; Fiber 1 g; Protein 30 g

> To make your own dipping sauce, mix 2 tablespoons each ketchup, Worcestershire sauce and sugar with 1 tablespoon water.

HAM AND CHEESE PIE WITH GREENS

ACTIVE: 30 min | TOTAL: 35 min | SERVES: 4

10   large eggs
Pinch of cayenne pepper
3   ounces ham, chopped
6   ounces muenster cheese, grated
4   tablespoons extra-virgin olive oil
3   bunches scallions, cut into 2-inch pieces
Kosher salt and freshly ground black pepper
1   large tomato, cut into wedges
1   teaspoon white wine vinegar
1   tablespoon sugar
4   ounces mesclun greens (about 4 cups)
½   head escarole, torn, or 1 bunch dandelion greens, trimmed

1. Position a rack in the center of the oven and preheat the broiler. Whisk the eggs, 2 tablespoons water and the cayenne in a large bowl. Fold in the ham and half of the cheese.
2. Heat 1 tablespoon olive oil in an ovenproof 6- to 8-inch nonstick skillet over medium-high heat, swirling to coat the pan. Add the scallions, ¼ teaspoon salt, and black pepper to taste; cook until soft, 4 to 5 minutes. Reduce the heat to medium low, pour in the egg mixture and stir gently with a rubber spatula to distribute the fillings. Cook until the bottom is just set, about 4 minutes. Sprinkle the remaining cheese on top, transfer to the oven and bake until puffed and golden, about 10 minutes. Let stand while you prepare the salad.
3. Season the tomato with salt and black pepper and toss with the vinegar, sugar and the remaining 3 tablespoons olive oil in a bowl. Add the greens and toss. Slice the pie and serve with the salad.

Per serving: Calories 555; Fat 39 g (Saturated 14 g); Cholesterol 590 mg; Sodium 901 mg; Carbohydrate 21 g; Fiber 6 g; Protein 32 g

Try using new types of greens in your salads, like this combination of mild-flavored mesclun and bitter escarole or dandelion greens.

GREEN EGGS AND HAM

ACTIVE: 40 min **I** TOTAL: 40 min **I** SERVES: 4

3   large eggs
⅓   cup diced half-sour pickles, plus 2 tablespoons pickling liquid
      from the jar
1   tablespoon whole-grain dijon mustard
3   tablespoons extra-virgin olive oil, plus more for frying
½   cup roughly chopped fresh parsley
2   tablespoons minced fresh chives
2   tablespoons minced fresh tarragon
Kosher salt and freshly ground pepper
1½   cups instant flour (such as Wondra)
1   cup milk
1   ham steak (about 1 pound), cut into 4 equal pieces
2   tablespoons capers, drained

1. Place 2 eggs in a saucepan, cover with water and bring to a boil. Cook
8 to 10 minutes. Cool in a bowl of ice water. Peel the eggs, then separate the
whites and chop them. Mash the yolks in a bowl, then whisk in 2 tablespoons
warm water, the pickling liquid and mustard. Gradually whisk in the olive oil.
Add 2 tablespoons parsley, the chives, tarragon, egg whites, pickles,
¼ teaspoon salt, and pepper to taste.
2. Combine the flour, the remaining 6 tablespoons parsley and a pinch of
pepper in a shallow dish. In another dish, beat the remaining egg with the
milk. Dip each piece of ham in the flour to coat both sides, then dip in the milk
mixture and re-dip in the flour mixture.
3. Heat ⅛ inch of olive oil in a large skillet over medium-high heat until sizzling.
Fry the ham in batches until golden, about 4 minutes per side. Transfer to a
paper towel–lined plate. Fry the capers in the skillet until crisp, about 1 minute.
Sprinkle the ham steaks with the capers, and serve the egg mixture on the side
to spoon on top.

Per serving: Calories 449; Fat 32 g (Saturated 6 g); Cholesterol 165 mg;
Sodium 1,981 mg; Carbohydrate 9 g; Fiber 1 g; Protein 29 g

> If you aren't usually a fan
> of capers, fry them in oil
> first. They'll get nice and
> crisp, and the intense briny
> flavor will mellow out.

HAM AND CHEESE PAN SOUFFLÉ

ACTIVE: 30 min **I** TOTAL: 40 min **I** SERVES: 4

2   russet potatoes, peeled and cut into ½-inch cubes
Kosher salt
6   large eggs, at room temperature, separated
8   ounces manchego or aged provolone cheese, grated (2 cups)
1   tablespoon all-purpose flour
Freshly ground pepper
4   tablespoons extra-virgin olive oil, plus more if needed
1   onion, halved and thinly sliced
2   Anaheim chile peppers, halved, seeded and thinly sliced
¼   pound boiled ham, cut into small cubes
1   teaspoon paprika
2   tablespoons chopped fresh parsley
1   clove garlic, minced

1. Preheat the oven to 400°. Cover the potatoes with water in a pot; season with salt, cover and boil until just tender, 2 minutes. Drain.
2. Whisk the egg yolks, cheese, flour, and pepper to taste in a bowl.
3. Heat a 10-inch ovenproof nonstick skillet over high heat. Add 2 tablespoons olive oil, the onion and chiles and cook until browned, 4 minutes. Add the ham and cook 3 minutes. Transfer the mixture to a bowl. Add the remaining 2 tablespoons oil and the potatoes to the skillet and cook until golden, 4 minutes. Add the paprika, parsley and garlic and cook 1 minute. Transfer to the same bowl.
4. Beat the egg whites, 2 tablespoons water and ½ teaspoon salt with a mixer until soft peaks form. Stir one-third of the whites into the yolk mixture, then gently fold in the rest. Oil the skillet, if dry, and place over medium-low heat. Add the egg mixture, cover and cook until the top just sets, 4 to 6 minutes. Top with the filling and transfer to the oven, uncovered, until set, 5 to 7 minutes.

Per serving: Calories 641; Fat 44 g (Saturated 19 g); Cholesterol 373 mg; Sodium 1,215 mg; Carbohydrate 32 g; Fiber 4 g; Protein 32 g

This dish makes a great weeknight meal or brunch, but you can also cut it into small pieces and serve it as an hors d'oeuvre for a party.

RICOTTA, HAM AND SCALLION TART

ACTIVE: 15 min **I** TOTAL: 40 min **I** SERVES: 4 to 6

3	tablespoons unsalted butter
1	13.8-ounce tube refrigerated pizza crust dough
¼	cup ricotta cheese
¼	cup heavy cream
1	large egg
2 to 3 bunches scallions	
3	tablespoons chopped fresh parsley
2	tablespoons chopped fresh dill or tarragon
Freshly ground pepper	
5	ounces deli-sliced ham, cut into ½-inch pieces

1. Place a baking sheet on the top rack of the oven; preheat to 425°. Grease a 9-inch fluted tart pan with 1 tablespoon butter. Line the pan with the pizza dough, carefully pressing it against the sides; trim the excess dough.
2. Whisk the ricotta, cream and egg in a medium bowl. Mince enough green scallion tops to make 2 tablespoons; add to the ricotta mixture along with the parsley and dill. Season with pepper. Slice the remaining scallions into ½-to-¾-inch pieces.
3. Heat the remaining 2 tablespoons butter in a large skillet over high heat. Add the sliced scallions and 2 tablespoons water; cook until the scallions are tender and start to sizzle, about 3 minutes. Remove from the heat and add the ham. Spread all but a few tablespoons of the scallion mixture on the prepared crust. Pour in the ricotta mixture, then scatter the remaining scallion mixture on top.
4. Bake the tart on the preheated baking sheet for 20 minutes, or until the crust is golden and the filling is set. Rest in the pan for 5 minutes, then remove and slice.

Per serving: Calories 460; Fat 22 g (Saturated 12 g); Cholesterol 115 mg; Sodium 1,165 mg; Carbohydrate 51 g; Fiber 2 g; Protein 18 g

Use the leftover parsley and dill to make your own herb butter: Just chop them and whip with soft butter, minced garlic and lemon juice. Using parchment or wax paper, roll the mixture into a log, twist the ends and refrigerate to harden.

LAMB CHOPS WITH FENNEL AND TOMATOES

ACTIVE: 35 min I TOTAL: 40 min I SERVES: 4

1   medium bulb fennel, trimmed and cut into 8 wedges
4   plum tomatoes, cored and halved lengthwise
2   tablespoons plus 1 teaspoon extra-virgin olive oil
Kosher salt and freshly ground pepper
2   cloves garlic, smashed
2   15-ounce cans cannellini or butter beans, drained and rinsed
2   tablespoons chopped fresh oregano or parsley
2   tablespoons grated parmesan cheese (optional)
4   5-ounce lamb chops, fat trimmed and bones frenched

1. Preheat the oven to 425°. Line a baking sheet with foil. Toss the fennel and tomatoes with 2 tablespoons olive oil and season with salt and pepper. Spread the vegetables on the baking sheet, with the tomatoes cut-side up. Roast until the tomatoes are soft and the fennel is golden, about 30 minutes, turning halfway through.

2. Meanwhile, cook the garlic in the remaining 1 teaspoon olive oil in a medium saucepan over medium heat until golden, about 3 minutes. Add the beans and 2½ cups water and cook, stirring occasionally, until the liquid thickens, about 15 minutes. Stir in the oregano and parmesan, if desired.

3. Heat a grill pan over medium-high heat. Season the lamb with salt and pepper and grill until marked on the bottom, about 4 minutes. Flip and cook until just firm to the touch, 4 to 5 more minutes for medium-rare. Divide the beans among plates and top with the lamb and roasted vegetables.

Per serving: Calories 416; Fat 17 g (Saturated 4 g); Cholesterol 62 mg; Sodium 442 mg; Carbohydrate 35 g; Fiber 11 g; Protein 30 g

Ask the butcher for frenched lamb chops: The excess fat has been removed, and the bone ends are clean.

Done in
15
minutes

STEAK WITH AVOCADO SAUCE AND TOMATO SALAD

ACTIVE: 15 min **I** TOTAL: 15 min **I** SERVES: 4

1¼   pounds beef eye round roast (in 1 piece)
2   tablespoons extra-virgin olive oil
1   tablespoon Mexican-style chili powder
Kosher salt
1   cup cherry or grape tomatoes, halved
7 to 8 canned hearts of palm, thickly sliced
2   tablespoons lime juice, plus lime wedges for serving
Freshly ground pepper
1   ripe Hass avocado
⅓   cup fresh cilantro
1   large clove garlic
Flour tortillas, warmed, for serving (optional)

1. Slice the roast crosswise into 3 even steaks. Heat a cast-iron skillet over medium-high heat. Brush the steaks all over with 1 tablespoon olive oil, season with the chili powder and add salt to taste. Cook until a thermometer inserted into the side registers 125° for medium-rare, 4 to 5 minutes per side. Let rest for 5 minutes.
2. Meanwhile, toss the tomatoes and hearts of palm in a bowl with the remaining 1 tablespoon olive oil, 1 tablespoon lime juice, and salt and pepper to taste.
3. Halve and pit the avocado; scoop the flesh into a blender or food processor. Add the cilantro, garlic, the remaining 1 tablespoon lime juice and ½ cup water; puree. Season with salt.
4. Thinly slice the steaks. Serve with the avocado sauce, tomato salad and tortillas for wrapping, if desired. Serve with lime wedges.

Per serving: Calories 325; Fat 17 g (Saturated 3 g); Cholesterol 58 mg; Sodium 337 mg; Carbohydrate 9 g; Fiber 5 g; Protein 35 g

> Save money on meat: Buy a whole roast and slice it into steaks yourself.

SPICY CHINESE BEEF

ACTIVE: 20 min **I** TOTAL: 35 min **I** SERVES: 4

1 tablespoon cornstarch
3 tablespoons Chinese rice wine, dry sherry or white vermouth
1 pound beef sirloin, thinly sliced against the grain into strips
Kosher salt and freshly ground pepper
2 tablespoons oyster sauce
2 teaspoons toasted sesame oil
3 to 4 tablespoons peanut oil
1 1-inch piece fresh ginger, thinly sliced
2 cloves garlic, smashed
5 to 7 dried red chiles, halved
1 small onion, thinly sliced
8 heads baby bok choy, halved
Pinch of sugar
Cooked rice, for serving (optional)

1. Whisk the cornstarch with 2 tablespoons rice wine in a medium bowl; add the beef, season with salt and pepper and toss to coat. Set aside for 15 minutes.
2. Mix the remaining 1 tablespoon rice wine, the oyster sauce and sesame oil in a large bowl; set the bowl near the stove.
3. Heat a wok or large nonstick skillet over high heat until very hot, about 1 minute. Add 3 tablespoons peanut oil, then the ginger, garlic and chiles; stir-fry until fragrant, about 1 minute. Add the beef and cook, stirring or shaking the skillet occasionally, 1 to 2 minutes. Transfer the beef with a slotted spoon to the sauce mixture and toss.
4. If the pan is dry, add 1 tablespoon peanut oil, then add the onion and stir-fry until just soft, about 2 minutes. Add the bok choy and sugar; stir-fry until just wilted, 1 to 2 minutes. Return the beef and any juices to the pan and stir to combine. Serve over rice, if desired.

Per serving (without rice): Calories 480; Fat 31 g (Saturated 9 g); Cholesterol 62 mg; Sodium 1,650 mg; Carbohydrate 42 g; Fiber 7 g; Protein 13 g

> You can use a large head of bok choy instead of the small ones; just slice and stir-fry the stems, then add the leaves at the end.

TANGERINE BEEF WITH SCALLIONS

ACTIVE: 20 min **I** TOTAL: 30 min (plus overnight marinating) **I** SERVES: 4

1½   pounds beef tri-tip steak, trimmed of excess fat
1   tangerine
4   scallions, sliced, plus more for topping
¼   cup soy sauce
2   tablespoons toasted sesame oil
2   teaspoons sugar
2   tablespoons chopped peeled ginger
3   cloves garlic, minced
Pinch of red pepper flakes
2   tablespoons orange preserves

1. Pierce the steak with a fork several times on each side. Remove a 2-inch strip of zest from the tangerine, halve the fruit and squeeze the juice into a resealable plastic bag. Add the zest, scallions, soy sauce, sesame oil, sugar, ginger, garlic, pepper flakes and ¼ cup water to the bag and mix well. Add the meat, seal the bag and turn to coat. Refrigerate overnight.
2. Preheat the broiler with a broiler pan in place. Remove the steak from the bag and reserve the marinade. Pat the meat dry and place on the preheated broiler pan. Cook, without turning, until the meat is golden brown and a thermometer inserted in the thickest part registers 130° for medium-rare, about 10 minutes. Let rest 5 to 10 minutes before slicing; reserve the drippings.
3. Meanwhile, boil the marinade in a small pot over medium-high heat until slightly thickened. Stir in the orange preserves and the drippings from the meat. Slice the meat against the grain and top with scallions. Serve with the sauce.

Per serving: Calories 341; Fat 18 g (Saturated 5 g); Cholesterol 91 mg; Sodium 994 mg; Carbohydrate 10 g; Fiber 1 g; Protein 38 g

> Broiling is a perfect indoor alternative to grilling. For best results, preheat your broiler pan: You'll get better browning, and the meat will cook more evenly.

MINI SKILLET MEATLOAVES

ACTIVE: 25 min **I** TOTAL: 40 min **I** MAKES: 6 meatloaves

⅓ cup breadcrumbs
⅓ cup milk
⅓ cup chopped fresh parsley
1 large egg
3 tablespoons Worcestershire sauce
1 small onion, finely minced
1 teaspoon chili powder
2 cloves garlic, grated or finely minced
1½ pounds meatloaf mix (ground beef, pork and/or veal)
Kosher salt and freshly ground pepper
1 tablespoon vegetable oil
½ cup ketchup
1 to 2 tablespoons packed light brown sugar
1 tablespoon apple cider vinegar

1. Mix the breadcrumbs, milk, parsley, egg, Worcestershire sauce, onion, chili powder and garlic in a large bowl. Add the meat, season with salt and pepper and mix with your hands until combined. Shape into six 3-to-4-inch oval loaves.
2. Heat the vegetable oil in a large nonstick skillet over high heat. Add the loaves and brown about 3 minutes per side.
3. Whisk the ketchup, sugar and vinegar together in a bowl and brush a few tablespoonfuls over the meat. Add ½ cup water to the skillet, cover and simmer over low heat until cooked through, about 15 minutes.
4. Transfer the loaves to a plate. Add the remaining ketchup mixture to the skillet and cook over high heat, stirring, until thick, 3 to 5 minutes. Serve the meatloaves with the hot glaze.

Per meatloaf: Calories 380; Fat 24 g (Saturated 8 g); Cholesterol 111 mg; Sodium 800 mg; Carbohydrate 16 g; Fiber 1 g; Protein 23 g

Try it with these sides...

Garlic Green Beans
page 330

Bacon-Cheddar Mashed Potatoes page 343

Corn Pudding
page 344

BEEF KEFTA WITH MELON SLAW

ACTIVE: 40 min **I** TOTAL: 40 min **I** SERVES: 4

½ cup lightly packed whole-wheat sourdough bread cubes
¼ cup walnuts
2 medium red onions; 1 grated, 1 halved and thinly sliced
1½ teaspoons paprika
½ teaspoon ground cinnamon
1½ teaspoons dried mint
½ teaspoon ground cumin
¼ teaspoon cayenne pepper
Kosher salt and freshly ground black pepper
2 tablespoons chopped fresh dill
½ cup fresh parsley
1½ pounds ground beef chuck
½ firm ripe cantaloupe, cut into matchsticks
1 tablespoon lemon juice
Extra-virgin olive oil, for brushing

1. Soak the bread in water for 10 minutes; squeeze dry and pulse in a food processor with the walnuts, grated onion, 1 teaspoon paprika, the cinnamon, mint, cumin, cayenne, 1½ teaspoons salt and ½ teaspoon black pepper. Add 1 tablespoon dill and the parsley; pulse until smooth.
2. Knead the spice paste and beef in a bowl. Form into 8 egg-shaped pieces, then flatten into ½-inch-thick oval patties. Refrigerate for 10 minutes. Meanwhile, soak the sliced red onion in ice water; drain.
3. Toss the cantaloupe, lemon juice, 1 teaspoon salt, the onion slices and the remaining 1 tablespoon dill and ½ teaspoon paprika in a bowl.
4. Preheat the grill to medium-high. Brush the patties with olive oil. Grill about 5 minutes; flip and continue grilling until cooked through but still moist, 4 more minutes. Serve with the melon slaw.

Per serving: Calories 416; Fat 24 g (Saturated 8 g); Cholesterol 104 mg; Sodium 1,336 mg; Carbohydrate 17 g; Fiber 3 g; Protein 33 g

Kefta (spiced meatballs or patties) are a popular Middle Eastern street food. They taste great with yogurt dip: Just mix Greek yogurt with lemon juice and salt.

FLANK STEAK WITH SALSA VERDE

ACTIVE: 25 min **I** TOTAL: 30 min **I** SERVES: 4

2   cups loosely packed fresh parsley
3   scallions, coarsely chopped
2   tablespoons capers, drained
Zest and juice of ½ lemon
2   anchovy fillets
2   cloves garlic, smashed
½   teaspoon dijon mustard
⅓   cup extra-virgin olive oil, plus more for the grill
Kosher salt
1   flank steak (about 1½ pounds)
Freshly ground pepper
2 or 3 medium tomatoes

1. Make the salsa verde: Pulse the parsley, scallions, capers, lemon zest and juice, anchovies, garlic, mustard and olive oil in a food processor until slightly chunky. Pour into a bowl and season with salt.
2. Preheat a grill to high or place a grill pan over high heat. Pierce the steak all over with a fork and season with salt and pepper. Oil the grill or pan; grill the steak, 4 to 5 minutes per side for medium-rare, turning once. Transfer to a cutting board and let rest for 5 minutes.
3. Slice the tomatoes and season with salt and pepper. Thinly slice the steak against the grain. Serve with the tomatoes and salsa verde.

Per serving: Calories 465; Fat 31 g (Saturated 8 g); Cholesterol 66 mg; Sodium 545 mg; Carbohydrate 7 g; Fiber 2 g; Protein 37 g

Anchovies are the secret ingredient to this dish: They add a deep, salty flavor to the salsa, but you can't detect any fishiness.

Done in
30
minutes

GRILLED STEAK WITH BLACK-EYED PEAS

ACTIVE: 40 min I TOTAL: 40 min I SERVES: 4

1   medium red onion, sliced into rings
1½   pounds skirt steak, patted dry
6   tablespoons extra-virgin olive oil
Kosher salt and freshly ground pepper
2   bunches baby turnips, trimmed and quartered, or 3 medium turnips,
     peeled and cut into chunks
1   12-ounce can black-eyed peas, drained and rinsed
2   plum tomatoes, seeded and diced
2 teaspoons red wine vinegar
4   fresh basil leaves, torn
1   tablespoon chopped fresh chives

1. Preheat a grill pan over high heat. Grill the onion rings until charred, about
2 minutes per side. If the steak is too large to fit in the pan, cut it in half.
Combine 3 tablespoons olive oil, 1 teaspoon salt and ½ teaspoon pepper
in a bowl, then brush over the meat. Grill the steak until slightly charred,
3 to 4 minutes per side for medium-rare. Transfer to a cutting board and
let rest at least 5 minutes.
2. Meanwhile, heat the remaining 3 tablespoons olive oil in a large skillet over
medium heat. Add the turnips and cook until fork-tender, about 8 minutes.
Add the black-eyed peas and tomatoes and cook until warmed through, about
3 minutes. Stir in the onion rings and vinegar and remove from the heat.
3. Cut the steak into 3-inch-long sections along the grain, then thinly slice
the meat against the grain. Stir the basil and chives into the black-eyed peas
and serve with the steak.

Per serving: Calories 705; Fat 46 g (Saturated 12 g); Cholesterol 90 mg;
Sodium 711 mg; Carbohydrate 33 g; Fiber 8 g; Protein 41 g

If a dish tastes a little flat, try
adding a splash of vinegar at
the end like we did here. The
acidity will brighten the flavors.

Turn your leftovers into this...

SLOW-COOKER CORNED BEEF AND CABBAGE

ACTIVE: 25 min **I** TOTAL: 25 min (plus 7-hr slow cooking) **I** SERVES: 6 (with leftovers for Corned Beef Hash, opposite)

4   pounds lean raw corned beef brisket

3   tablespoons pickling spice (often included with brisket)

1   medium rutabaga, halved and cut into wedges

1   pound large carrots, cut into 4-inch pieces

1¼   pounds large fingerling potatoes

1   leek, white and light green parts only, cut into 3-inch pieces

½   head Savoy cabbage, cut into wedges

⅓   cup horseradish, drained

⅓   cup crème fraîche or sour cream

1. Place the corned beef in a large slow cooker and scatter the pickling spice on top. Layer the rutabaga, carrots, potatoes and leek in the cooker (in this order for even cooking). Add enough hot water (4 to 5 cups) to cover the meat by at least 1 inch, put the lid on the slow cooker and cook on high, 7 to 8 hours.

2. Remove the meat and vegetables from the slow cooker and keep warm. Put the cabbage in a microwave-safe dish with 2 cups cooking liquid from the slow cooker, cover and microwave until tender, 7 to 10 minutes. Meanwhile, boil another cup of cooking liquid in a small skillet until reduced by half, about 10 minutes. Mix with the horseradish and crème fraîche in a small bowl.

3. Slice the corned beef and serve with the slow-cooked vegetables, cabbage and sauce; reserve about a quarter each of the meat and vegetables and 1½ cups cooking liquid for Corned Beef Hash (opposite).

Per serving: Calories 639; Fat 35 g (Saturated 12 g); Cholesterol 175 mg; Sodium 2,075 mg; Carbohydrate 44 g; Fiber 11 g; Protein 37 g

CORNED BEEF HASH

ACTIVE: 25 min **I** TOTAL: 25 min **I** SERVES: 4

2 to 4 tablespoons
  unsalted butter
1 tablespoon vegetable oil
1 small onion, chopped
Kosher salt and freshly
  ground pepper
2 cups diced leftover rutabaga,
  carrots, potatoes and leek
  (opposite)
2 cups chopped leftover
  corned beef (opposite)
2 tablespoons chopped
  parsley
1 to 1½ cups leftover corned beef
  cooking liquid (opposite)

1. Heat 2 tablespoons butter with the vegetable oil in a large cast-iron skillet over medium-high heat until almost smoking. Add the onion, season with salt and pepper and cook until translucent, about 4 minutes. Add half of the vegetables and cook, stirring occasionally, until golden, about 5 minutes. Add the corned beef and cook until slightly brown, about 2 minutes.

2. Meanwhile, mash the remaining vegetables in a bowl with the parsley and ¾ cup cooking liquid. Add to the skillet and stir to make a large pancake, adding up to ½ cup more cooking liquid, if needed.

3. Cook until the hash is dark on the bottom, about 2 minutes. Flip and continue cooking, turning occasionally and adding more butter if needed, until the hash is crunchy on the outside but still moist in the middle, 5 to 7 minutes. Add ¼ cup cooking liquid 1 minute before serving.

Per serving: Calories 343; Fat 25 g (Saturated 9 g); Cholesterol 98 mg; Sodium 1,050 mg; Carbohydrate 12 g; Fiber 2 g; Protein 17 g

SEARED STEAK WITH CHARD SALAD

ACTIVE: 35 min **I** TOTAL: 35 min **I** SERVES: 4

1   bunch Swiss chard, stems removed, leaves thinly sliced
4   tablespoons extra-virgin olive oil
2   cups large crusty bread cubes
Kosher salt and freshly ground pepper
3 to 4 anchovy fillets
1   clove garlic, smashed
1   cup grape tomatoes, halved
Juice of 1 lemon
1½   pounds boneless beef sirloin steak
1   teaspoon dried mint
½   cup crumbled feta cheese

1. Put the chard in a bowl. Heat a large skillet over medium-high heat. Add 1 tablespoon olive oil and the bread cubes and season with salt and pepper. Cook, tossing, until toasted, 4 to 5 minutes. Add to the chard.
2. Add the anchovies to the skillet, mashing them with a whisk. Add the garlic and 2 tablespoons olive oil and cook until the garlic is golden, about 45 seconds. Add the tomatoes and warm slightly, then whisk in the lemon juice and season with salt and pepper. Pour the warm dressing over the chard, toss and set aside to wilt.
3. Wipe out the skillet and place over high heat. Sprinkle the steak on both sides with the mint, and salt and pepper to taste. Add the remaining 1 tablespoon olive oil to the skillet. Sear the steak until browned on the bottom, about 5 minutes. Turn and cook until browned on the other side, 3 to 4 more minutes for medium-rare. Transfer to a cutting board and let rest 5 minutes.
4. Add the feta to the chard salad and toss. Thinly slice the steak and serve with the chard salad.

Per serving: Calories 484; Fat 26 g (Saturated 8 g); Cholesterol 88 mg; Sodium 1,304 mg; Carbohydrate 18 g; Fiber 3 g; Protein 44 g

Use the leftover anchovy fillets in...

Parisian Tuna Sandwiches page 63

Grilled Chicken Caesar Salad page 149

Flank Steak with Salsa Verde page 206

STEAK WITH BLUE CHEESE BUTTER AND CELERY SALAD

ACTIVE: 35 min **I** TOTAL: 40 min **I** SERVES: 4

½   small red onion, thinly sliced
4   6-to-7-ounce top blade steaks
Kosher salt and freshly ground pepper
2   tablespoons Worcestershire sauce
1   tablespoon hot sauce
2   tablespoons unsalted butter, softened
3   tablespoons crumbled blue cheese
3   tablespoons chopped fresh parsley
4   stalks celery, thinly sliced
1   tablespoon plus 2 teaspoons extra-virgin olive oil
1   lemon

1. Soak the onion slices in a bowl of cold water, about 10 minutes. Pierce the steaks with a fork and season with salt and pepper. Mix the Worcestershire and hot sauce in a baking dish, add the steaks and turn to coat; set aside while you prepare the butter and salad.
2. Mash the butter, blue cheese and 1 tablespoon parsley in a small bowl and season with salt and pepper. Drain the onion and pat dry, then toss with the celery, 1 tablespoon olive oil and the remaining 2 tablespoons parsley in another bowl. Grate the zest from half of the lemon into the celery mixture and squeeze in all of the juice. Season with salt and pepper and toss.
3. Heat a large cast-iron skillet over high heat, then add the remaining 2 teaspoons olive oil and cook the steaks until browned on the bottom, 3 to 5 minutes. Flip and continue to cook 3 to 5 more minutes for medium-rare. Transfer to a plate and let rest 5 minutes. Top with the blue cheese butter and serve with the celery salad.

Per serving: Calories 448; Fat 31 g (Saturated 12 g); Cholesterol 132 mg; Sodium 448 mg; Carbohydrate 6 g; Fiber 1 g; Protein 34 g

> Make extra blue cheese butter and store it in the fridge—it tastes great on mashed potatoes or crusty bread.

Mix & Match

STIR-FRIES

Beef with Broccoli and
Brown Sauce

PICK A PROTEIN

- ¾ pound flank steak, trimmed and thinly sliced against the grain
- ¾ pound pork tenderloin, thinly sliced
- ¾ pound medium or large shrimp, peeled and deveined
- ¾ pound skinless, boneless chicken breasts or thighs, thinly sliced against the grain
- 12-ounce package extra-firm silken tofu, cubed

MARINATE

Whisk 1 egg white, 1 tablespoon Chinese rice wine or dry sherry and 1 tablespoon cornstarch.
Toss with your protein; cover and refrigerate, 1 hour.

PREP 3 CUPS VEGETABLES (IN ANY COMBINATION)

- sliced carrots
- sliced celery
- sliced bell peppers
- 1-inch scallion pieces
- sliced onions or shallots

- quartered mushroom caps
- sliced bok choy or cabbage
- sliced leeks

- whole snow peas
- sliced asparagus
- halved cherry tomatoes
- baby spinach

- blanched broccoli or- cauliflower florets
- thawed frozen peas or edamame

CHOOSE A SAUCE

CLEAR SAUCE
Mix ¾ cup chicken broth, 1 tablespoon cornstarch, 2 tablespoons Chinese rice wine or dry sherry, ½ teaspoon sesame oil, 1 teaspoon salt and ½ teaspoon sugar.

SWEET-AND-SOUR SAUCE
Mix ¾ cup chicken broth, 2 teaspoons cornstarch, ¼ cup ketchup, 2 teaspoons soy sauce, 3 tablespoons rice vinegar, ¼ cup sugar, ½ teaspoon salt and 1 teaspoon sesame oil.

BROWN SAUCE
Mix ½ cup chicken broth, 1 tablespoon cornstarch, 1 tablespoon soy sauce, 1 tablespoon hoisin sauce and 1 tablespoon Chinese rice wine or dry sherry.

SPICY SAUCE
Mix ¾ cup chicken broth, 1 tablespoon cornstarch, 2 tablespoons each soy sauce, rice vinegar and Chinese rice wine or dry sherry, ½ teaspoon sesame oil, 1 tablespoon sugar and 2 teaspoons Asian chili sauce.

STIR-FRY

- Drain the excess marinade from the protein. Place your sauce, vegetables and protein near the stove.
- Heat ¼ inch peanut or vegetable oil in a wok or skillet over medium heat. Add the protein; slowly stir until almost opaque, 30 seconds to 1 minute (for tofu, brown on both sides—do not stir). Transfer to a plate; discard the oil and wipe out the pan.
- Heat the pan over high heat, 1 to 2 minutes. Add 2 tablespoons oil, then 2 cloves minced garlic (or 4 cloves if using Spicy Sauce), 1 to 2 tablespoons minced ginger, 2 minced scallions and a pinch each of salt and sugar; stir-fry about 30 seconds. Add the vegetables, starting with the ones that take the longest to cook; stir-fry until crisp-tender.
- Add the protein and sauce and stir until the sauce is thick and the vegetables and protein are cooked through, about 3 minutes. Thin with chicken broth, if needed. Garnish with sliced scallions, peanuts, sesame seeds, sliced jalapeños and/or cilantro.

Michael says...

" We cook a lot at home, especially on weekends—we have lots of family close by. My wife, Liz, is a great cook, too. We love to make pastas, grill and roast meats and make simple salads from our garden."

—MICHAEL SYMON, ONE OF FOOD NETWORK'S IRON CHEFS, IS THE HOST OF *FOOD FEUDS* AND COOKING CHANNEL'S *COOK LIKE AN IRON CHEF.*

KITCHEN SECRET

Michael is ready for anything at home: He keeps a giant industrial fridge in a separate room off the kitchen, where he also stores his collection of 50 pots and pans.

Shrimp Scampi
with Garlic Toasts,
page 261

Fish & Seafood

For faster prep, use a 16-ounce bag of shredded coleslaw mix in place of the cabbage and carrot.

PAN-FRIED COD WITH SLAW

ACTIVE: 30 min **I** TOTAL: 30 min **I** SERVES: 4

FOR THE SLAW
½   cup mayonnaise
2   tablespoons apple cider vinegar
1   tablespoon whole-grain mustard, plus more for serving
1   tablespoon sugar
¼ to ½ teaspoon caraway or celery seeds
Kosher salt and freshly ground pepper
½   head light green cabbage, thinly sliced (about 6 cups)
1   small carrot, shredded
1   gala apple, julienned
1   bunch scallions, white and green parts, thinly sliced

FOR THE FISH
1   large egg
½   cup milk
4   6-ounce cod or other white-fleshed fish fillets
⅓   cup all-purpose flour
⅓   cup cracker meal or crushed saltine crackers
¼   teaspoon cayenne pepper
Kosher salt
Vegetable oil, for shallow frying

1. Prepare the slaw: Whisk the mayonnaise, vinegar, mustard, sugar, caraway seeds, 1½ teaspoons salt, and pepper to taste in a large bowl. Toss in the cabbage, carrot, apple and scallions; cover and refrigerate.
2. Prepare the fish: Whisk the egg and milk in a medium bowl; add the cod and set aside to soak. Mix the flour, cracker meal, cayenne pepper and a pinch of salt on a plate.
3. Heat 1 inch of oil in a heavy-bottomed skillet over medium-high heat. Remove the fish from the milk mixture and dredge in the flour mixture, turning to coat. Fry in the hot oil until golden, 2 to 4 minutes per side. Transfer to a paper towel–lined plate to drain; season with salt and pepper. Serve with the slaw and extra mustard.

Per serving: Calories 640; Fat 40 g (Saturated 7 g); Cholesterol 140 mg; Sodium 1,125 mg; Carbohydrate 35 g; Fiber 4 g; Protein 37 g

MOROCCAN GRILLED SALMON

ACTIVE: 20 min **I** TOTAL: 40 min **I** SERVES: 4

½ cup plain yogurt
Juice of 1 lemon, plus lemon wedges for serving
1 tablespoon extra-virgin olive oil, plus more for the grill
2 to 3 cloves garlic, smashed
1½ teaspoons ground coriander
1½ teaspoons ground cumin
Kosher salt and freshly ground pepper
4 6-ounce skinless center-cut salmon fillets
¼ cup chopped fresh cilantro or parsley

1. Stir together the yogurt, lemon juice, olive oil, garlic, coriander, cumin, ¼ teaspoon salt, and pepper to taste in a small bowl. Pour half of the sauce into a large resealable plastic bag; cover and refrigerate the remaining sauce. Add the salmon to the bag and turn to coat with the marinade. Refrigerate for 20 to 30 minutes, turning the bag over once.
2. Preheat a grill to medium-high. Remove the salmon from the marinade and blot off excess yogurt with paper towels. Lightly oil the grill and add the salmon; cook, turning once, until browned on the outside and opaque in the center, 4 to 6 minutes per side, depending on the thickness. Sprinkle with the parsley and serve with the reserved yogurt sauce and lemon wedges.

Per serving: Calories 365; Fat 22 g (Saturated 4 g); Cholesterol 101 mg; Sodium 120 mg; Carbohydrate 4 g; Fiber 1 g; Protein 36 g

Buy wild salmon instead of farmed; it's better for the environment (and it's leaner, too).

Low-calorie dinner

SMOKED TROUT AND POTATO SALAD

ACTIVE: 30 min **I** TOTAL: 30 min **I** SERVES: 4

½   small red onion, thinly sliced
1   pound red-skinned potatoes, cut into 1-inch chunks
Kosher salt
¼   cup crème fraîche or sour cream
1   tablespoon white wine vinegar
1   tablespoon extra-virgin olive oil
1½   teaspoons grainy mustard
3   tablespoons chopped fresh dill
½   small seedless cucumber, halved lengthwise and thinly sliced
Freshly ground pepper
1   large bunch watercress, stems trimmed
12   ounces smoked trout, skin removed
Pumpernickel bread and/or pickled beets, for serving (optional)

1. Soak the onion slices in a bowl of ice water. Cover the potatoes with water in a pot; add a pinch of salt, cover and bring to a boil. Reduce to a simmer and cook, uncovered, until tender, 8 to 10 minutes. Drain, let cool slightly and pat dry.
2. Meanwhile, whisk the crème fraîche, vinegar, olive oil and mustard in a large bowl to make a smooth dressing. Stir in the dill. Drain the onion, pat dry and add to the dressing. Add the potatoes and cucumber, season with salt and pepper and toss to coat.
3. Divide the watercress among 4 plates and add some potato salad to each. Flake the trout with your fingers and scatter on top. Serve with pumpernickel bread and/or pickled beets, if desired.

Per serving: Calories 344; Fat 15 g (Saturated 6 g); Cholesterol 67 mg; Sodium 296 mg; Carbohydrate 22 g; Fiber 3 g; Protein 27 g

Smoked trout is sold in vacuum packages like smoked salmon. Just use salmon if trout isn't available.

TILAPIA WITH ESCAROLE AND LEMON-PEPPER OIL

ACTIVE: 15 min **I** TOTAL: 30 min **I** SERVES: 4

½   cup extra-virgin olive oil
12   ounces baby fingerling potatoes, halved, or small
      red-skinned potatoes, quartered
4   cloves garlic, smashed
1   head escarole (about 1¼ pounds), torn into pieces
Kosher salt and freshly ground pepper
1¼   pounds tilapia fillets, patted dry
2   sprigs fresh oregano, leaves torn
Juice of 1 lemon

1. Heat ¼ cup of the olive oil in a large deep skillet with a lid over medium heat. Place the potatoes in the pan cut-side down. Add the garlic and cook until the potatoes are slightly golden and crisp, 4 to 5 minutes. Add the escarole, season with salt and pepper, then add about ⅓ cup water. Cover and steam until the escarole wilts, about 5 minutes.
2. Season the fish with salt and pepper; place on top of the greens in the pan and sprinkle with the oregano leaves. Cover and steam until the fish is just cooked through, about 5 more minutes.
3. Meanwhile, whisk the lemon juice in a bowl with the remaining ¼ cup olive oil; season with 1 teaspoon salt and plenty of pepper.
4. Carefully lift the fish off the greens and transfer to rimmed plates or bowls. Distribute the greens, potatoes and pan juices around the fish. Drizzle with the lemon-pepper oil.

Per serving: Calories 465; Fat 30 g (Saturated 5 g); Cholesterol 70 mg; Sodium 590 mg; Carbohydrate 20 g; Fiber 6 g; Protein 32 g

> Tilapia is a smart fish choice for weeknight meals—it's mild, inexpensive and easy to find fresh or frozen.

One-pan meal

Done in
25
minutes

BROILED HALIBUT WITH RICOTTA-PEA PUREE

ACTIVE: 25 min | TOTAL: 25 min | SERVES: 4

3	small carrots, quartered lengthwise
1	medium red onion, thinly sliced
3	tablespoons extra-virgin olive oil

Kosher salt and freshly ground pepper

4	6-ounce center-cut skinless halibut fillets (1¾ inches thick)
½	teaspoon smoked paprika
1	10-ounce package frozen peas
⅓	cup ricotta cheese
1	tablespoon unsalted butter

1. Preheat the broiler. Line a broiler pan with foil and preheat 5 minutes.
2. Meanwhile, brush the carrots and onion with 1 tablespoon olive oil and season with salt and pepper. Brush the fish with the remaining 2 tablespoons olive oil, season with salt and pepper and sprinkle with the paprika; brush to coat the fish evenly with paprika.
3. Carefully remove the pan from the oven, place the fish in the center and scatter the onion and carrots around. Broil until the fish is golden and just cooked through, 8 to 10 minutes.
4. Meanwhile, microwave the peas in a bowl with ¼ cup water until just tender, about 4 minutes. Transfer the peas and liquid to a food processor and pulse with the ricotta, butter and a pinch of salt to make a slightly chunky puree. Divide the puree among plates and top with the fish, carrots, onion and pan juices.

Per serving: Calories 429; Fat 20 g (Saturated 6 g); Cholesterol 72 mg; Sodium 484 mg; Carbohydrate 18 g; Fiber 5 g; Protein 42 g

Pureed peas are an easy and healthful alternative to mashed potatoes.

TILAPIA WITH GREEN BEANS

ACTIVE: 30 min I TOTAL: 30 min I SERVES: 4

2	tablespoons all-purpose flour
2	teaspoons chopped fresh oregano, plus more for sprinkling
2	tablespoons chopped fresh parsley

Kosher salt and freshly ground pepper

4	6-ounce tilapia fillets
4	tablespoons unsalted butter
½	pound haricots verts or thin green beans
1	clove garlic, chopped
1	cup grape or cherry tomatoes, halved

Juice of 1 lemon

1. Combine the flour, oregano and parsley in a shallow dish. Season with salt and pepper.

2. Place a large skillet over medium-high heat. Dredge the fish in the flour mixture, shaking off the excess. Melt 3 tablespoons butter in the skillet, then add 2 fillets and cook until golden brown on the bottom, about 4 minutes. Flip and cook through, 1 to 2 more minutes. Transfer to a plate and keep warm. Repeat with the remaining 2 fillets.

3. Add the green beans and garlic to the skillet and cook about 2 minutes. Season with salt and pepper, then add the tomatoes and cook until just softened, about 1 more minute. Stir in the lemon juice and ¼ cup water, then cover and cook until the beans are tender, about 3 more minutes. Remove from the heat and stir in the remaining 1 tablespoon butter until just melted.

4. Divide the fish and vegetables among plates. Sprinkle with oregano.

Per serving: Calories 306; Fat 14 g (Saturated 8 g); Cholesterol 115 mg; Sodium 155 mg; Carbohydrate 10 g; Fiber 3 g; Protein 36 g

> Haricots verts are thin French green beans. The ends aren't as tough as regular green beans, so you don't have to trim them.

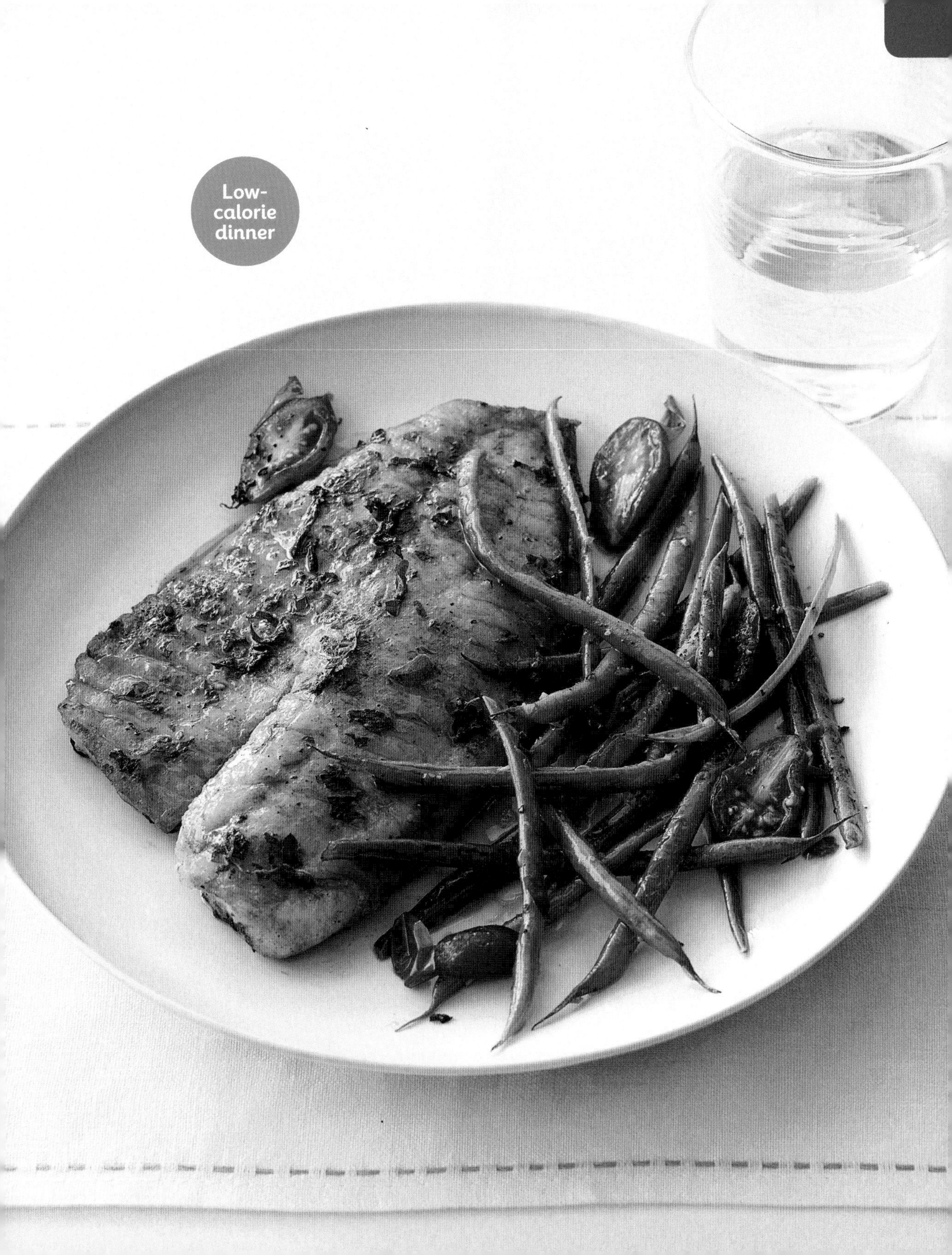
Low-calorie dinner

STRIPED BASS WITH MUSHROOMS

ACTIVE: 35 min | TOTAL: 35 min | SERVES: 4

3   tablespoons unsalted butter
5   large shallots, thinly sliced
2   sprigs thyme
Kosher salt and freshly ground pepper
10   ounces white mushrooms, trimmed and quartered
4   6-ounce skin-on striped bass fillets (about 1 inch thick)
2   tablespoons extra-virgin olive oil
¾   cup dry white wine
¾   cup heavy cream
Chopped fresh parsley or chives, for topping (optional)

1. Heat the butter in a large skillet over medium heat. Add the shallots and thyme and cook until the shallots are translucent, about 7 minutes; season with salt and pepper. Add the mushrooms and cook, stirring occasionally, until brown and tender, about 8 minutes.
2. Meanwhile, season the fish with salt and pepper. Heat the oil in another large skillet over medium-high heat. Add the fish, skin-side down, and cook until the skin is crisp, 3 to 4 minutes; transfer to a plate. Add the wine to the skillet and scrape up any browned bits with a wooden spoon. Boil over high heat until syrupy, 2 to 3 minutes. Add the cream and simmer to thicken slightly, 2 to 3 minutes. Season with salt and pepper.
3. Pour the cream sauce over the mushrooms in the skillet, then add the fish, skin-side up. Simmer until the fish is just firm and translucent, 5 to 7 minutes. Top with parsley, if desired.

Per serving: Calories 546; Fat 35 g (Saturated 17 g); Cholesterol 197 mg; Sodium 300 mg; Carbohydrate 21 g; Fiber 0 g; Protein 31 g

Try it with these sides...

Tomato Gratin
page 333

Lemon Potatoes
page 337

Braised Celery
page 344

CURRIED SALMON CAKES

ACTIVE: 40 min **I** TOTAL: 40 min **I** SERVES: 4

1   pound skinless salmon fillet, halved crosswise
2   teaspoons curry powder, preferably hot
Kosher salt and freshly ground pepper
8   tablespoons store-bought tartar sauce
¼   cup cracker meal or crushed saltines, plus more for sprinkling
2   tablespoons grated peeled ginger
1   bunch scallions, finely chopped
1   large egg, lightly beaten
½   red bell pepper, seeded and diced
2   stalks celery, thinly sliced
1   mango, peeled, pitted and diced
Juice of 1 lime
Vegetable oil, for frying

1. Combine the salmon, 1 tablespoon water, 1½ teaspoons curry powder, ½ teaspoon salt, and pepper to taste in a microwave-safe bowl. Cover with plastic wrap and microwave until the fish is opaque, 2 to 3 minutes. Flake with a fork and cool slightly. Stir in 1 tablespoon tartar sauce, the cracker meal, ginger, half of the scallions and the egg. Form into 4 patties and freeze until firm, about 10 minutes.

2. Meanwhile, whisk the remaining 7 tablespoons tartar sauce and ½ teaspoon curry powder in a bowl. In a separate bowl, mix 1 tablespoon of the curried tartar sauce with the bell pepper, celery, mango, remaining scallions, lime juice, ¼ teaspoon salt, and pepper to taste.

3. Heat ¼ inch of vegetable oil in a nonstick skillet over medium heat. Sprinkle the patties with cracker meal on both sides and fry until golden, 2 to 3 minutes per side. Drain on paper towels. Serve with the mango salad and curried tartar sauce.

Per serving: Calories 536; Fat 34 g (Saturated 7 g); Cholesterol 112 mg; Sodium 767 mg; Carbohydrate 30 g; Fiber 3 g; Protein 27 g

> Turn these salmon cakes into burgers: Serve them on crusty rolls with the tartar sauce as a topping.

PESTO SALMON AND SMASHED POTATOES

ACTIVE: 15 min **I** TOTAL: 35 min **I** SERVES: 4

1	pound new potatoes, halved
1	bunch fresh basil leaves, plus more for serving
¼	cup hazelnuts
1	clove garlic
4	tablespoons extra-virgin olive oil, plus more for drizzling
1	lemon, plus wedges for serving

Kosher salt and freshly ground pepper

2	tablespoons plain low-fat yogurt
4	6-ounce skinless wild salmon fillets
2	tablespoons grated pecorino cheese

1. Set up a 2-layer bamboo steamer in a skillet and add enough water to reach the bottom rim; bring the water to a simmer. Or set up a 2-layer electric steamer according to the manufacturer's instructions. Put the potatoes in the bottom tray of the steamer and cook until just tender, about 15 minutes.

2. Meanwhile, put the basil (reserving some for topping), hazelnuts, garlic and 2 tablespoons olive oil in a blender. Finely grate in the zest from half the lemon and squeeze in all of the juice. Add 3 to 4 tablespoons water and puree. Season with salt and pepper. Transfer to a bowl and stir in the yogurt.

3. After the potatoes have cooked 15 minutes, place the salmon in the top tray of the steamer. Season with salt and pepper and cook until the salmon is opaque, 6 to 8 minutes. Let the fish sit in the steamer off the heat while you transfer the potatoes to a bowl and smash with the remaining 2 tablespoons olive oil and the pecorino; season with salt and pepper. Remove the salmon and top with the pesto and the reserved basil. Serve with the potatoes and lemon wedges.

Per serving: Calories 486; Fat 26 g (Saturated 4 g); Cholesterol 101 mg; Sodium 198 mg; Carbohydrate 18 g; Fiber 3 g; Protein 43 g

We used a stackable steamer to cook the salmon and potatoes at the same time. If you don't have one, just cook them separately.

BAJA FISH TACOS

ACTIVE: 30 min **I** TOTAL: 30 min **I** SERVES: 4

Vegetable oil, for frying
¼   red cabbage, thinly sliced (about 1½ cups)
½   cup fresh cilantro, roughly chopped
Juice of 1 lime, plus wedges for serving
2   tablespoons honey or agave nectar
½   cup mayonnaise
Kosher salt
12   corn tortillas
¾   cup all-purpose flour
½   teaspoon chili powder
Freshly ground pepper
1¼   pounds skinless halibut fillet, cut into 2-by-½-inch pieces
1   Hass avocado
½   cup fresh salsa

1. Heat about 3 inches vegetable oil in a medium pot over medium-low heat until a deep-fry thermometer registers 375°. Meanwhile, toss the cabbage, cilantro, lime juice, honey and mayonnaise in a bowl. Season the slaw with salt.
2. Warm the tortillas in a skillet over medium-low heat or wrap in a damp cloth and microwave 25 seconds. Wrap in a towel to keep warm.
3. Mix the flour, chili powder, and salt and pepper to taste in a shallow bowl. Dredge the fish in the flour mixture, then fry in batches until golden and just cooked through, 2 to 3 minutes. Transfer with a slotted spoon to a paper towel–lined plate to drain. Season with salt.
4. Halve, pit and slice the avocado. Fill the tortillas with the fish, avocado, slaw and salsa. Serve with lime wedges.

Per serving: Calories 777; Fat 45 g (Saturated 7 g); Cholesterol 103 mg; Sodium 529 mg; Carbohydrate 66 g; Fiber 9g; Protein 31 g

> To pit an avocado, slice it in half vertically around the pit, then twist the halves in opposite directions to separate. Hold the half containing the pit in a kitchen towel and carefully knock the bottom end of a knife blade into the pit, then twist the knife to remove the pit.

Done in
30
minutes

Turn your leftovers into this...

THAI RED CURRY MAHI MAHI SALAD

ACTIVE: 30 min ▮ TOTAL: 40 min ▮ SERVES: 4 (or 2, with leftovers for Mahi Mahi Banh Mi, opposite)

Vegetable oil, for the pan
1   13.5-ounce can coconut milk
1   tablespoon red curry paste
1¼   pounds skinless mahi mahi fillet, dark flesh trimmed
⅓   cup fresh lime juice, plus lime wedges for serving
2   tablespoons sugar
2   tablespoons fish sauce
1   teaspoon Asian chili sauce (such as sambal oelek)
1   clove garlic, minced
1   head Boston lettuce, leaves separated
1   bunch watercress, woody stems removed
1   Kirby cucumber, thinly sliced
3   scallions, thinly sliced
1   red or yellow bell pepper, stemmed, seeded and thinly sliced
1   bunch fresh cilantro or mint
1   handful roasted peanuts or cashews

1. Preheat the broiler. Line a broiler pan with foil and lightly oil.
2. Skim 2 tablespoons cream from the top of the coconut milk (reserve the milk to flavor rice as a side dish, if desired). Fry the coconut cream in a small skillet over medium heat until glossy, about 2 minutes. Stir in the curry paste and cook until fragrant, 2 minutes. Spread the mixture over the fish in the broiler pan; broil until browned and just cooked through, about 15 minutes. Cut the fish into 4 pieces.
3. Whisk the lime juice, sugar, 2 tablespoons water and fish sauce in a bowl until the sugar dissolves. Stir in the chili sauce and garlic.
4. Arrange the lettuce, watercress, cucumber, scallions, pepper, herbs, nuts and lime wedges with 4 pieces of fish on a platter; drizzle with the Thai salad dressing. (Or save 2 fillets and some dressing to make Mahi Mahi Banh Mi, opposite.)

Per serving: Calories 249; Fat 7 g (Saturated 2 g); Cholesterol 103 mg; Sodium 953 mg; Carbohydrate 16 g; Fiber 3 g; Protein 31 g

MAHI MAHI BANH MI (VIETNAMESE SANDWICHES)

ACTIVE: 10 min **I** TOTAL: 10 min **I** SERVES: 2

½ baguette, cut into 2 pieces, or 2 ciabatta rolls
1 tablespoon unsalted butter, melted
2 tablespoons mayonnaise
2 scallions, sliced lengthwise and cut into 2-inch pieces
½ carrot, shredded or julienned
½ Kirby cucumber, julienned
1 tablespoon leftover Thai Salad Dressing (opposite)
2 leftover Thai Red Curry Mahi Mahi fillets (opposite)
½ bunch fresh cilantro or mint
½ bunch watercress, woody stems removed
Asian chili sauce (such as sambal oelek; optional)

1. Preheat the broiler to high. Split the baguette or rolls and brush both sides lightly with butter. Broil until lightly toasted, about 2 minutes.

2. Remove from the broiler and spread both sides with mayonnaise. Toss the scallions, carrot and cucumber in the dressing. Stack the sandwiches with fish, the tossed vegetables, herbs, watercress and chili sauce, if desired.

Per serving: Calories 500; Fat 20 g (Saturated 7 g); Cholesterol 123 mg; Sodium 980 mg; Carbohydrate 42 g; Fiber 2 g; Protein 34 g

RICE AND PEAS WITH TROUT

ACTIVE: 30 min **I** TOTAL: 40 min **I** SERVES: 4

2	tablespoons extra-virgin olive oil, plus more for drizzling
1	small onion, chopped
2	teaspoons chopped fresh thyme
1	cup arborio rice
¼	cup dry white wine

Kosher salt and freshly ground pepper

1½	cups low-sodium chicken broth
1½	cups fresh or frozen peas
2	tablespoons horseradish
½	cup grated parmesan cheese
6	ounces smoked trout fillet, flaked

Baby greens or pea shoots, for serving (optional)

1. Preheat the oven to 375°. Heat the olive oil in an ovenproof pot over medium heat. Add the onion and thyme and cook until the onion is slightly softened, about 2 minutes. Stir in the rice and cook, stirring, until glossy, 1 to 2 minutes. Add the wine and cook, stirring, until it's absorbed, about 1 minute. Add 1 teaspoon salt, and pepper to taste.

2. Pour the broth and 1½ cups water over the rice and bring to a simmer, about 4 minutes. Stir, then cover and transfer to the oven. Bake 20 minutes, stirring halfway through.

3. Meanwhile, cook the peas in 4 cups salted boiling water until tender, about 5 minutes. Reserve 1 cup cooking water, then drain.

4. Remove the rice from the oven. Stir in the peas, 1 tablespoon horseradish, the parmesan, and salt and pepper to taste. Stir in enough of the reserved cooking water until the rice is creamy. Divide among bowls. Top with the trout, the remaining tablespoon horseradish, and baby greens, if desired. Drizzle with olive oil.

Per serving: Calories 370; Fat 16 g (Saturated 5 g); Cholesterol 63 mg; Sodium 925 mg; Carbohydrate 29 g; Fiber 4 g; Protein 2 g

> You can replace the trout with shredded rotisserie chicken or leftover salmon.

POPCORN SHRIMP SALAD

ACTIVE: 25 min **I** TOTAL: 25 min **I** SERVES: 4

FOR THE DRESSING
¼ cup mayonnaise
2 tablespoons chopped
    cornichons, plus 2 tablespoons
    pickling liquid from the jar
2 teaspoons whole-grain mustard
½ teaspoon hot sauce
Kosher salt and freshly
    ground pepper

FOR THE SALAD
½ pound medium shrimp,
    peeled and deveined

1 large egg
1 cup instant flour
    (such as Wondra)
1 tablespoon Cajun seasoning
Kosher salt
Vegetable oil, for frying
2 romaine hearts, torn into
    bite-size pieces
1 medium tomato, chopped
1 small red onion, thinly sliced
1 green bell pepper,
    cut into strips
Freshly ground pepper

1. Make the dressing: Whisk the mayonnaise, cornichons and their liquid, mustard, hot sauce, and salt and pepper to taste in a bowl.
2. Prepare the salad: Halve the shrimp lengthwise. Whisk the egg and 2 tablespoons water in a medium bowl. In another bowl, whisk the flour, Cajun seasoning and 2 teaspoons salt.
3. Heat about 1 inch of vegetable oil in a deep skillet until a deep-fry thermometer registers 350°. (A piece of shrimp will sizzle on contact.) Dip each shrimp in the egg mixture, then dredge in the flour mixture. Working in batches, fry the shrimp until crisp and golden, turning once, about 2 minutes. Remove with a slotted spoon and drain on a paper towel–lined plate; season with salt.
4. Toss the romaine, tomato, onion and bell pepper with the dressing in a large bowl; season with salt and pepper. Divide the salad among plates and scatter the shrimp on top.

Per serving: Calories 319; Fat 21 g (Saturated 3 g); Cholesterol 139 mg; Sodium 593 mg; Carbohydrate 16 g; Fiber 2 g; Protein 18 g

Try it with these sides...

Cheesy Chile Rice
page 341

Patatas Bravas
page 347

Herb Toasts
page 352

Done in
25
minutes

HOME-STYLE SHRIMP CURRY

ACTIVE: 35 min **I** TOTAL: 40 min **I** SERVES: 4

1   cup basmati rice, rinsed
2   teaspoons Madras curry powder
Kosher salt
3½   tablespoons vegetable oil
1   medium white onion, quartered
3   cloves garlic
1   2-inch piece ginger, peeled
1   14.5-ounce can diced tomatoes
1 to 2 serrano chile peppers, halved (remove seeds for less heat)
1   pound medium shrimp, peeled and deveined
½   cup whole or low-fat plain yogurt
⅓   cup chopped fresh cilantro

1. Combine the rice, 1⅓ cups water, 1 teaspoon curry powder, ¼ teaspoon salt and ½ tablespoon oil in a saucepan. Cover and cook, undisturbed, over medium-low heat, about 15 minutes; keep warm.
2. Meanwhile, chop the onion in a food processor, drain the excess liquid and set the onion aside. Mince the garlic and ginger in the processor and set aside, then puree the tomatoes with 1 cup water.
3. Heat the remaining 3 tablespoons oil in a Dutch oven or deep skillet over medium-high heat. Add the onion and cook until golden, about 12 minutes. Add the garlic-ginger mixture, chiles, 1 teaspoon salt and the remaining 1 teaspoon curry powder and stir-fry until slightly browned, about 3 minutes. Add the tomato puree and simmer until thickened, about 8 minutes. Add the shrimp, cover and cook over medium-low heat until the shrimp are firm, 3 to 4 minutes. Remove from the heat, then stir in the yogurt and half the cilantro. Serve with the rice and top with the remaining cilantro.

Per serving: Calories 387; Fat 13 g (Saturated 2 g); Cholesterol 171 mg; Sodium 847 mg; Carbohydrate 43 g; Fiber 3 g; Protein 24 g

Use Madras-style curry powder for this dish: It's full of aromatic spices like cumin and coriander.

CAJUN SHRIMP AND RICE

ACTIVE: 20 min **I** TOTAL: 20 min **I** SERVES: 4

1   tablespoon unsalted butter
2   tablespoons extra-virgin olive oil
3   cloves garlic, minced
2   teaspoons Cajun seasoning
1   pound large shrimp, peeled and deveined, tails intact
Kosher salt and freshly ground pepper
4   plum tomatoes, chopped
2   bunches scallions, chopped
3   cups cooked white rice
3   tablespoons chopped fresh parsley
Lemon wedges, for serving (optional)

1. Heat the butter, olive oil and garlic in a large skillet over medium-high heat until fragrant, about 1 minute. Add the Cajun seasoning and shrimp and cook, stirring, until the shrimp begin to curl, about 1 minute. Season with salt and pepper.
2. Add the tomatoes and scallions to the skillet and cook, stirring, about 1 minute. Add the rice and ¼ cup water and continue to cook until the rice is warmed through and the shrimp are opaque, about 3 more minutes. Stir in the parsley and serve with lemon, if desired.

Per serving: Calories 357; Fat 11 g (Saturated 3 g); Cholesterol 176 mg; Sodium 537 mg; Carbohydrate 40 g; Fiber 3 g; Protein 23 g

This dish is a great way to use up leftover takeout rice.

Done in
20
minutes

Low-calorie dinner

SCALLOPS WITH CITRUS AND QUINOA

ACTIVE: 40 min | TOTAL: 40 min | SERVES: 4

¾ cup quinoa, rinsed well
Kosher salt
3 oranges
4 tangerines
2 tablespoons sugar
1 tablespoon apple cider vinegar
1 teaspoon coriander seeds, crushed
2 tablespoons cold unsalted butter, cut into pieces
1¼ pounds sea scallops, tough foot muscles removed
Freshly ground pepper
1 teaspoon extra-virgin olive oil
1 tablespoon chopped fresh parsley or chives

1. Combine the quinoa, 2 cups water and ½ teaspoon salt in a saucepan and bring to a boil over high heat. Reduce the heat to low and simmer, uncovered, until the water is absorbed, 12 to 14 minutes.
2. Meanwhile, grate 1 teaspoon orange zest, then juice all 3 oranges and the tangerines into a bowl. Sprinkle the sugar in a skillet and cook over medium-high heat until dark amber, about 5 minutes. Remove from the heat and whisk in the vinegar, citrus juices and zest, and the coriander. Return to medium heat and boil until thick, about 8 minutes. Remove from the heat and whisk in the butter; keep warm.
3. Season the scallops on one side with salt and pepper. Heat the oil in a large cast-iron skillet over medium heat. Add the scallops seasoned-side down and sear until golden, 4 to 5 minutes. Flip and cook until golden on the other side, 2 to 3 more minutes.
4. Fluff the quinoa with a fork and divide among plates. Top with the scallops, drizzle with the citrus sauce and sprinkle with the parsley.

Per serving: Calories 335; Fat 10 g (Saturated 4 g); Cholesterol 62 mg; Sodium 475 mg; Carbohydrate 34 g; Fiber 2 g; Protein 28 g

> Quinoa is a high-protein grain available at health-food stores and many supermarkets. If you can't find it, use whole-wheat couscous.

CLAMS AND MUSSELS IN THAI CURRY SAUCE

ACTIVE: 30 min **I** TOTAL: 30 min **I** SERVES: 4

2   tablespoons vegetable oil
1   3-inch piece ginger, peeled and finely chopped
3   cloves garlic, finely chopped
1 to 2 Thai chile peppers or jalapeños, seeded and chopped
2   tablespoons Thai red curry paste
½   cup ketchup
Juice of 2 limes, plus lime wedges for serving
16   littleneck clams, scrubbed
1¾   pounds mussels, scrubbed
1   small red bell pepper, cut into thin strips
¾   cup fresh cilantro
¾   cup fresh basil
Crusty bread, for serving (optional)

1. Heat the oil in a large pot over medium-high heat. Add the ginger, garlic and chiles and stir-fry until fragrant, 1 to 2 minutes. Add the curry paste and ketchup and fry until slightly browned, 3 to 4 more minutes. Add the lime juice and 3 cups water, cover and bring to a boil.
2. Add the clams; cover and steam until they open slightly, about 3 minutes. Add the mussels; cover and steam until they open slightly, 3 to 4 minutes. Stir in the bell pepper and half of the cilantro and basil. Cook, covered, until the pepper is crisp-tender, about 2 minutes.
3. Transfer the clams and mussels to serving bowls and ladle the broth on top. Sprinkle with the remaining cilantro and basil and serve with lime. Serve with crusty bread, if desired.

Per serving: Calories 216; Fat 10 g (Saturated 1 g); Cholesterol 38 mg; Sodium 489 mg; Carbohydrate 18 g; Fiber 2 g; Protein 17 g

> Tap any mussels or clams that do not open after cooking; if they still don't open, discard them.

Done in
25
minutes

SPINACH-ORZO SALAD WITH SHRIMP

ACTIVE: 25 min **I** TOTAL: 25 min **I** SERVES: 4

Kosher salt
½   cup orzo
4   cups spinach, thinly sliced
10   medium radishes, quartered
1   small cucumber, peeled, seeded and diced
½   red onion, quartered and thinly sliced
¼   cup pitted oil-cured olives, chopped
½   cup packed fresh mint, chopped
½   cup packed fresh parsley, chopped
⅓   cup plus 2 tablespoons fresh lemon juice
⅓   cup plus 2 tablespoons extra-virgin olive oil
Freshly ground pepper
1   pound medium shrimp, peeled and deveined
½   cup crumbled feta cheese

1. Preheat the broiler. Bring a pot of salted water to a boil. Add the orzo and cook until al dente, about 8 minutes. Drain, rinse with cold water and shake dry.
2. Meanwhile, toss the spinach, radishes, cucumber, onion, olives, mint, parsley and ⅓ cup each lemon juice and olive oil in a large bowl. Add the orzo and season with salt and pepper.
3. Toss the shrimp with the remaining 2 tablespoons each lemon juice and olive oil in a bowl. Arrange on a foil-lined broiler pan and broil until slightly pink, 1 to 2 minutes. Turn and broil until just cooked through, 2 to 3 more minutes.
4. Divide the salad among plates. Top with the shrimp, sprinkle with the feta and season with pepper.

Per serving: Calories 672; Fat 35 g (Saturated 7 g); Cholesterol 238 mg; Sodium 576 mg; Carbohydrate 54 g; Fiber 5 g; Protein 36 g

Use the leftover parsley in...

Bacon-and-Egg Soup
page 11

**Shrimp Scampi with
Garlic Toasts**
page 261

**Whole-Grain Pasta with
Chickpeas and Escarole**
page 269

SHRIMP BOIL

ACTIVE: 40 min **I** TOTAL: 40 min **I** SERVES: 4

2   lemons, halved, plus wedges for serving
½   cup Old Bay Seasoning
8   cloves garlic, smashed
1   large red onion, quartered
6   sprigs thyme
1   pound baby red potatoes
4   ears corn, husked and snapped in half
1¼   pounds large shrimp, unpeeled
2   tablespoons unsalted butter
Hot sauce, for serving (optional)

1. Fill a large pot with 4 quarts of water. Squeeze the lemon juice into the water and add the squeezed lemon halves. Add the Old Bay, garlic and onion. Tie the thyme sprigs together with kitchen twine and add to the pot. Cover and bring to a boil, then reduce to a simmer and cook about 5 minutes.
2. Add the potatoes to the pot and cook until just tender, about 10 minutes. Add the corn and cook 5 more minutes.
3. Meanwhile, slice along the back of each shrimp through the shells; remove the veins and rinse the shrimp. Add to the pot, cover and cook until the shrimp curl and are just opaque, 2 to 3 minutes.
4. Transfer the shrimp and vegetables with a slotted spoon or skimmer to a large bowl. Add the butter and about 1 cup broth to the bowl and toss until the butter is melted. Transfer the shrimp and vegetables to a platter. Serve with the remaining broth, lemon wedges and hot sauce, if desired.

Per serving: Calories 379; Fat 10 g (Saturated 5 g); Cholesterol 225 mg; Sodium 735 mg; Carbohydrate 41 g; Fiber 9 g; Protein 30 g

No need to peel your shrimp—the shells are useful: They help flavor the broth, and they protect the inside of the shrimp from the heat, so you're much less likely to overcook them.

Low-calorie dinner

Done in
25
minutes

SHRIMP SCAMPI WITH GARLIC TOASTS

ACTIVE: 25 min I TOTAL: 25 min I SERVES: 4

3   tablespoons extra-virgin olive oil
3   tablespoons unsalted butter
5   cloves garlic, chopped
Kosher salt
Pinch of red pepper flakes
8   ½-inch-thick slices crusty bread
1¼   pounds large shrimp, peeled and deveined, tails intact
¾   cup dry white wine or low-sodium chicken broth
Grated zest and juice of ½ lemon, plus lemon wedges for serving
⅓   cup chopped fresh parsley
⅓   cup chopped fresh chives

1. Preheat the broiler. Heat the olive oil and 2 tablespoons butter in a large ovenproof skillet over medium heat. Add the garlic, ½ teaspoon salt and the red pepper flakes and cook 1 to 2 minutes; remove from the heat. Brush both sides of the bread with some of the garlic mixture and arrange on a baking sheet. Broil the bread until toasted, about 1 minute per side. Divide the bread among 4 bowls.
2. Place the skillet with the remaining garlic mixture over high heat. Add the shrimp and toss to coat, then stir in the wine and lemon zest and juice. Transfer to the broiler and cook until the shrimp are pink, about 3 minutes. Transfer the shrimp with a slotted spoon to the bowls.
3. Return the skillet to high heat and boil the cooking liquid until slightly thickened, 1 to 2 minutes. Stir in the parsley and chives. Whisk in the remaining 1 tablespoon butter and simmer 1 to 2 more minutes; pour over the shrimp. Serve with lemon wedges.

Per serving: Calories 578; Fat 22 g (Saturated 7 g); Cholesterol 299 mg; Sodium 963 mg; Carbohydrate 44 g; Fiber 4 g; Protein 38 g

Leave the tail end of the shell on your shrimp so you can eat them with your hands.

Mix & Match

FOIL-PACKET FISH

Salmon with Corn,
Cherry Tomatoes and
Citrus-Basil Oil

PICK A FISH

- four 6-ounce skinless salmon fillets
- four 6-ounce skinless striped bass fillets
- four 6-ounce skinless halibut fillets
- four 6-ounce skinless cod fillets
- 1½ pounds large shrimp, peeled and deveined
- 3 pounds mussels, cleaned

PREP YOUR VEGETABLES

Choose 2 vegetables (½ cup of each) per packet.

- boiled potato chunks
- fresh corn kernels
- thawed frozen lima beans
- halved cherry tomatoes
- 1-inch scallion pieces
- thinly sliced yellow squash
- thinly sliced red onion
- thinly sliced mushrooms
- thinly sliced celery
- thinly sliced bell pepper
- thinly sliced leeks
- shaved carrots

MAKE A TOPPING

CITRUS-BASIL OIL

Cook 10 basil leaves in salted boiling water, about 10 seconds; drain and run under cold water, then squeeze dry. Puree the basil with ½ cup olive oil, 1 tablespoon orange juice and a pinch each of sugar and salt in a blender.

FENNEL SPICE BLEND

Toast 2 tablespoons fennel seeds and 1 teaspoon coriander seeds in a skillet, about 2 minutes. Add ¼ teaspoon red pepper flakes and toast for 30 seconds. Grind in a spice grinder or with a knife; toss with salt and pepper.

SPICY CHIPOTLE BUTTER

Pulse ½ stick softened butter, 1 minced chipotle pepper in adobo sauce, the juice of ½ lime, ½ teaspoon grated lime zest and ¼ teaspoon salt in a food processor, or mash with a wooden spoon.

④ FILL THE PACKETS

- Preheat the oven to 450°. Lay out a large sheet of heavy-duty foil for each packet. Mound 1 cup vegetables in the center of each, season with salt and pepper and top with a sprig of parsley or basil.
- Put a fish fillet or portion of seafood on top of the vegetables, season with salt and pepper and drizzle with olive oil. Add a splash of water or white wine, then fold up the ends of the foil and seal into packets, leaving room inside for steam.
- Put the packets on a baking sheet and bake until just cooked through, about 12 minutes for the fillets and shrimp and 15 minutes for mussels. Let sit about 5 minutes, then carefully open the packets and add your topping.

Ellie says...

    One of the biggest joys in my life is cooking and enjoying food with my daughter, Isabella. I have always involved her in the kitchen and have approached healthy eating as a sensory adventure, celebrating all of food's wonderful colors, textures, tastes and aromas rather than pushing a bunch of 'shoulds.' I knew I had done something right when, at age 3, while heading downtown on a city bus, Isabella said excitedly, 'I smell basil!' Sure enough, a woman behind her had a big bunch of the fragrant herb in her shopping bag. All I could think was, 'That's my girl!'"

—ELLIE KRIEGER IS THE HOST OF HEALTHY APPETITE WITH ELLIE KRIEGER AND THE AUTHOR OF THE FOOD YOU CRAVE: LUSCIOUS RECIPES FOR A HEALTHY LIFE AND SO EASY: LUSCIOUS, HEALTHY RECIPES FOR EVERY MEAL OF THE WEEK.

KITCHEN SECRET
The queen of healthy cooking keeps a stash of candy, including Tootsie Rolls, in a cabinet over her fridge.

Garlic-and-
Greens Spaghetti,
page 277

Pasta & Grains

WHOLE-GRAIN PASTA WITH CHICKPEAS AND ESCAROLE

ACTIVE: 30 min **I** TOTAL: 30 min **I** SERVES: 4

2	cups whole-grain penne
1	head escarole, roughly chopped
4	tablespoons extra-virgin olive oil, plus more to taste
¼	cup capers, drained and patted dry (optional)
5	cloves garlic, sliced
½	cup roughly chopped fresh parsley
¼	teaspoon red pepper flakes
1	28-ounce can whole peeled tomatoes, crushed slightly, liquid reserved
1	15.5-ounce can chickpeas, drained, rinsed and patted dry

Kosher salt and freshly ground pepper

2	bay leaves
½	cup freshly grated parmesan cheese, plus more for sprinkling

1. Cook the pasta according to the package directions; add the escarole during the last 2 minutes, cover and do not stir. Remove the escarole with tongs; set aside. Drain the pasta, reserving ½ cup cooking liquid. Meanwhile, if you're using capers, heat 1 tablespoon olive oil in a large skillet over medium-high heat. Add the capers and fry until crisp, about 2 minutes. Transfer to a paper towel–lined plate.

2. Add the remaining 3 tablespoons oil to the skillet. Cook the garlic, parsley and red pepper flakes until the garlic toasts slightly, 1 minute. Add the tomatoes, chickpeas, a pinch of salt and the bay leaves. Cook until the tomatoes and chickpeas brown, about 6 minutes. Add the escarole and reserved tomato juice and cook until the sauce thickens slightly, about 4 more minutes. Remove and discard the bay leaves.

3. Add the cooked pasta to the skillet and toss with the sauce; season with salt and pepper. (If the sauce is thick, add some reserved pasta water.) Stir in the cheese, top with fried capers, if using, and more cheese.

Per serving: Calories 499; Fat 22 g (Saturated 5 g); Cholesterol 20 mg; Sodium 548 mg; Carbohydrate 55 g; Fiber 15 g; Protein 21 g

> Use your hands to crush the tomatoes directly into the skillet, or chop the tomatoes right in the can with a pair of kitchen shears.

CREAMY CHICKEN AND PASTA SALAD

ACTIVE: 15 min | TOTAL: 25 min | SERVES: 4

Kosher salt
8   ounces tubetti or other small tube-shaped pasta
1¼ cups low-fat plain Greek yogurt
½   cup mayonnaise
2   teaspoons apple cider vinegar
1   teaspoon dijon mustard
⅓   cup chopped fresh dill
1   tablespoon chopped fresh chives
1   rotisserie chicken
2   stalks celery, chopped
1   Kirby cucumber, peeled, halved lengthwise, seeded and chopped
Freshly ground pepper
8   cups mesclun greens

1. Bring a pot of salted water to a boil. Add the pasta and cook as the label directs. Drain and rinse under cold water to stop the cooking.
2. Meanwhile, whisk the yogurt, mayonnaise, ¼ cup water, the vinegar, mustard, dill, chives and 2 teaspoons salt in a medium bowl. Remove the skin from the chicken and shred the meat into large pieces. Add the chicken, celery and cucumber to the dressing and gently stir to combine.
3. Shake the excess water from the pasta and add it to the chicken salad. Season with pepper and toss. Serve over the greens.

Per serving: Calories 672; Fat 32 g (Saturated 6 g); Cholesterol 114 mg; Sodium 1,724 mg; Carbohydrate 56 g; Fiber 6 g; Protein 44 g

You normally shouldn't rinse pasta—the residual starch helps sauce cling to the noodles—but pasta salads are an exception. Rinsing keeps the pasta from overcooking and prevents it from clumping together when it cools.

Done in
25
minutes

We tossed the cooked pasta with milk to keep it from getting gummy.

CROQUE MONSIEUR MAC AND CHEESE

ACTIVE: 20 min **I** TOTAL: 40 min **I** SERVES: 4

½ pound ziti
2 cups milk
2 cups coarsely grated gruyère cheese (about 6 ounces)
1 cup finely grated parmesan cheese (about 4 ounces)
2 large eggs
3 slices white sandwich bread, roughly diced
2 tablespoons unsalted butter, plus more for greasing
1 medium onion, diced
1 clove garlic, minced
3 tablespoons all-purpose flour
Pinch of cayenne pepper
⅛ teaspoon freshly grated nutmeg
Kosher salt
8 ounces deli-sliced boiled ham

1. Preheat the oven to 425°. Bring a large pot of salted water to a boil. Add the ziti and cook until al dente, about 6 minutes. Drain and transfer to a large bowl; toss with ¼ cup milk.
2. Meanwhile, combine both cheeses in a bowl. Beat ¼ cup milk and the eggs in another bowl; fold in the bread and add half of the cheese.
3. Melt the butter in a saucepan over high heat. Add the onion and garlic; cook, stirring, until just brown, 2 minutes. Sprinkle in the flour, cayenne, nutmeg and 1 teaspoon salt; cook, stirring, about 2 minutes. Slowly add ¾ cup water and the remaining 1½ cups milk; bring to a boil, stirring until thickened. Remove from the heat and whisk to cool slightly. Whisk in the remaining cheese, then add the pasta and toss.
4. Butter a shallow casserole dish. Add half of the pasta, top with some of the ham and cover with the remaining pasta. Top with the remaining ham, then cover with the bread mixture. Bake until golden and bubbly, about 20 minutes. Let rest a few minutes before serving.

Per serving: Calories 835; Fat 37 g (Saturated 20 g); Cholesterol 242 mg; Sodium 1,996 mg; Carbohydrate 71 g; Fiber 3 g; Protein 48 g

Turn your leftovers into this...

FONTINA RISOTTO WITH CHICKEN

ACTIVE: 35 min ▎ TOTAL: 35 min ▎ SERVES: 4 (with leftovers for Risotto Cakes with Mixed Greens, opposite)

4   cups low-sodium chicken broth
5   tablespoons unsalted butter
1   medium onion, finely chopped
2½ cups arborio rice
3   sprigs thyme
1   cup dry white wine
Kosher salt
1   cup finely grated
    parmesan cheese
Freshly ground pepper
1   cup coarsely grated fontina
    cheese, plus more for topping
8   ounces deli smoked chicken
    breast, diced (about 1¼ cups)
¼   cup roughly chopped
    fresh parsley

1. Bring the broth and 4 cups water to a simmer in a saucepan; keep warm.
2. Meanwhile, melt 4 tablespoons butter in a pot over medium-high heat. Add the onion; cook until translucent, about 4 minutes. Add the rice and thyme; cook, stirring, until the rice is glossy, about 1 minute. Add the wine and cook, stirring, until the liquid is absorbed. Add 1 teaspoon salt. Ladle in the hot broth, about ½ cup at a time, stirring constantly, allowing all of the liquid to be absorbed before adding more. Continue until the rice is just tender, 20 to 25 minutes.
3. Remove the thyme. Stir in the parmesan, the remaining 1 tablespoon butter, ½ teaspoon salt and pepper to taste. Gently stir in the fontina and chicken. Reserve about 2 cups risotto for Risotto Cakes with Mixed Greens, opposite. Divide the rest among bowls; top with parsley and more fontina.

Per serving: Calories 790; Fat 27 g (Saturated 15 g); Cholesterol 101 mg; Sodium 902 mg; Carbohydrate 90 g; Fiber 2 g; Protein 42 g

If you don't have panko, just coarsely grind stale or crusty bread in a food processor.

RISOTTO CAKES WITH MIXED GREENS

ACTIVE: 15 min I TOTAL: 35 min I SERVES: 4

2 tablespoons chopped chives or scallion greens

2 cups leftover Fontina Risotto with Chicken, chilled (opposite)

8 small cubes fontina cheese (about 1½ ounces)

½ cup panko (Japanese breadcrumbs)

2 tablespoons extra-virgin olive oil, plus more for shallow frying

Kosher salt and freshly ground pepper

8 cups mesclun greens (about 6 ounces)

½ bulb fennel, very thinly sliced

1 tablespoon fresh lemon juice

1. Stir the chives into the chilled risotto. Form into 8 patties, using about ¼ cup risotto for each. Press a hole in the center of each patty and stuff with a cube of fontina; pat risotto around each hole to cover.

2. Place the breadcrumbs in a shallow bowl. Lightly dredge each risotto cake in the crumbs, turning to coat evenly. Place on a plate, cover with plastic wrap and refrigerate for 20 minutes.

3. Heat about ¼ inch of oil in a medium nonstick skillet over medium-high heat. Fry the cakes, 2 or 3 at a time, until evenly browned, about 1½ minutes per side. Transfer to a paper towel–lined plate to drain; season with salt and pepper.

4. Combine the greens and fennel in a bowl; drizzle with 2 tablespoons olive oil and the lemon juice, season with salt and pepper and toss. Divide the risotto cakes and salad among 4 plates.

Per serving: Calories 445; Fat 22 g (Saturated 8 g); Cholesterol 46 mg; Sodium 430 mg; Carbohydrate 41 g; Fiber 4 g; Protein 20 g

Try three ounces of pasta per serving, rather than the usual four, to keep calories in check. High-fiber greens make the dish plenty filling.

GARLIC-AND-GREENS SPAGHETTI

ACTIVE: 25 min **I** TOTAL: 35 min **I** SERVES: 4

16   cloves garlic, thinly sliced
⅓   cup extra-virgin olive oil
2   medium onions, halved and sliced
⅛   teaspoon red pepper flakes, or more to taste
Kosher salt
12   cups torn winter greens, such as kale, chard, escarole or mustard greens
     (about 2½ pounds)
12   ounces spaghetti
¼   cup grated pecorino romano cheese

1. Bring a large pot of salted water to a boil. Meanwhile, cook the garlic in the olive oil in a large skillet over medium-high heat, stirring occasionally, until golden brown and crisp, about 3 minutes. (Be careful not to overbrown the garlic or it will taste bitter.) Using a slotted spoon, transfer the garlic chips to a paper-towel-lined plate. Pour off all but 2 tablespoons oil into a small bowl to use as a dip for crusty bread, if desired. Add the onions and red pepper flakes to the oil in the pan; cook, stirring, until the onions are light brown, about 10 minutes. Season with 1½ teaspoons salt.
2. When the onions are almost done, add the greens to the boiling water and cook, uncovered, until just tender, about 2 minutes. Using tongs, remove the greens, shaking off the excess water; add them to the skillet with the onions (set the pot of water aside). Cook, stirring occasionally, until tender, about 5 minutes.
3. Return the cooking water to a boil. Add the spaghetti and cook until al dente, 8 to 10 minutes. Remove and reserve about 1 cup cooking water; drain the pasta and transfer to a serving bowl. Add the cheese and toss. Add the greens and some of the reserved pasta water and toss, adding more water as necessary to keep the pasta from clumping. Top with the garlic chips.

Per serving: Calories 565; Fat 16 g (Saturated 4 g); Cholesterol 8 mg;
Sodium 940 mg; Carbohydrate 28 g; Fiber 4 g; Protein 28 g

GNOCCHI NIÇOISE

ACTIVE: 20 min **I** TOTAL: 40 min **I** SERVES: 4

1   tablespoon extra-virgin olive oil
4   ounces bacon, diced
4   cloves garlic, smashed
½   pound coarsely ground beef (look for "chili grind")
2   tablespoons brandy or red wine
3   shallots, chopped
1   cup diced carrots
1   stalk celery, sliced
1   tablespoon tomato paste
Kosher salt and freshly ground pepper
1   15-ounce can plum tomatoes
1   cup low-sodium chicken broth
1   bay leaf
2   1-inch strips orange peel
⅔   cup niçoise olives, pitted and chopped
1   package (about 1 pound) vacuum-packed gnocchi

1. Heat the oil in a medium skillet over medium-high heat. Add the bacon and garlic; cook until the bacon starts to brown, about 4 minutes. Add the ground beef; cook, stirring, 3 minutes. Add the brandy, shallots, carrots, celery and tomato paste; cook until the vegetables soften, about 4 minutes. Season with salt and pepper.
2. Crush the tomatoes into the pan with your hands and add any juices from the can. Stir in the broth, bay leaf, orange peel and olives. Bring to a simmer and lower the heat; cover and cook 20 minutes. Uncover, increase the heat and bring to a boil to thicken the sauce.
3. Bring a large pot of salted water to a boil. Just before serving, boil the gnocchi until one floats to the top, about 1 minute. Drain immediately to prevent the gnocchi from becoming mushy. Remove the orange peel and bay leaf from the sauce and season with salt and pepper. Toss the gnocchi with the sauce.

Per serving: Calories 615; Fat 25 g (Saturated 8 g); Cholesterol 57 mg; Sodium 1,155 mg; Carbohydrate 70 g; Fiber 7 g; Protein 24 g

> Brandy or wine makes this quick sauce taste like it has simmered for hours.

Done in
25
minutes

BLT PASTA SALAD

ACTIVE: 25 min I TOTAL: 25 min I SERVES: 4

12	ounces corkscrew-shaped pasta
½	cup milk
12	ounces lean bacon
3	ripe medium tomatoes, cut into chunks
1	tablespoon chopped fresh thyme
1	clove garlic, minced

Kosher salt and freshly ground pepper

½	cup mayonnaise
¼	cup sour cream
4	tablespoons chopped chives or scallion greens
5	heads Bibb lettuce, quartered, or 5 cups chopped romaine hearts

1. Cook the pasta in a large pot of salted boiling water as the label directs. Drain and toss with the milk in a large bowl; set aside.

2. Meanwhile, cook the bacon in a large skillet over medium-high heat until crisp. Drain on paper towels. Discard all but 3 tablespoons drippings from the pan. Add the tomatoes, thyme and garlic to the pan and toss until warmed through; season with salt and pepper. Crumble the bacon into bite-size pieces; set aside ¼ cup for topping. Toss the remaining bacon and the tomato mixture with the pasta.

3. Mix the mayonnaise, sour cream and 3 tablespoons chives with the pasta until evenly combined. Season with salt and pepper. Add the lettuce; toss again to coat. Top with the reserved bacon and the remaining 1 tablespoon chives. Serve at room temperature.

Per serving: Calories 960; Fat 56 g (Saturated 20 g); Cholesterol 125 mg; Sodium 2,114 mg; Carbohydrate 73 g; Fiber 5 g; Protein 44 g

Use the leftover sour cream in...

Poppy Seed–Chicken Pitas page 76

Pork with Potato-Bean Salad page 178

Smoked Trout and Potato Salad page 227

SPANISH-STYLE NOODLES
WITH CHICKEN AND SAUSAGE

ACTIVE: 40 min **I** TOTAL: 40 min **I** SERVES: 4

¾   pound skinless, boneless chicken thighs, cut into ½-inch chunks
½   pound sweet or hot Italian sausage, cut into ½-inch chunks
Kosher salt and freshly ground pepper
1   teaspoon dried marjoram or oregano
⅓   cup extra-virgin olive oil
2   medium onions, diced
3   cloves garlic, chopped
2   bay leaves
¾   cup tomato puree
12   ounces spaghetti, broken into 3-inch pieces
Grated manchego or parmesan cheese, for topping (optional)

1. Bring a large kettle or pot of water to a boil. Season the chicken and sausage with 2 teaspoons salt, 1 teaspoon pepper and the marjoram. Heat the olive oil in a heavy-bottomed pot over high heat. Add the chicken and sausage and brown on all sides, about 5 minutes. Transfer to a plate with a slotted spoon.
2. Add the onions, garlic, bay leaves and tomato puree to the pot. Reduce the heat and cook, stirring, until the oil turns deep red and the onions are tender, 6 to 8 minutes. If the onions are sticking, add a splash of water and scrape the bottom of the pan with a wooden spoon.
3. Add the spaghetti to the onion mixture and stir-fry until golden, about 6 minutes. Add the chicken and sausage and enough boiling water to cover the pasta by ½ inch. Simmer, stirring once or twice, until the pasta is al dente and the sauce thickens, about 10 minutes. Season with salt and pepper and top with cheese, if desired.

Per serving: Calories 776; Fat 36 g (Saturated 8 g); Cholesterol 102 mg; Sodium 1,600 mg; Carbohydrate 76 g; Fiber 5 g; Protein 30 g

> This is the ultimate one-pot meal: The spaghetti cooks right in the sauce with the chicken and sausage.

Done in
15
minutes

UDON WITH TOFU AND ASIAN GREENS

ACTIVE: 15 min I TOTAL: 15 min I SERVES: 4

1   8-ounce package udon noodles
4   tablespoons roasted peanut oil, or 3 tablespoons sesame oil mixed
     with 1 tablespoon vegetable oil
1   12-ounce package firm tofu, cut into 12 pieces
Kosher salt and freshly ground pepper
1   11-ounce package Asian cooking greens or baby spinach
1   bunch scallions, thinly sliced diagonally
Large pinch of red pepper flakes
3   tablespoons soy sauce
Pinch of sugar

1. Cook the udon noodles as the label directs. (Don't overcook or they will get mushy.) Drain, reserving about ⅓ cup of the cooking water.
2. Meanwhile, heat 2 tablespoons oil in a medium skillet over medium heat. Pat the tofu dry and season all over with salt and pepper. Add the tofu to the skillet and sear until golden brown, about 2 minutes per side. Set aside and keep warm.
3. Add 1 tablespoon oil and the greens to the skillet. Cook, tossing, until just wilted. Add the scallions, red pepper flakes, the remaining 1 tablespoon oil, the soy sauce and sugar. Add the reserved cooking water; heat to create a broth. Divide the noodles and greens among 4 bowls and top with the tofu.

Per serving: Calories 430; Fat 19 g (Saturated 3 g); Cholesterol 0 mg; Sodium 990 mg; Carbohydrate 51 g; Fiber 8 g; Protein 18 g

Asian noodles like udon and ramen are lighter than Italian pasta, so they cook quickly. They taste great hot or cold.

VEGETABLE COUSCOUS WITH MOROCCAN PESTO

ACTIVE: 40 min **I** TOTAL: 40 min **I** SERVES: 4

FOR THE PESTO
1   cup fresh cilantro (leaves and some stems)
½   cup fresh parsley (stems reserved for couscous)
2   tablespoons whole almonds
½   clove garlic
¼   cup extra-virgin olive oil
Kosher salt

FOR THE COUSCOUS
4   tablespoons unsalted butter
Kosher salt
1   onion, cut into 8 wedges
1   cinnamon stick
1   14-ounce can peeled tomatoes, halved
2   small carrots, cut into chunks
1   zucchini and/or 1 bunch Swiss chard, chopped
⅓   cup raisins
Freshly ground pepper
1½ cups whole-wheat couscous

1. Make the pesto: Combine the cilantro, parsley leaves, almonds and garlic in a food processor; pulse until coarsely chopped. Add the olive oil and ½ teaspoon salt; process until smooth.
2. Prepare the vegetables for the couscous: Heat a wide heavy-bottomed pot over medium heat. Add 3 tablespoons butter and 1 teaspoon salt; cook until the butter begins to brown. Add the onion. Tie the reserved parsley stems and cinnamon stick together with twine; add to the pot. Cook, stirring occasionally, until the onion is lightly browned, about 5 minutes. Add the tomatoes, 1 cup water, carrots, zucchini and/or Swiss chard, raisins, 1½ teaspoons salt, and pepper to taste. Cook, stirring occasionally, until the vegetables are crisp-tender, about 15 minutes. Remove the parsley and cinnamon.
3. Meanwhile, cook the couscous as the label directs. Add the remaining 1 tablespoon butter, season with salt and pepper and fluff with a fork. Top the couscous with the vegetables and pesto.

Per serving: Calories 525; Fat 29 g (Saturated 9 g); Cholesterol 30 mg; Sodium 1,364 mg; Carbohydrate 60 g; Fiber 11 g; Protein 11 g

Even if you're not a vegetarian, cutting out meat every once in a while is a smart way to make dinner healthier and cheaper. Grains like couscous, bulgur wheat or quinoa make a perfectly filling meal.

One-pan
meal

SKILLET LASAGNA

ACTIVE: 20 min I TOTAL: 40 min I SERVES: 4

¼ cup extra-virgin olive oil, plus more for drizzling
4 cloves garlic, sliced
1½ pounds ripe tomatoes, diced
4 tablespoons chopped fresh basil and/or parsley, plus more for topping
Kosher salt and freshly ground pepper
1 cup ricotta cheese
1 large egg
2 tablespoons grated parmesan cheese, plus more for topping
6 sheets no-bake lasagna noodles
1 carrot, peeled into ribbons
1 zucchini, peeled into ribbons
3½ cups baby spinach
⅓ pound mozzarella cheese, thinly sliced

1. Heat the ¼ cup olive oil in a large skillet over medium-high heat. Add the garlic; cook until golden, 1 minute. Add the tomatoes, 1 tablespoon herbs, ½ teaspoon salt, and pepper to taste; cook until saucy, about 5 minutes. Transfer to a blender and puree. Return 1 cup of the sauce to the skillet and reduce the heat to low; reserve the remaining sauce.
2. Meanwhile, mix the ricotta, egg, parmesan, the remaining 3 tablespoons herbs, ½ teaspoon salt, and pepper to taste in a bowl.
3. Place 2 lasagna noodles over the sauce in the skillet. Layer half of the carrot and zucchini on top; drizzle with olive oil and season with salt and pepper. Cover with half of the spinach, half of the ricotta mixture, a few pieces of mozzarella and 2 to 3 tablespoons of the reserved tomato sauce. Repeat the layers, ending with noodles. Top with the remaining sauce and mozzarella. Cover and simmer until the lasagna is cooked and the cheese melts, 20 to 25 minutes. Let rest a few minutes before slicing. Top with more parmesan and fresh herbs.

Per serving: Calories 564; Fat 35 g (Saturated 14 g); Cholesterol 108 mg; Sodium 924 mg; Carbohydrate 38 g; Fiber 4 g; Protein 24 g

Try it with these sides...

Mushroom Salad
page 333

Creamy Bibb Salad
page 334

Tomato-Basil Lima Beans
page 346

SPINACH RAVIOLI WITH TOMATO SAUCE

ACTIVE: 20 min **|** TOTAL: 25 min **|** SERVES: 4

2   tablespoons extra-virgin olive oil
1   ounce Italian salami, finely diced, or pulsed in a food processor
4   cloves garlic, minced
1   28-ounce can San Marzano plum tomatoes, drained, juices reserved
5 or 6 fresh basil leaves, plus more for topping
Pinch of sugar
Kosher salt and freshly ground pepper
1½   pounds frozen spinach-and-cheese ravioli
1   ounce ricotta salata or parmesan cheese, grated

1. Bring a large pot of water to a boil. Meanwhile, heat the olive oil in a large skillet over medium-high heat. Add the salami and garlic and cook, about 1 minute. Crush the tomatoes into the pan with your hands and cook until slightly dry, about 5 minutes. Add the reserved tomato juice, basil, sugar, and salt and pepper to taste. Increase the heat to high and cook until the sauce thickens, about 5 minutes. Stir in ¾ cup water and reduce the heat to medium-low. Let simmer while you cook the ravioli.
2. Add salt to the boiling water, then add the ravioli and cook as the label directs; drain. Divide the ravioli among shallow bowls, spoon the sauce on top and sprinkle with the cheese. Top with more basil.

Per serving: Calories 482; Fat 20 g (Saturated 7 g); Cholesterol 60 mg; Sodium 1,007 mg; Carbohydrate 54 g; Fiber 7 g; Protein 25 g

> Ricotta salata is firm, not soft like regular ricotta. Grate it onto pasta and pizza instead of parmesan.

Done in
25
minutes

Done in
25
minutes

WHOLE-WHEAT SPAGHETTI WITH LEEKS AND HAZELNUTS

ACTIVE: 25 min I TOTAL: 25 min I SERVES: 4

Kosher salt
12 ounces whole-wheat spaghetti
4   tablespoons extra-virgin olive oil
3   large leeks, white and light-green parts only, thinly sliced
2   teaspoons sugar
2   teaspoons balsamic vinegar (preferably aged)
1   small head radicchio, halved, cored and thinly sliced
6   ounces creamy Italian cheese, such as fontina or taleggio, cubed
¼ to ⅓ cup hazelnuts, toasted and chopped

1. Bring a large pot of salted water to a boil. Add the spaghetti and cook as the label directs.
2. Meanwhile, heat a large skillet over medium-low heat and add 2 tablespoons olive oil. Scatter the leeks in the skillet and season with 1 teaspoon each salt and sugar. Cook, stirring occasionally, until tender, about 10 minutes.
3. Drain the pasta, reserving about 1 cup of the cooking liquid. Add the pasta and the reserved cooking liquid to the skillet with the leeks. Add the remaining 2 tablespoons oil, 1 teaspoon sugar and the balsamic vinegar. Increase the heat to medium-high and add the radicchio and cheese. Toss until the cheese melts, 3 to 5 minutes. Season with salt and top with the hazelnuts.

Per serving: Calories 692; Fat 34 g (Saturated 11 g); Cholesterol 49 mg; Sodium 966 mg; Carbohydrate 78 g; Fiber 13 g; Protein 26 g

To clean the sand off your leeks, slice them first, then soak the slices in cold water, remove and dry in a salad spinner.

BAKED PENNE WITH FENNEL

ACTIVE: 25 min **I** TOTAL: 40 min **I** SERVES: 6

Kosher salt
3   tablespoons extra-virgin olive oil, plus more for greasing
½   pound pancetta, trimmed of excess fat and diced
1   medium onion, chopped
1   fennel bulb, trimmed and thinly sliced
1   28-ounce can whole plum tomatoes
½   cup heavy cream
12   ounces penne
½   cup chopped fresh basil
1   cup grated parmesan cheese (about 2½ ounces)
2   cups grated mozzarella cheese (about 8 ounces)
1¾   cups grated fontina cheese (about 6 ounces)

1. Position a rack in the upper third of the oven and preheat to 450°. Bring
a large pot of salted water to a boil. Heat 1 tablespoon olive oil in a large
skillet over medium-high heat. Add the pancetta and cook, stirring, until
the fat renders, 2 to 3 minutes. Pour off the fat, leaving about 1 tablespoon
in the pan. Add the onion and fennel and cook until the fennel is soft, about
5 minutes. Crush the tomatoes into the pan with your hands, then pour in
the juices from the can and bring to a simmer. Fill the empty can with ½ cup
of the boiling water and add to the sauce. Stir in the cream and simmer
while you cook the pasta.
2. Add the pasta to the boiling water and cook until al dente. Drain and add
to the sauce. Stir in the basil and ½ cup parmesan. Drizzle with 1 tablespoon
olive oil, season with salt and toss.
3. Oil a 9-by-13-inch baking dish. Layer the pasta, mozzarella, fontina and
the remaining ½ cup parmesan in the dish, alternating pasta and cheese.
Drizzle with the remaining 1 tablespoon olive oil. Bake, uncovered, until
browned and bubbly, about 15 minutes.

Per serving: Calories 757; Fat 45 g (Saturated 22 g); Cholesterol 117 mg;
Sodium 939 mg; Carbohydrate 56 g; Fiber 6 g; Protein 33 g

> Save drippings from bacon
> or pancetta in a heavy plastic
> container; they'll keep in the
> fridge for a week or in the
> freezer for up to a month. Use
> them in place of oil for sautéing.

Done in
20
minutes

LINGUINE WITH TUNA PUTTANESCA

ACTIVE: 20 min **I** TOTAL: 20 min **I** SERVES: 4

Kosher salt
12   ounces linguine
2   tablespoons extra-virgin olive oil
4   cloves garlic, thinly sliced
¼ to ½ teaspoon red pepper flakes
2   tablespoons capers, drained
½   cup roughly chopped kalamata olives
1   28-ounce can San Marzano plum tomatoes
4   basil leaves, torn, plus more for topping
1   5-ounce can albacore tuna, packed in olive oil
Freshly ground pepper

1. Bring a large pot of salted water to a boil. Add the linguine and cook
until al dente.
2. Meanwhile, heat the olive oil in a large skillet over medium heat. Add
the garlic and red pepper flakes and cook, stirring, until slightly toasted,
1 to 2 minutes. Add the capers and olives and fry 2 more minutes. Crush the
tomatoes into the skillet with your hands and reserve the juices. Cook until
the tomatoes are slightly dry, about 2 minutes. Add the reserved tomato juices,
the basil, and salt to taste and cook until the sauce thickens, 1 to 2 minutes.
Add the tuna with its oil, breaking it up with a fork, and season with salt.
3. Drain the pasta, reserving ½ cup cooking water, and return it to the pot.
Add the sauce and the reserved cooking water and toss. Season with
pepper and top with more basil.

Per serving: Calories 524; Fat 16 g (Saturated 2 g); Cholesterol 6 mg;
Sodium 641 mg; Carbohydrate 73 g; Fiber 7 g; Protein 24 g

> Chefs swear by Italian San
> Marzano tomatoes, sold in a can.
> They're grown in mineral-rich
> soil and have more pronounced
> acidity and sweetness. Look
> for "D.O.P." on the label: That
> indicates the real deal.

STEAMED VEGETABLES WITH CHICKPEAS AND RICE

ACTIVE: 20 min | TOTAL: 40 min | SERVES: 4

1   cup brown rice
1   small kabocha or buttercup squash (about 2 pounds), seeded and cut into 1-inch-thick wedges
½   head cauliflower, sliced into florets
1   2-inch piece ginger, peeled and thinly sliced
Kosher salt
4   cups snow peas (about 8 ounces)
½   teaspoon coriander seeds, crushed
2   tablespoons toasted sesame oil
1   15-ounce can chickpeas, drained and rinsed
3   tablespoons unsalted butter
4   scallions, thinly sliced
Freshly ground pepper
¼   cup thinly sliced fresh mint
Toasted sesame seeds, for sprinkling

1. Prepare the brown rice as the label directs. Meanwhile, place the squash, cauliflower and ginger in a large steamer basket over a saucepan of simmering water and season with salt. Cover and steam until the vegetables are tender, about 25 minutes. Add the snow peas, remove the pan from the heat and keep covered until the peas are crisp-tender, about 5 minutes.
2. Meanwhile, toast the coriander seeds in a skillet over medium-low heat until fragrant, about 1 minute. Add the sesame oil and increase the heat to medium-high. Add the chickpeas and cook until crisp, about 5 minutes. Add the butter and scallions; remove from the heat. Season with salt and pepper.
3. Divide the rice among plates and top with the vegetables and chickpea mixture. Sprinkle with the mint and sesame seeds.

Per serving: Calories 548; Fat 17 g (Saturated 6 g); Cholesterol 23 mg; Sodium 795 mg; Carbohydrate 85 g; Fiber 13 g; Protein 15 g

> Toast the coriander and sesame seeds to bring out their flavor. Shake the pan or stir the seeds so they don't burn, and remove them from the pan as soon as they smell nutty.

SPAGHETTI CARBONARA

ACTIVE: 30 min I TOTAL: 30 min I SERVES: 4

Kosher salt
6   slices thick-cut bacon, cut into ½-inch pieces
2   tablespoons extra-virgin olive oil
3   cloves garlic, crushed
½   teaspoon minced fresh rosemary
2   red jalapeño peppers, seeded and minced
¼   cup cognac or brandy (optional)
12   ounces spaghetti
3   large eggs
¾   cup freshly grated parmesan cheese, plus more for topping
½   cup freshly grated pecorino romano cheese
2   tablespoons chopped fresh parsley
Freshly ground pepper

1. Bring a large pot of salted water to a boil. Combine the bacon, olive oil, garlic, rosemary, jalapeños and ¼ cup water in a large skillet. Cook over medium-high heat, stirring occasionally, until the water evaporates and the bacon crisps, about 12 minutes. Discard the garlic. Add the cognac, if desired, and cook until it evaporates. Remove from the heat and set aside ¼ cup bacon mixture for topping.
2. Meanwhile, cook the spaghetti in the boiling water as the label directs. Mix the eggs, cheeses, parsley and 1 teaspoon pepper in a bowl. Drain the pasta, reserving ¼ cup cooking water.
3. Return the skillet to medium-high heat. Add the pasta and toss until heated through, 1 to 2 minutes. Remove from the heat. Whisk the reserved pasta water into the egg mixture, then quickly pour over the pasta and toss to gently cook the eggs and make a creamy **sauc**e. Top with the reserved bacon mixture and more parmesan.

Per serving: Calories 888; Fat 50 g (Saturated 18 g); Cholesterol 219 mg; Sodium 1,223 mg; Carbohydrate 65 g; Fiber 3 g; Protein 35 g

> Get into the habit of removing a mugful of cooking water before you drain your pasta. You can add the starchy water to your sauce to adjust the consistency.

SWISS CHARD LASAGNA

ACTIVE: 15 min | TOTAL: 40 min | SERVES: 4

6   no-boil lasagna noodles
3   tablespoons extra-virgin olive oil, plus more for brushing
1   bunch Swiss chard, finely chopped, leaves and stems separated
4   cloves garlic, sliced
1   cup ricotta cheese
¼   cup heavy cream
1   large egg
2   tablespoons grated parmesan cheese
2   tablespoons chopped fresh basil
Kosher salt and freshly ground pepper
7   ounces asiago cheese, shredded (about 2 cups)
2   ounces fresh mozzarella cheese, shredded (about ¼ cup)

1. Preheat the oven to 350˚. Soak the lasagna noodles in a bowl of hot water until they begin to soften, about 10 minutes. Meanwhile, heat the olive oil in a large skillet over medium heat. Add the chard stems and garlic and cook until golden, about 4 minutes. Add the chard leaves and cook until wilted, about 3 more minutes.
2. Mix the ricotta, cream, egg, parmesan, basil, ½ teaspoon salt, and pepper to taste in a small bowl.
3. Brush a 2-quart baking dish with oil and add 3 noodles in a single layer. Top with half of the ricotta mixture, chard and asiago. Repeat with the remaining noodles, ricotta mixture, chard and asiago. Cover with foil and bake until the cheese melts, about 20 minutes. Remove the foil, sprinkle with mozzarella and bake until bubbly and golden, about 5 more minutes.

Per serving: Calories 664; Fat 50 g (Saturated 23 g); Cholesterol 160 mg; Sodium 1,110 mg; Carbohydrate 24 g; Fiber 3 g; Protein 30 g

Use the leftover ricotta cheese in...

Chicken with Sun-Dried Tomato, Eggplant and Basil page 137

Ricotta, Ham and Scallion Tart page 193

Broiled Halibut with Ricotta-Pea Puree page 231

VEGETABLE FRIED RICE WITH BACON

ACTIVE: 25 min | TOTAL: 25 min | SERVES: 4

1	tablespoon vegetable oil
¼	pound thick-cut bacon, cut into ¼-inch pieces
¾	teaspoon sugar
2¼	teaspoons soy sauce
3	cloves garlic, thinly sliced
1	2-inch piece ginger, peeled and minced
¼ to ½ teaspoon red pepper flakes
½	head broccoli, florets and stalks cut into ¼-inch pieces
5	cups cooked long-grain white rice
¼	cup low-sodium chicken broth
4	large eggs
1	bunch watercress, stems removed
Spicy mustard or chili sauce, for serving (optional)

1. Place a wok or large skillet over high heat. Add the vegetable oil and bacon and stir-fry until golden and crisp, about 2 minutes. Sprinkle the sugar over the bacon and toss. Add ¼ teaspoon soy sauce (watch out—the oil will bubble up) and continue to stir-fry until the bacon is glazed, about 30 seconds. Transfer the bacon to a bowl with a slotted spoon. Add the garlic, ginger and red pepper flakes to the drippings in the pan and stir-fry until fragrant, about 30 seconds. Add the broccoli and cook until crisp, 2 to 3 minutes. Add the rice, the remaining 2 teaspoons soy sauce, the broth and glazed bacon. Toss to heat through.
2. Push the fried rice to one side of the pan, crack the eggs into the other side and scramble until set, about 1 minute. Mix the eggs into the rice and stir in the watercress. Divide among bowls and serve with mustard or chili sauce, if desired.

Per serving: Calories 513; Fat 21 g (Saturated 6 g); Cholesterol 201 mg; Sodium 456 mg; Carbohydrate 61 g; Fiber 2 g; Protein 17 g

> Assemble all of your ingredients by the stove before you start cooking—this dish comes together quickly.

ROASTED PEPPER PASTA SALAD

ACTIVE: 30 min **I** TOTAL: 30 min **I** SERVES: 4

Kosher salt
12   ounces mezzi rigatoni or other short tube-shaped pasta
2   bell peppers (red and/or yellow), halved, stemmed and seeded
6   cloves garlic, unpeeled
¼   cup almonds
⅓   cup extra-virgin olive oil
1   lemon
8   ounces bocconcini (small mozzarella balls)
1   bunch fresh basil, leaves torn
Freshly ground pepper

1. Preheat the broiler. Bring a pot of salted water to a boil. Add the pasta and cook as the label directs. Drain and rinse under cold water to stop the cooking. Shake off the excess water.
2. Meanwhile, place the bell peppers cut-side down on a foil-lined broiler pan, add the garlic and broil until charred, 7 to 8 minutes. Transfer the peppers to a bowl, cover and set aside about 5 minutes.
3. Heat a dry skillet over medium-high heat. Add the almonds and toast, shaking the pan, 4 to 5 minutes. Let cool, then coarsely chop.
4. Squeeze the garlic from its skin onto a cutting board. Add ½ teaspoon salt; mince and mash the garlic into a paste with a large knife. Peel the roasted peppers and slice into strips; transfer to a large bowl. Add the garlic paste and drizzle with the olive oil. Finely grate about 1 teaspoon lemon zest into the bowl and squeeze in all of the lemon juice. Add the bocconcini, basil, almonds, pasta, 1 teaspoon salt, and pepper to taste; toss.

Per serving: Calories 731; Fat 37 g (Saturated 11 g); Cholesterol 41 mg; Sodium 845 mg; Carbohydrate 73 g; Fiber 6 g; Protein 26 g

> To easily peel roasted peppers, transfer to a bowl and cover with plastic wrap until cool enough to handle. The trapped steam helps loosen the skins so you can pull them off with your fingers.

Done in
20
minutes

LEMON-PEPPER FETTUCCINE

ACTIVE: 20 min **I** TOTAL: 20 min **I** SERVES: 4

Kosher salt
12   ounces fettuccine
1   tablespoon unsalted butter
1   large shallot, minced
1¼   cups heavy cream
1   large egg yolk
1 to 2 teaspoons finely grated lemon zest
⅓   cup grated pecorino cheese, plus more for topping
Freshly ground pepper
Crusty bread, for serving (optional)

1. Bring a large pot of salted water to a boil. Add the fettuccine and cook as
the label directs. Drain, reserving about ½ cup cooking water.
2. Meanwhile, melt the butter in a skillet over medium heat. Add the shallot and a
pinch of salt and cook, stirring occasionally, until lightly golden, about 3 minutes.
Whisk the cream, egg yolk and lemon zest in a bowl. Reduce the heat to low and
add the cream mixture and cheese to the skillet. Cook, whisking, until slightly
thickened, about 2 minutes. Season with salt and 2 to 3 teaspoons pepper.
3. Add the pasta to the skillet and toss, adding enough of the reserved
cooking water to loosen the sauce. Divide among bowls and top with more
pecorino. Serve with crusty bread, if desired.

Per serving: Calories 680; Fat 38 g (Saturated 23 g); Cholesterol 178 mg;
Sodium 386 mg; Carbohydrate 67 g; Fiber 3 g; Protein 21 g

ungent
emony
re you
the

PASTA WITH ESCAROLE

ACTIVE: 25 min **I** TOTAL: 30 min **I** SERVES: 4

Kosher salt
12   ounces gemelli, fusilli or spaghetti
1   head escarole, roughly chopped
1   tablespoon pine nuts
2   tablespoons extra-virgin olive oil, plus more for drizzling
2   tablespoons breadcrumbs
Freshly ground pepper
¼   pound pancetta, cut into thin strips
2   cloves garlic, thinly sliced
1   red jalapeño pepper, thinly sliced (remove seeds for less heat)
2   tablespoons grated parmesan cheese

1. Bring a large pot of salted water to a boil. Add the pasta and cook until just al dente, about 10 minutes. Add the escarole and cook, stirring occasionally, until tender, about 2 more minutes.
2. Meanwhile, toast the pine nuts in a large skillet over medium-high heat, about 1 minute. Add 1 tablespoon olive oil, the breadcrumbs, and salt and pepper to taste; cook until golden, about 2 minutes. Transfer the mixture to a plate. Wipe out the skillet, add the pancetta and cook until crisp, about 5 minutes. Transfer to paper towels and blot dry.
3. Add the remaining 1 tablespoon olive oil to the skillet, then add the garlic and jalapeño and cook until fragrant, about 1 minute. Drain the pasta and escarole, reserving 1 cup cooking water, and add to the skillet. Add half of the pancetta and toss, drizzling in enough pasta water to moisten. Season with salt and pepper.
4. Divide the pasta among bowls, top with the breadcrumb mixture, remaining pancetta and the parmesan. Drizzle with olive oil.

Per serving: Calories 568; Fat 23 g (Saturated 6 g); Cholesterol 20 mg; Sodium 140 mg; Carbohydrate 71 g; Fiber 3 g; Protein 21 g

Instead of finishing this dish with tons of cheese, we used toasted breadcrumbs. They add a nice crunch without all the fat.

Done in
25
minutes

ORECCHIETTE SALAD WITH ROAST BEEF

ACTIVE: 25 min **I** TOTAL: 25 min **I** SERVES: 4

Kosher salt
8   ounces orecchiette pasta
1   cup bocconcini (small mozzarella balls), halved
1   cup marinated artichoke hearts, quartered
8   small sweet marinated peppers (such as Peppadew), quartered
3   tablespoons chopped fresh mint or basil
3   tablespoons extra-virgin olive oil
1   teaspoon finely grated lemon zest
2   tablespoons fresh lemon juice
Freshly ground pepper
4   cups baby arugula
6   ounces deli-sliced roast beef, cut into strips

1. Bring a large pot of salted water to a boil. Add the pasta and cook as
the label directs; drain but don't rinse.
2. Meanwhile, combine the bocconcini, artichokes, marinated peppers
and mint in a serving bowl. Add the olive oil, lemon zest and juice, and salt
and pepper to taste and toss. Add the pasta and toss again.
3. Just before serving, stir in the arugula and roast beef. Season the salad
with pepper.

Per serving: Calories 500; Fat 22 g (Saturated 7 g); Cholesterol 49 mg;
Sodium 548 mg; Carbohydrate 51 g; Fiber 3 g; Protein 26 g

> Shop at the deli case for this
> recipe. It's a great place to
> find prepared ingredients,
> like marinated vegetables.

POLENTA WITH ROASTED TOMATOES

ACTIVE: 35 min | TOTAL: 40 min | SERVES: 4

1   28-ounce can San Marzano plum tomatoes, drained
1   tablespoon extra-virgin olive oil
Kosher salt
1   cup instant polenta
Freshly ground pepper
2   bunches Swiss chard (about 2 pounds)
4   tablespoons unsalted butter
1   7.5-ounce package farmer cheese, crumbled

1. Position a rack in the upper third of the oven and preheat to 450°. Toss the tomatoes, olive oil and ¼ teaspoon salt in a large ovenproof skillet. Roast in the oven until the tomatoes are charred around the edges, about 25 minutes. Reduce the oven temperature to 300° but keep the tomatoes inside.
2. Meanwhile, bring 5 cups water to a boil in a saucepan over medium heat. Slowly whisk in the polenta until smooth and creamy. Add 1 teaspoon salt, and pepper to taste. Remove from the heat, cover and keep warm.
3. Bring a pot of salted water to a boil. Slice the chard leaves into wide strips and the stems into 1-inch pieces. Boil the stems until almost tender, about 5 minutes, then add the leaves and cook until both are tender, about 3 more minutes. Drain the chard.
4. Remove the skillet from the oven and place over medium-high heat. Push the tomatoes to one side, add the butter and swirl until the butter is golden brown. Add the chard and toss to coat. Divide the polenta among 4 bowls. Top with the tomatoes and chard. Season the cheese with salt and sprinkle over the top.

Per serving: Calories 456; Fat 23 g (Saturated 11 g); Cholesterol 51 mg; Sodium 1,056 mg; Carbohydrate 47 g; Fiber 9 g; Protein 18 g

> Farmer cheese is mild and firm with a slight tang. If you can't find it, use ricotta or queso fresco.

Vegetarian
dinner

Done in
25
minutes

TORTELLINI WITH PEAS AND PROSCIUTTO

ACTIVE: 25 min **I** TOTAL: 25 min **I** SERVES: 4

Kosher salt
1   pound meat-filled tortellini
2   tablespoons extra-virgin olive oil
4   ounces prosciutto or pancetta, finely chopped
3   cloves garlic, thinly sliced
1   tablespoon tomato paste
¼   cup heavy cream
1   cup frozen peas, thawed
2   tablespoons chopped fresh parsley
½   cup grated parmesan cheese

1. Bring a large pot of salted water to a boil. Add the tortellini and cook as the label directs.
2. Meanwhile, heat a large skillet over medium heat. Add the olive oil and prosciutto and cook until crisp, 3 to 4 minutes. Stir in the garlic and tomato paste and cook until fragrant, about 1 minute. Ladle in about 1 cup of the pasta cooking water and simmer until reduced by about half, 3 to 4 minutes. Add the cream and simmer until slightly thickened, 2 to 3 minutes.
3. About 2 minutes before the tortellini are done, add the peas to the boiling water and cook until just tender. Drain the tortellini and peas and add to the skillet, tossing to coat with the sauce. Stir in the parsley. Sprinkle with the parmesan cheese.

Per serving: Calories 475; Fat 27 g (Saturated 10 g); Cholesterol 195 mg; Sodium 1,237 mg; Carbohydrate 28 g; Fiber 3 g; Protein 29 g

Chop and fry prosciutto to use as a topping for salads and soups; it makes a delicious BLT, too.

PAPPARDELLE WITH SNAP PEAS

ACTIVE: 30 min I TOTAL: 30 min I SERVES: 4

Kosher salt
1   tablespoon extra-virgin olive oil
3   tablespoons unsalted butter
1   bunch scallions, cut into ½-inch pieces
½   pound sugar snap peas, roughly chopped
1   jalapeño pepper, seeded and minced
1   cup roughly chopped fresh parsley
1   bunch fresh chives, thinly sliced
½   pound dry pappardelle pasta
¾   cup crumbled ricotta salata or grated pecorino cheese

1. Bring a large pot of salted water to a boil. Heat the olive oil and 1 tablespoon butter in a large skillet over medium-high heat. Add the scallions, snap peas, jalapeño and ¼ teaspoon salt and cook, stirring, until soft, about 4 minutes. Transfer to a serving bowl and toss with the parsley and chives; reserve the skillet.
2. Meanwhile, cook the pappardelle in the boiling water until al dente, about 6 minutes. Reserve ⅔ cup of the cooking water, then drain the pasta and toss with the vegetables.
3. Pour the reserved cooking water into the skillet and add the remaining 2 tablespoons butter. Bring to a boil, whisking until the butter melts, then cook until reduced slightly, about 2 minutes. Pour the sauce over the pasta, sprinkle with ½ cup cheese and toss. Top with the remaining ¼ cup cheese.

Per serving: Calories 409; Fat 18 g (Saturated 9 g); Cholesterol 32 mg; Sodium 451 mg; Carbohydrate 49 g; Fiber 5 g; Protein 14 g

Try it with these sides...

Glazed Radishes
page 331

Coriander Roasted Carrots page 335

Summer Squash Carpaccio page 339

PASTA WITH ZUCCHINI AND HAM

ACTIVE: 35 min **I** TOTAL: 35 min **I** SERVES: 4

Kosher salt
10 ounces gemelli or cavatelli pasta
1 medium zucchini
3 tablespoons extra-virgin olive oil
2 cloves garlic, thinly sliced
Pinch of red pepper flakes
2 medium tomatoes, cut into chunks
¼ pound thinly sliced Black Forest ham, cut into strips
Freshly ground pepper
⅓ cup crumbled goat or feta cheese
3 tablespoons chopped fresh parsley
6 fresh mint leaves, torn

1. Bring a large pot of salted water to a boil. Add the pasta and cook as
the label directs. Drain, reserving 1 cup cooking water.
2. Trim the zucchini, then coarsely grate into a colander set in the sink.
Toss the zucchini with ¼ teaspoon salt and let sit 10 minutes.
3. Meanwhile, heat the olive oil in a large skillet over medium heat. Add the
garlic, red pepper flakes and ¼ teaspoon salt and cook, stirring, until the garlic
is golden, 3 to 4 minutes. Add the tomatoes and cook until slightly softened,
3 to 4 minutes. Squeeze any excess moisture from the zucchini, then add to
the skillet. Add the pasta, ham and the reserved cooking water and toss until
warmed through, 2 to 3 minutes. Season with salt and pepper. Remove from
the heat and fold in the cheese, parsley and mint.

Per serving: Calories 447; Fat 16 g (Saturated 4 g); Cholesterol 22 mg;
Sodium 578 mg; Carbohydrate 60 g; Fiber 3 g; Protein 17 g

> Draining the zucchini helps
> concentrate the flavor and
> speeds up the browning process.

COLD CURRY-PEANUT NOODLES

ACTIVE: 35 min **I** TOTAL: 35 min **I** SERVES: 4

Kosher salt
12 ounces whole-wheat spaghetti
⅔ cup crunchy peanut butter
1 to 2 tablespoons red curry paste
2 teaspoons rice wine vinegar
Juice of 1 lime, plus wedges for serving
⅓ cup fresh cilantro leaves, plus more for sprinkling
2 scallions, thinly sliced
1 cucumber, peeled, seeded and cut into thin strips
1 large carrot, coarsely grated
Red pepper flakes or chili paste, for serving (optional)

1. Bring a large pot of salted water to a boil. Add the spaghetti and cook as
the label directs. Reserve about ½ cup cooking water, then drain in a colander
and rinse under cold water. Shake off the excess water.
2. Meanwhile, puree the peanut butter, curry paste, vinegar, lime juice, cilantro,
½ cup water and 1 teaspoon salt in a food processor or blender until smooth.
Toss the spaghetti with the peanut sauce, scallions, cucumber and carrot in
a large bowl until coated. Season with salt and stir in some of the reserved
cooking water to loosen the sauce, if necessary. Transfer to bowls and top with
more cilantro and pepper flakes, if desired. Serve with lime wedges.

Per serving: Calories 574; Fat 23 g (Saturated 4 g); Cholesterol 0 mg;
Sodium 576 mg; Carbohydrate 79 g; Fiber 16 g; Protein 24 g

> Look for jars of red curry
> paste in the Asian condiment
> aisle. One spoonful adds a
> variety of spices to the dish.

Mix & Match

MAC AND CHEESE

Rigatoni with Monterey
Jack, Cheddar, Broccoli,
Bacon and Herbed Panko

① PICK A PASTA

Cook 1 pound pasta as the label directs, then drain. Meanwhile, preheat the oven to 450°.

- fusilli
- medium shells
- elbows
- rigatoni

② MAKE THE SAUCE

Heat 5 cups milk in a saucepan. In a separate saucepan, melt 5 tablespoons butter over medium heat. Whisk in 6 tablespoons flour and cook, stirring, about 1 minute (do not let the flour brown). Slowly whisk in the hot milk, then bring to a simmer and cook 5 minutes. Season with salt, pepper and nutmeg. Pour into a bowl.

③ STIR IN CHEESE

Add the hot cooked pasta to the sauce and mix in 1 pound grated cheese (about 4 cups) in any combination until melted.

- cheddar
- fontina
- gruyère
- mozzarella
- monterey jack
- gouda

④ ADD PROTEIN AND VEGETABLES

Mix in 2 cups (in any combination).

- shredded rotisserie chicken
- cooked sausage
- crumbled cooked bacon
- diced deli ham
- drained canned tuna
- thawed frozen peas
- thawed frozen spinach (squeezed dry)
- sliced roasted red peppers
- blanched broccoli
- boiled butternut squash cubes
- sautéed zucchini
- sautéed mushrooms
- chopped thawed frozen artichokes
- chopped pitted green olives

⑤ MAKE A TOPPING

PARMESAN BREADCRUMBS
Heat 3 tablespoons olive oil in a skillet. Add ½ cup breadcrumbs and toast, stirring, 3 to 4 minutes. Let cool slightly, then stir in ½ cup grated parmesan. Sprinkle on the pasta before baking.

FRIED SHALLOTS
Toss ½ pound thinly sliced shallots with 3 tablespoons instant flour. Fry in ½ inch hot vegetable oil until crisp, 2 to 3 minutes. Drain on paper towels and season with salt. Sprinkle on the pasta in the last 2 minutes of baking.

BUTTERED ALMONDS
Melt 2 tablespoons butter in a skillet. Add 1 cup sliced almonds and ½ teaspoon paprika; toast 4 to 5 minutes. Remove from the heat; add ¼ cup chopped parsley and season with salt. Sprinkle on the pasta before baking.

HERBED PANKO
Melt 3 tablespoons butter in a skillet. Add 1 cup panko, season with salt and toast 4 to 5 minutes. Remove from the heat and stir in ½ cup chopped herbs. Sprinkle on the pasta in the last 5 minutes of baking.

⑥ BAKE

Spread the pasta in a buttered 3-to-4-quart baking dish, top as directed and bake, uncovered, until browned, about 15 minutes.

Ted says...

❝ My idea of perfect happiness: A glass of wine, *All Things Considered* and a sauté pan buzzing with olive oil, carrots, celery and onions. My partner, Barry, and I cook at least three or four nights a week, unless I'm shooting *Chopped*, in which case we mostly eat our own cooking out of the freezer. And we cook everything from scratch. So many people suffer from the misconception that the only way to eat quickly and conveniently is to buy packaged, processed food, which is terrible. There are so many fast, *real* dishes—baked fish fillets with vinaigrette, stir-fries, main-dish salads. The freezer is really the best tool in the arsenal. Anything you cook, make extra and freeze it in those stackable plastic take-out containers. And remember to label and date it. You recognize it now, but in six months, it's going to be something mysterious."

—TED ALLEN IS THE HOST OF *CHOPPED* AND THE AUTHOR OF *THE FOOD YOU WANT TO EAT*.

KITCHEN SECRET
Ted's the cook and Barry, his partner, is the pastry chef. Barry designed the kitchen so they'd each have their own work spaces. Barry says Ted's not allowed to touch his baking zone—or roast big, messy meats in the convection oven where Barry bakes cakes and other desserts.

→

Parmesan
Broccoli,
page 337

Side Dishes

GARLIC GREEN BEANS

Toast 4 sliced **garlic cloves** and a pinch of **cayenne pepper** in a skillet with **butter.** Add 1¼ pounds **green beans,** season with **salt** and a pinch of **sugar** and cook 2 minutes. Add ¼ cup water, cover and cook 6 minutes, then uncover and boil until the water evaporates. Season with salt and **pepper** and toss with chopped **pecans.**

ROASTED RUTABAGA

Toss 1 large peeled and cubed **rutabaga** with 3 tablespoons **olive oil,** and **salt** and **pepper** on a baking sheet. Roast at 425˚ until golden and soft, 40 minutes. Toss with ½ teaspoon **apple cider vinegar** and chopped **parsley.**

GLAZED RADISHES

Place trimmed **radishes** in a sauté pan and add water until it comes a third of the way up the vegetables. Add a slab of **butter** and a hearty pinch of **salt** and **sugar,** bring to a boil, then simmer over medium-high heat until most of the liquid evaporates; toss the radishes in the buttery glaze.

ISRAELI COUSCOUS WITH RAISINS

Cook 2 cups **Israeli couscous** as the label directs; drain. Sauté 1 diced **onion** in **olive oil** with a pinch of **cinnamon** until golden, 5 minutes. Add 1 cup **golden raisins** and 2 tablespoons water and cook 2 minutes; toss with the couscous and a handful each of sliced **almonds** and chopped **parsley.** Season with **salt** and **pepper.**

MUSHROOM SALAD
Combine 1 pound thinly sliced **button mushrooms** with 3 tablespoons **lemon juice,** 2 tablespoons **olive oil** and 2 tablespoons each chopped **parsley, dill** and **chives** in a bowl. Season with **salt** and **pepper;** toss.

TOMATO GRATIN
Toss 2 pints **grape tomatoes,** 4 smashed **garlic cloves,** ¼ cup **olive oil** and 2 teaspoons **fresh thyme** in an ovenproof skillet; cook over medium-high heat until the tomatoes are soft, 8 minutes. Mix 2 tablespoons olive oil and ½ cup each **breadcrumbs** and **parmesan cheese;** sprinkle over the tomatoes and broil until golden, 3 minutes.

TARRAGON SNAP PEAS
Cook 1 pound **sugar snap peas** in boiling salted water until crisp-tender, about 4 minutes. Drain and toss with 2 tablespoons chopped **tarragon,** 1 tablespoon **olive oil,** and **salt** and **pepper.**

CAULIFLOWER TABOULI
Grate 1 head **cauliflower** into grain-size pieces with a box grater. Toss with 2 diced **plum tomatoes,** ⅓ cup **lemon juice,** 3 tablespoons **olive oil,** 2 tablespoons **soy sauce,** 2 chopped **scallions,** 1 bunch chopped **parsley** and 2 tablespoons chopped **mint** in a large bowl. Season with **salt** and **pepper.**

CREAMY BIBB SALAD

Rinse 2 or 3 **anchovy fillets,** then puree in a blender with a handful each of chopped **chives** and **parsley** and the juice of 1 **lemon.** Add ½ cup **mayonnaise** and ½ cup **sour cream** and blend until smooth. Season with **salt** and **pepper,** then drizzle over **Bibb lettuce.**

GARLIC-SESAME SPINACH

Cook 8 to 10 **garlic cloves** and a pinch of **red pepper flakes** in a skillet with **vegetable oil** until the garlic is golden. Add 10 cups **baby spinach** and cook until wilted; add a big splash of water and some **salt.** Top with **toasted sesame seeds;** drizzle with **sesame oil.**

CORIANDER ROASTED CARROTS

Toss 1½ pounds **carrots,** 2 tablespoons **olive oil,** the juice of 2 **lime wedges,** ¾ teaspoon cracked **coriander seeds** and **salt** and **pepper** on a sheet of foil. Seal into a tight package and roast at 425° until tender, 30 minutes. Sprinkle with **cilantro** and serve with lime.

ROASTED PEPPERS WITH BASIL

Halve, stem and seed 2 **red** and 2 **yellow bell peppers.** Broil, cut-side down, until blackened, 5 minutes. Place in a bowl, cover and cool; peel and cut into pieces. Sauté sliced **garlic** in **olive oil;** drizzle the oil over the peppers. Top with **basil, lemon juice, salt** and **pepper.**

LEMON POTATOES

Slice 4 peeled **potatoes** into 1½-inch rounds. Toss in an ovenproof skillet with ⅓ cup **lemon juice,** ¼ cup **olive oil,** 4 smashed **garlic cloves,** 4 **oregano sprigs,** and **salt** and **pepper.** Add enough water to come halfway up the sides of the potatoes. Cover, bring to a boil and cook 5 minutes. Uncover and roast at 500° for 30 more minutes.

PARMESAN BROCCOLI

Preheat the oven to 450° with a baking sheet on the lower rack. Blanch 1 head chopped **broccoli** in boiling water with **salt** and sliced **garlic** for 1 minute; drain. Toss with a splash of **olive oil,** a handful each of **breadcrumbs** and **parmesan cheese,** and salt and **pepper.** Place on the hot baking sheet. Top with more cheese and breadcrumbs; roast until golden, 15 minutes.

CAULIFLOWER GRATIN

Place 1 head **cauliflower florets** in a 2-quart baking dish. Whisk ½ cup **heavy cream,** ½ teaspoon **dry mustard** and 1 teaspoon **salt,** then pour over the cauliflower. Sprinkle 1 cup shredded **gruyère** and ⅓ cup **breadcrumbs** on top. Bake at 350° until tender, about 45 minutes.

GLAZED SNOW PEAS

Melt 2 tablespoons **butter** in a large skillet over medium-high heat. Add 8 ounces **snow peas,** 1 bunch chopped **scallions,** a pinch of **sugar** and ¼ cup water. Cover and simmer 2 minutes, then uncover and boil until the water evaporates, 2 more minutes. Season with **salt.**

BABY BROCCOLI WITH OYSTER SAUCE

Steam 2 bunches **baby broccoli** until bright green and tender, 5 minutes. Drizzle with 1 teaspoon **sesame oil.** Whisk 2 tablespoons **oyster sauce** with a splash of water and **lemon juice** and serve with the broccoli for dipping.

WATERMELON-CUCUMBER SALAD

Soak ½ thinly sliced **red onion** in cold water. Pat dry 4 cups diced **watermelon** and 1 seeded and sliced **cucumber;** toss with a handful of thinly sliced **mint.** Drain the onion, squeeze dry and add to the salad along with some chopped **cashews.** Add ¼ cup **olive oil** and the juice of ½ **lemon;** season with **salt** and toss. Top with crumbled **goat cheese.**

SUMMER SQUASH CARPACCIO

Thinly slice 1 **yellow squash** and 1 **zucchini** lengthwise (a mandoline works best); arrange a few slices on a plate in a single layer. Sprinkle with minced **shallots** and chopped **mixed herbs,** drizzle with **lemon juice** and **olive oil,** and season with **salt** and **pepper.** Repeat to make about 5 layers. Top with grated **pecorino;** let marinate for 20 minutes.

CURRIED WINTER SQUASH

Slice any **winter squash** in half, discard the seeds and cut into wedges. Brush all over with **butter** or **olive oil** and season the flesh with **curry powder.** Roast on a baking sheet at 400° until softened, about 30 minutes. Season with **salt.**

CARROT-MUSTARD SLAW

Soak a thinly sliced **red onion** in water for 15 minutes; drain. Whisk 1½ tablespoons **dijon mustard,** 2 tablespoons **white wine vinegar** and 1 tablespoon **capers** in a large bowl. Whisk in ⅓ cup **olive oil,** and **salt** and **pepper** to taste. Toss in 1 pound shredded **carrots,** 2 thinly sliced **celery stalks,** the onion slices and ¼ cup chopped **dill.**

CHEESY CHILE RICE

Mix 2 cups cooked **rice,** ½ cup **sour cream,** 1 cup chopped **scallions,** a 4-ounce can chopped **green chiles** (drained), 1 cup shredded **cheddar,** and **salt** and **cayenne** to taste. Butter a casserole dish and sprinkle with **parmesan cheese.** Spread the rice mixture in the dish, sprinkle with more parmesan and dot with **butter.** Bake 20 minutes at 450°.

SPICY SWEET-POTATO FRIES

Toss 2 pounds **sweet potatoes** (cut into wedges) with 3 tablespoons **olive oil,** 1½ teaspoons each **brown sugar** and **salt,** ¼ teaspoon each **cumin** and **chili powder,** and a pinch of **cayenne.** Roast cut-side down on a baking sheet in a 425° oven until crisp, 30 minutes, turning once.

ROASTED ASPARAGUS

Toss 2 pounds trimmed **asparagus,** 1 tablespoon **olive oil,** and **salt** and **pepper** on a baking sheet. Roast at 450° until lightly browned, 15 minutes. Mix ⅓ cup toasted **pine nuts,** ½ cup chopped **parsley,** the grated zest of 1 **lemon** and salt and pepper. Sprinkle over the asparagus.

FRIED PICKLES

Beat 1 **egg,** ¾ cup **milk** and a pinch of **cayenne.** Place ½ cup **cornstarch** in a shallow dish. In another dish, mix ½ cup each cornstarch and **cornmeal** with 2 tablespoons chopped **dill,** 2 teaspoons **paprika** and **salt** and **pepper.** Dip about 3 dozen cold **pickle slices** in the plain cornstarch, then the egg wash, then the cornmeal mixture. Fry in 2 inches of 375° **canola oil** until golden, about 3 minutes. Drain on paper towels and serve with **ranch dressing.**

BACON-CHEDDAR MASHED POTATOES

Simmer 2 pounds small **russet potatoes** in salted water until tender, about 20 minutes; drain. Cool slightly, then peel. Heat 1 cup **milk** with ½ stick **butter.** Mash the potatoes with the hot milk and stir in 1 cup shredded **cheddar.** Top with crumbled cooked **bacon** and sliced **scallions.**

BLACK BEAN SALAD

Heat 2 smashed **garlic cloves,** 1 diced **jalapeño** and 1 teaspoon **cumin seeds** in a skillet with **olive oil** over low heat, 5 minutes. Toss a 15-ounce can **black beans,** 1½ cups each diced **cucumber** and halved **grape tomatoes,** 4 chopped **scallions,** a squeeze of **lime juice** and some chopped **cilantro** in a bowl. Mash the hot garlic mixture and add to the beans. Season with **salt** and toss with **watercress.**

GLAZED TURNIPS AND EDAMAME

Simmer 1 bunch peeled and quartered **baby turnips** with 2 tablespoons **butter,** a pinch each of **sugar** and **salt,** and ⅓ cup water, covered, 5 minutes. Add 1 pound shelled **edamame,** 1 tablespoon **butter** and the white parts of 3 sliced **scallions;** cover and cook 2 minutes, then uncover and cook until the water evaporates. Add the scallion greens and let wilt.

CORN PUDDING

Beat 4 ounces softened **cream cheese,** a 15-ounce can **creamed corn,** ¾ cup thawed **frozen corn,** ½ cup **cornmeal** and ½ chopped **onion.** Stir in ⅔ cup **milk,** 3 tablespoons melted **butter,** 1 beaten **egg,** 1 tablespoon **sugar,** ½ cup shredded **cheddar,** and **salt** and **pepper.** Spread in a buttered 1-quart casserole dish and bake 50 minutes at 350°. Let stand 10 minutes before serving.

BRAISED CELERY

Sauté 1 sliced **onion** in a skillet with **butter** until golden. Add 1 chopped **carrot, fresh oregano, salt** and **pepper;** cook 2 minutes. Peel 1 bunch **celery;** cut into long pieces and add to the skillet with 1 cup **chicken broth.** Cover and simmer until just tender, 20 minutes; uncover and boil to thicken. Stir in more butter and chopped **parsley.**

SPICY ESCAROLE WITH GARLIC

Cook 3 minced **garlic cloves** in a skillet with **olive oil** until golden. Add a few pinches of **red pepper flakes.** Stir in 1 head torn **escarole** in batches, season with **salt** and toss. Cover and cook until the greens are wilted, 5 minutes.

ROASTED BEET SALAD
Toss 4 **beets** in a baking dish with **olive oil, salt** and **pepper.** Cover and roast at 425° until tender, about 40 minutes; let cool, then rub off the skins. Cut into wedges; toss with any juices from the baking dish, **capers,** chopped **pickles,** a dash each of **Worcestershire** and **hot sauce,** and chopped **parsley.**

TOMATO-BASIL LIMA BEANS
Toast 3 sliced **garlic cloves** and a pinch of **red pepper flakes** in a large skillet with **olive oil**. Add **salt,** then stir in a 10-ounce box thawed frozen **lima beans;** cook about 7 minutes. Remove from the heat; add halved **cherry tomatoes,** sliced **basil** and a splash of **white wine vinegar.** Drizzle with olive oil and top with shaved **parmesan cheese.**

PATATAS BRAVAS

Toss 2 pounds diced **potatoes** and 1 pound grated **plum tomatoes** in a baking dish with **olive oil.** Add a spoonful of **sugar** and 2 **bay leaves;** season with **salt, paprika** and **cayenne pepper.** Bake at 425° until the potatoes are tender, about 40 minutes. Thin a little **mayonnaise** with water; drizzle over the potatoes and sprinkle with sliced **scallions.**

CURRIED BROWN RICE PILAF

Cook 1 cup **brown rice** in a pot of salted boiling water for 30 minutes; drain. Melt ½ stick **butter** in the same pot. Add ½ cup finely broken thin **spaghetti,** some chopped **almonds** and **raisins, curry powder, salt** and **pepper;** cook 3 minutes. Stir in the rice, along with sliced **scallions.**

SNOW PEA AND AVOCADO SLAW

Thinly slice 10 ounces **snow peas** lengthwise. Toss with 2 thinly sliced **celery stalks** (add the leaves, too) and some toasted **walnuts.** Dress with **olive oil** and **lemon juice,** and season with **salt** and **pepper.** Gently stir in a thinly sliced **avocado** and minced **chives.**

GRILLED SCALLIONS

Place a grill pan over high heat. Toss 3 bunches **scallions** with 2 tablespoons **olive oil** in a bowl and season with **salt** and **pepper.** Brush the pan with oil. When the pan is almost smoking, add the scallions and grill until slightly charred, 2 minutes per side. Serve with **lemon wedges.**

BUTTERED EGG NOODLES

Cook 12 ounces wide **egg noodles** in salted boiling water until al dente. Transfer ¼ cup cooking water to a skillet. Stir in 4 tablespoons **butter,** one at a time. Add some chopped **parsley** and/or **dill,** a squeeze of **lemon juice,** and **salt** and **pepper.** Drain the noodles and toss with the sauce.

EGGPLANT WITH PEANUT DRESSING

Puree 2 tablespoons **peanut butter,** 1 **garlic clove,** the juice of 1 **lemon** and some fresh **oregano** in a blender. Blend in 3 tablespoons each **olive oil** and water; add **salt** and **pepper.** Brush 2 thinly sliced **eggplants** with olive oil, season with salt and pepper and grill 3 minutes per side. Top with the peanut dressing, more oregano and **red pepper flakes.**

ROASTED RED ONIONS
Halve 2 pounds unpeeled **red onions;** toss in a large
bowl with ¼ cup **olive oil,** 1 teaspoon **sweet smoked
paprika** and a pinch each of **sugar** and **salt.** Place
the **onions** cut-side down on a baking sheet; roast at
450° until soft and browned, 30 minutes.

ROASTED BRUSSELS SPROUTS

Toss 1½ pounds halved **Brussels sprouts** with ¼ cup **olive oil** and a pinch each of **red pepper flakes, salt** and **pepper.** Roast cut-side down on a baking sheet at 450° until caramelized, 25 to 30 minutes. Drizzle with **white wine vinegar** and **honey.**

OKRA WITH TOMATOES

Sauté 4 smashed **garlic cloves** in 3 tablespoons **olive oil** over medium heat until golden. Add 4 cups **okra** (halved lengthwise) and 1 small **onion** (cut into wedges); season with **salt** and **pepper** and cook until the okra is tender and bright, 10 to 12 minutes. Add 1 pint halved **cherry tomatoes;** cook until just bursting, 3 minutes. Finish with a splash of **cider vinegar.**

GREEN BEAN AND CELERY SALAD

Whisk 2 tablespoons **lemon juice,** 1 tablespoon **dijon mustard,** a pinch of **salt** and 3 tablespoons **olive oil** in a bowl. Add 1 minced **shallot,** 2 tablespoons **capers,** a handful each of chopped **parsley** and **celery leaves,** and a pinch of **pepper.** Boil ¾ pound halved **green beans** until crisp-tender, 4 minutes; drain and add to the dressing along with a few thinly sliced **celery stalks.**

CHARM CITY CORN

Bring 2 cups water, 1 cup **milk** and a pinch of **salt** to a boil in a pot. Cut 4 ears **corn** into thirds; add to the pot and cook until crisp-tender, 5 minutes, then drain. In the same pot, melt 4 tablespoons **butter** with 2 teaspoons **Old Bay Seasoning,** a dash of **green hot sauce** and some salt. Toss the corn in the spicy butter.

CELERY ROOT AND PARSNIP PUREE

Peel and chop 1 pound **celery root** and 1 pound **parsnips;** cook in salted boiling water until tender, about 20 minutes. Drain, then puree in a blender with 1 cup **milk,** ⅔ cup **sour cream** and 2 tablespoons **butter.** Season with **salt** and **pepper.**

HERB TOASTS

Slice a **baguette** in half crosswise, then cut each half lengthwise into 4 sticks. Cook 3 tablespoons minced **red onion** in 4 tablespoons **butter** until soft. Season with **salt** and **pepper** and add ¼ cup minced **mixed herbs.** Brush onto the bread and sprinkle with **parmesan cheese.** Bake at 400° until golden, 10 to 15 minutes.

CARROTS WITH CHICKPEAS AND PINE NUTS

Fry 1 sliced **red onion** and a 15-ounce can **chickpeas** in ⅓ cup **olive oil** until browned. Add 4 shaved **carrots** (use a peeler), 2 smashed **garlic cloves** and a handful of **pine nuts;** cook until the nuts are toasted. Drizzle with **white wine vinegar;** add **parsley** and **salt** and **pepper** to taste.

BRUSSELS SPROUT HASH

Thaw 1 cup frozen **pearl onions** and cook in a skillet with **butter** and **honey** until golden and glazed. Add 1½ pounds thinly sliced **Brussels sprouts,** season with **salt** and **pepper** and cook until crisp-tender. Finish with a splash of **chicken broth** or **white wine** and a drizzle of honey.

MEDITERRANEAN BULGUR

Toast 1 cup **bulgur** in a dry skillet until fragrant, about 5 minutes. Pour 2½ cups boiling water over the bulgur in a heat-resistant bowl and cover tightly with plastic wrap. Let stand for 15 minutes, then toss with a little **olive oil,** some chopped dried **apricots** and **olives,** and **salt** and **pepper** to taste.

GARLICKY BOK CHOY

Preheat 1 to 2 tablespoons **peanut oil** in a wok or large pan until rippling. Halve 6 heads **baby bok choy** lengthwise, keeping the stems and leaves intact, and place in the wok with sliced **garlic** and fresh **ginger.** Stir-fry until fragrant; season with **salt.**

Berry
Toast Tartlets,
page 374

10-Minute Desserts

CHOCOLATE-GLAZED POUND CAKE

Microwave 6 ounces chopped **bittersweet chocolate** with 1 stick cut-up **butter** and 1 tablespoon **honey** on 75% power until melted, about 2 minutes. Whisk until smooth. Place a loaf of **pound cake** on a rack and drizzle with the glaze.

MICROWAVE FUDGE

Microwave 12 ounces **semisweet chocolate chips** and a 14-ounce can **sweetened condensed milk,** 5 minutes. Stir vigorously, then add 1½ cups chopped **nuts** and 1 teaspoon **vanilla extract.** Spread into an 8-inch square pan lined with buttered parchment paper. Refrigerate, then cut into squares.

AFFOGATO

Beat ⅓ cup **heavy cream** with 2 teaspoons **confectioners' sugar** until soft peaks form. Put a scoop of **vanilla ice cream** into each glass or bowl. Pour hot **espresso** over the ice cream and top with the whipped cream and **chocolate shavings.**

CARAMEL APPLES

Combine 1 cup **sugar** and 2 teaspoons **lemon juice** in a saucepan. Bring to a boil over medium-high heat and cook, swirling the pan but not stirring, until amber. Remove from the heat and carefully stir in ¾ cup **heavy cream** and 1 tablespoon **bourbon** (it will bubble). Bring to a boil, whisking until smooth. Swirl in 2 tablespoons **butter.** Drizzle over sliced **apples.**

LEMON CRÊPES

Warm pre-made **crêpes** in a skillet with a little **butter.** Sprinkle with **sugar** and a squeeze of **lemon juice.** Spread with **lemon curd** and fold into triangles. Dust with **confectioners' sugar.**

INSTANT CHOCOLATE CAKE

Whisk ¼ cup **flour**, 5 tablespoons **sugar,** 2 tablespoons **cocoa powder,** 1 **egg,** 3 tablespoons **milk,** 3 tablespoons **vegetable oil** and a dash each of **vanilla extract** and **salt** in a large mug until smooth. Microwave until puffed, about 2 minutes.

CINNAMON-ANISE POACHED PEARS

Peel, halve and core 2 **pears.** Put in a shallow dish with 1 cup water, ⅓ cup **sugar,** 1 **cinnamon stick** and 1 **star anise pod.** Cover with plastic wrap and microwave until the pears are soft, 8 minutes. Meanwhile, beat ½ cup **heavy cream** with 1 tablespoon sugar and ¼ teaspoon **ground cinnamon** until soft peaks form. Serve the pears with the syrup and cinnamon cream.

COOKIES-AND-CREAM PARFAITS
Make two layers of **vanilla pudding,** crushed **chocolate wafer cookies** and **whipped cream** in tall glasses. Top with a cookie.

CHOCOLATE CRÈME BRÛLÉE
Spoon prepared **chocolate pudding** into ramekins. Sprinkle each with 1 heaping tablespoon **turbinado** or **raw sugar.** Caramelize the sugar with a kitchen torch. Top with **raspberries.**

PEARS WITH CHOCOLATE SAUCE

Microwave 6 ounces chopped **bittersweet chocolate** with 6 tablespoons cut-up **butter** and ¼ cup **honey** on 75% power until melted, about 2 minutes. Whisk until smooth. Peel, halve and core 2 **pears.** Top each half with **chocolate ice cream** and the chocolate sauce.

QUICK APPLE CRISP

For each crisp, put 1 peeled chopped **apple** and 2 tablespoons **butter** on a large sheet of heavy-duty foil. Sprinkle with ½ teaspoon chopped **crystallized ginger** and a pinch each of **cinnamon, ground cloves** and **salt.** Seal to make a packet, leaving room for steam. Bake 8 minutes at 500°. Serve topped with **vanilla ice cream** and **granola.**

CHOCOLATE-NUT BUTTONS

Microwave 3 ounces chopped **bittersweet chocolate** on 75% power until melted, about 2 minutes. Beat ¼ cup **peanut butter,** 2 tablespoons softened **butter** and ½ cup **confectioners' sugar** until smooth. Roll into balls. Dip in the melted chocolate, place on a parchment-lined baking sheet and freeze 3 minutes.

PEACH MELBA

Puree 3 cups **raspberries,** ¼ cup **sugar** and 1 tablespoon **lemon juice** in a blender. Strain and discard the seeds. Serve the raspberry sauce over **vanilla ice cream** with fresh or canned **peach halves.**

FIGS AND CREAM

Stir 1 cup **dark brown sugar** and 2 teaspoons **lemon juice** in a saucepan. Bring to a boil over medium-high heat and cook, swirling the pan but not stirring, until the sugar melts. Off the heat, carefully add ½ cup **heavy cream** and 1 tablespoon **bourbon** (it will bubble). Bring to a boil, whisking until smooth, then swirl in 2 tablespoons **butter.** Spoon over **vanilla ice cream** and top with quartered fresh **figs.**

CRISPY-CRUNCHY BARS

Melt 3 tablespoons **butter,** 10 ounces **marshmallows** and ½ cup **peanut butter** (or other nut butter) in a large saucepan over low heat. Stir in 4 cups **crisp brown rice cereal,** 1 cup **granola** and 1 cup chopped **almonds.** Stir in ½ cup **chocolate chips.** Press into a buttered 9-inch square pan; let cool, then cut into bars.

GRAPEFRUIT MOUSSE

Cut the peel and pith from 1 large **pink grapefruit** with a paring knife, then cut into segments and chop. Whip 1½ cups **heavy cream** with 6 tablespoons **sugar** and 1 tablespoon **Campari** until soft peaks form. Fold in the grapefruit, then divide among bowls.

ICE CREAM WAFFLEWICHES

Toast **frozen waffles,** then let cool. Sandwich
scoops of **ice cream** (any flavor) between the waffles.
Dust with **confectioners' sugar,** if desired.

CANDY SHAKES
Blend 1 pint **vanilla ice cream** with ¾ cup **milk** and ⅓ cup chopped **candy-coated chocolates, peanut butter cups** or chopped **peppermint patties.** Divide among chilled glasses.

CHOCOLATE CROSTINI
Brush thick slices of **baguette** with **butter** on both sides and toast in a skillet until golden. Microwave 3 ounces chopped **bittersweet chocolate** on 75% power until melted, about 2 minutes. Spread on the toast and sprinkle with **sea salt,** if desired.

CARAMEL PINEAPPLE CAKE
Top sliced **angel food** or **pound cake** with **dulce de leche ice cream,** a drizzle of **caramel sauce** and some chopped fresh **pineapple** and **macadamia nuts.**

GRAPEFRUIT BRÛLÉE
Cut a **grapefruit** in half, then cut between the membranes to loosen the segments, but keep them in place. Sprinkle each half with 2 teaspoons **superfine sugar.** Caramelize the sugar with a kitchen torch. Top with **raspberries.**

COCONUT PINEAPPLE SUNDAE

Heat 2 tablespoons **rum,** 2 tablespoons **brown sugar** and 1 tablespoon **butter** in large skillet until the sugar dissolves. Add 3½ cups cubed fresh **pineapple** and cook over medium-high heat until caramelized, about 6 minutes. Remove from the heat and stir in ½ tablespoon butter and 1 teaspoon rum. Serve the pineapple in bowls topped with **coconut sorbet** and **shredded coconut.**

CHOCOLATE FONDUE

Microwave 6 ounces chopped **bittersweet chocolate** with ¼ cup **heavy cream** on 75% power until melted, about 2 minutes. Whisk until smooth. Serve with fresh **fruit** and/ or cubed **angel food cake,** for dipping.

CHOCOLATE CREAM PIE

Beat 8 ounces softened **cream cheese,** ½ cup **sugar,** ⅓ cup **cocoa powder,** ⅓ cup **milk** and 1 teaspoon **vanilla extract** until fluffy. Spread in a **chocolate cookie crust.** Beat 1 cup **heavy cream** with 2 tablespoons sugar until soft peaks form, then spread over the cream cheese layer. Top with shaved **chocolate.**

TIRAMISU TRIFLES

Mix ½ pound **mascarpone** with 3 tablespoons **sugar.** Dip 12 **ladyfingers** in a mix of ¾ cup **espresso** and 1 tablespoon **rum.** Layer the mascarpone and ladyfingers in glasses, breaking the cookies to fit, if necessary. Top with **whipped cream** and dust with **cocoa powder.**

MEXICAN CHOCOLATE S'MORES

Put 1 square **dark chocolate** on a **cinnamon graham cracker** and top with a **marshmallow;** microwave until the marshmallow puffs, about 10 seconds. Sprinkle with **cinnamon** and top with another cinnamon graham.

RICOTTA WITH BALSAMIC BERRIES

Boil 1 cup **balsamic vinegar,** 2 tablespoons **honey** and a sprig of **mint** in a small saucepan until syrupy, about 7 minutes. Cool slightly, then drizzle over sliced **strawberries** and/or **blackberries** and **ricotta.**

CHILLED HONEYDEW SOUP

Puree 1 cubed ripe **honeydew melon** in a blender until smooth. Add 2 tablespoons **honey** and ½ cup water and puree. Add a splash of **seltzer.** Pour into chilled bowls and top with **crème fraîche** and **fresh mint.**

CARAMELIZED BANANAS

Melt 2 tablespoons **butter** in a skillet. Add 2 sliced **bananas** and 2 tablespoons **brown sugar.** Cook until golden and syrupy, about 5 minutes. Sprinkle the bananas with **cinnamon** and spoon over **rum raisin ice cream.**

369

MANGO CLOUD

Puree 2 ripe peeled and pitted **mangoes,** ¼ cup **confectioners' sugar,** 2 teaspoons **lime juice,** and a pinch each of **ground cinnamon** and **cloves** in a blender until smooth. Transfer to a bowl and refrigerate. Whip ¾ cup **heavy cream** with ¼ teaspoon **coconut extract** until stiff peaks form, then gently fold into the mango puree. Spoon into glasses.

CHEESECAKE POPS

Microwave 6 ounces chopped **bittersweet chocolate** on 75% power until melted, about 3 minutes. Cut a **frozen cheesecake** into 1-inch cubes. Gently press lollipop sticks halfway into each cube. Dip in the chocolate and roll in **sprinkles** and/or **coconut,** if desired.

RHUBARB CRUMBLE

Mix 2 cups chopped **rhubarb,** ½ cup **sugar,** 1 teaspoon **lemon juice** and a splash of **vanilla extract** in a small skillet. Cook until the rhubarb is soft, 5 to 7 minutes. Stir in 1 cup sliced **strawberries.** Divide among bowls, top with **Greek yogurt** and sprinkle with chopped toasted **almonds.**

YOGURT WITH APRICOTS

Mix ¾ cup **apricot preserves** with 3 diced **fresh apricots.** Divide **Greek yogurt** among bowls; top with the apricot mixture, drizzle with **honey** and sprinkle with chopped **pistachios.**

SHORTCAKE ROYALE

Microwave ¼ cup **orange liqueur** with 3 tablespoons **sugar** until the sugar dissolves, about 4 minutes. Cut 1 **pound cake** horizontally into 4 thin rectangles. Toss 2 cups **mixed berries** with the orange syrup and 2 tablespoons sugar. Beat 1 cup **heavy cream** with 2 tablespoons sugar until soft peaks form. Make a 4-layer cake with the whipped cream and berries between each layer. Dust with **confectioners' sugar.**

BLUE CHEESE AND PEARS
Spread **soft blue cheese** on **pear slices**
and drizzle with **honey.**

STRAWBERRY-MERINGUE FOOLS

Beat 1 cup **heavy cream** with 2 tablespoons **confectioners' sugar** until stiff peaks form. Fold in 1 cup finely chopped **strawberries** (with their juice). Layer in bowls with crushed **meringue cookies.**

PEACHES AND CREAM

Beat 1 cup **heavy cream,** 2 teaspoons **vanilla extract** and 2 teaspoons **confectioners' sugar** until soft peaks form. Spoon jarred **peaches** and some of their juices into bowls. Top with the whipped cream and **blackberries.**

RICE PUDDING WITH PLUMS

Halve and pit 2 **plums,** then cut into thin wedges. Toss with 1 tablespoon **butter** and 1 to 2 teaspoons **honey** in a small skillet. Cook over medium-high heat until bubbling, about 6 minutes. Cool slightly, then spoon over prepared **rice pudding.** Top with freshly ground **black pepper.**

BERRY TOAST TARTLETS

Whisk 2 tablespoons each **almond butter** and **sugar,** 1 tablespoon softened **butter,** 1 **egg yolk** and ⅛ teaspoon **almond extract.** Spread on 2 pieces **sandwich bread.** Bake in a toaster oven at 400° until crusty on top, about 6 minutes. Top with **blueberries** or **raspberries** and dust with **confectioners' sugar.**

SWEET-AND-SALTY SHORTBREAD

Microwave 6 ounces chopped **bittersweet chocolate** with 1 tablespoon **butter** at 75% power until melted, about 3 minutes. Whisk until smooth. Dip **shortbread cookies** halfway into the melted chocolate and transfer to a rack. Sprinkle with **coarse sea salt.**

GRAPE SODA FLOATS

Put 2 scoops **vanilla ice cream** in a chilled glass. Add ⅓ cup **pure grape juice** and top with **seltzer.**

CHEESECAKE PARFAITS

Beat 8 ounces softened **cream cheese** with 3 tablespoons **sugar** and
3 tablespoons **heavy cream**. Put a heaping teaspoon of **graham cracker crumbs** in each glass. Top with the cream cheese mixture, chopped
canned or fresh **pears** and sliced **crystallized ginger.**

CHERRIES JUBILEE
Toss 1 pound pitted **cherries,** ½ cup **sugar,** 2 strips
lemon zest and the juice of ½ **lemon** in a large skillet.
Cover and cook until the sugar dissolves, 4 minutes,
then uncover and cook until juicy, 2 more minutes.
Carefully add ⅓ cup **rum,** ignite and let it burn until
the flame dies out. Spoon over **vanilla ice cream.**

WAFFLE CAKE

Toast 3 **frozen waffles** until crisp. Stack the waffles with 3 tablespoons **chocolate-hazelnut spread** and 2 sliced **strawberries** between each layer. Top with more strawberries and dust with **cocoa powder.**

CHOCOLATE–PEANUT BUTTER PIE

Microwave 4 ounces chopped **semisweet chocolate** at 75% power until melted, about 3 minutes; whisk in 3 tablespoons softened **butter.** Spread in a **graham cracker crust.** Beat 8 ounces **mascarpone cheese,** ½ cup **peanut butter,** ⅓ cup **sugar** and 1 teaspoon **vanilla extract** until fluffy, then spoon into the crust. Beat 2 cups **heavy cream** with ¼ cup **sugar** until it holds soft peaks, then spread over the peanut butter layer. Top with chopped **peanuts.**

BERRY ICE CREAM SANDWICHES

Fold 1 pint mixed fresh **berries** into 1 quart softened **vanilla ice cream.** Sandwich scoops of the ice cream between **chocolate wafer cookies.**

PEARS WITH YOGURT

Spoon jarred **pears** and their juices into bowls; top with a dollop of **Greek yogurt** and some chopped **almonds** or **hazelnuts.** Drizzle with **honey.**

BUTTER PECAN BROWNIE SUNDAE

Top prepared **brownies** with scoops of **butter-pecan ice cream.** Drizzle with **caramel sauce** and sprinkle with **chopped pecans.**

PEANUT BUTTER– BANANA MOUSSE

Puree 3 frozen chopped **bananas,** ⅓ cup **peanut butter,** 2 tablespoons **honey** and a pinch of **salt** in a food processor until smooth. Scoop into bowls and top with chopped **peanuts** and **chocolate sauce.**

BLACK-AND-WHITE SHAKES

Blend 1 pint **vanilla ice cream** with ¾ cup **milk** in a blender until smooth. Pour half into the bottom of 4 chilled glasses. Add 2 tablespoons **chocolate syrup** to the remaining vanilla shake and blend. Pour into the glasses. Top with **whipped cream** and **shaved chocolate.**

Food Network Kitchens'
Secret Ingredients...

Spice up your cooking every night by keeping these test-kitchen favorites at home. You'll use them again and again!

☐ Anchovies

These tiny fish add great salty punch to sauces and dressings. Buy the fillets in a can, then rinse and chop them. Or pick up a tube of anchovy paste—it'll keep for months in the fridge. Try them in:

- **Grilled Chicken Caesar Salad** page 149
- **Flank Steak with Salsa Verde** page 206

☐ Toasted sesame oil

This dark, nutty oil is used mostly for flavoring food, not frying it (it has a low smoke point); it's great in salad dressing or drizzled onto roasted vegetables. It's more expensive than olive or vegetable oil, but a bottle will last you a while because most recipes call for only a tablespoon or so. Try it in:

- **Chinese Dumpling Soup** page 16
- **Poached Ginger Chicken** page 97

☐ Instant flour

The granular texture of this flour makes it ideal for breading meat and fish. And it doesn't clump up in liquids, so it's perfect for thickening sauce and gravy. Try it in:

- **Chicken and Waffles** page 109
- **Popcorn Shrimp Salad** page 246

☐ Ginger

You'll find assorted sizes of this knobby root near the garlic. Don't worry about buying too much: It will keep in your fridge, unpeeled in a sealed plastic bag, for about 3 weeks. Peel off the skin with a vegetable peeler or scrape it off with a spoon before chopping (a 1-inch piece yields about 1 tablespoon minced); sauté to include in soup or stir-fry. Try it in:

- **Carrot-Ginger Soup with Tofu** page 8
- **Garlicky Bok Choy** page 353

☐ Panko

These Japanese-style breadcrumbs are coarse and light—perfect for creating a crunchy crust. Use them in place of regular breadcrumbs in recipes for breading. Try them in:

- **Japanese-Style Crispy Pork** page 185
- **Risotto Cakes with Mixed Greens** page 275

☐ Greek yogurt

This strained yogurt is extra thick and creamy and is a good nonfat or low-fat substitute for sour cream or mayonnaise. Try it in:

- **Poppy Seed–Chicken Pitas** page 76
- **Oven-Fried Chicken** page 129

☐ Curry paste

Look for this tasty Thai staple in the international aisle. It's a blend of chiles, spices, vinegar and clarified butter, sold in jars and available in green (hot), red (medium-hot) and yellow (mild). You can mix it with coconut milk, broth or water to make a quick spicy curry sauce. Try it in:

- **Clams and Mussels in Thai Curry Sauce** page 254
- **Cold Curry-Peanut Noodles** page 322

☐ Chipotle peppers in adobo sauce

Chipotle chile peppers are dried smoked jalapeños. They're sold in cans, packed in a smoky, spicy adobo sauce, and will add tons of flavor to salsa or chili. After you open the can, you can keep leftovers in an airtight container in the refrigerator for a month. Try them in:

- **Mexican Chicken Soup** page 41
- **Chicken and Black Bean Tostadas** page 102

☐ Rice vinegar

If you regularly make Asian dishes, keep a bottle of this mild, slightly sweet vinegar on hand. (It's sometimes labeled rice wine vinegar.) We like the unseasoned kind; seasoned rice vinegar has added salt and sugar. Try it in:

- **Hoisin Chicken with Cucumber Salad** page 113
- **Udon with Tofu and Asian Greens** page 285

☐ Fish sauce

This tasty, pungent sauce, sold near the soy sauce, is made from salted, fermented fish, but we promise it won't make your food taste fishy. Add a splash to your favorite stir-fry—it tends to bring out the other great flavors in the dish. Try it in:

- **Vietnamese Noodle Soup** page 3
- **Mahi Mahi Banh Mi (Vietnamese Sandwiches)** page 243

☐ Horseradish

Keep a jar of grated horseradish in the fridge to give burgers and mashed potatoes an instant kick. The spicy root is packed in vinegar, so remember to drain it before using. Try it in:

- **Slow-Cooker Corned Beef and Cabbage** page 210
- **Rice and Peas with Trout** page 245

☐ Asian chili sauce

Use this spicy chile pepper–based condiment like hot sauce: It comes in many different varieties—we like sriracha and sambal oelek. Look for it in the international aisle (but don't confuse it with sweet chili sauce, found near the ketchup). It's delicious mixed with mayonnaise as a spread for burgers and sandwiches. Try it in:

- **Poached Ginger Chicken** page 97
- **Vegetable Fried Rice with Bacon** page 305

☐ Kosher salt and freshly ground pepper

Replace your old salt and pepper shakers with a small bowl of kosher salt and a pepper mill filled with whole peppercorns so you can add salt by the pinch and grind in pepper to taste when you're cooking. This is how we season almost every dish in the test kitchen!

☐ Dijon mustard

This French mustard is much sharper than regular yellow mustard. We like using the whole-grain variety to add flavor and texture to sauces and dressings. Try it in:

- **Green Eggs and Ham** page 189
- **Carrot-Mustard Slaw** page 341

☐ queso fresco

Use this crumbly, tangy cheese, sold in wedges or rounds near the packaged cheeses, as a topping for tacos and other Mexican dishes. It gets soft when heated, but it doesn't melt. Try it in:

- **Mexican Meatball Subs** page 60
- **Chicken-and-Cheese Enchiladas** page 106

☐ Hoisin sauce

Thick, sweet and spicy, this popular Chinese sauce is great as an ingredient and on its own as a dipping sauce—think of it as hot Asian ketchup. Try it in:

- **Hoisin Chicken with Cucumber Salad** page 113
- **Teriyaki Hens with Bok Choy** page 126

☐ Crème fraîche

Look for this smooth, tangy cream near the sour cream and swirl some into soups and stews—it won't curdle! Try it in:

- **Slow-Cooker Corned Beef and Cabbage** page 210
- **Smoked Trout and Potato Salad** page 227

☐ Italian cured meats

Add prosciutto (top) and pancetta (bottom) to your order at the deli counter: Pancetta is unsmoked Italian-style bacon and can be fried like regular bacon; prosciutto is cured for much longer, so it's fine to eat raw or cooked. You can fry either into salty, crunchy toppings for soups and salads. Try them in:

- **Apple-Cheddar-Squash Soup** page 15
- **Pasta with Escarole** page 310

☐ Capers

These tiny dried flower buds, sold in jars near the olives and pickles, are super salty and will punch up a salad or sauce. To mellow them out, just rinse them before using. Try them in:

- **Linguine with Tuna Puttanesca** page 297
- **Roasted Beet Salad** page 345

☐ Chinese rice wine

Made from fermented rice, this Chinese cooking staple has an acidic, nutty flavor that is similar to dry sherry. Shaoxing is a good-quality rice wine; look for it at Asian markets. (Don't substitute mirin, a Japanese rice wine that's much sweeter.) Try it in:

- **Japanese-Style Crispy Pork** page 185
- **Spicy Chinese Beef** page 198

METRIC CHARTS

Conversions by Ingredient

A standard cup measure of a dry or solid ingredient will vary in weight depending on the type of ingredient. A standard cup of liquid is the same volume for any type of liquid. Use this chart to convert standard cup measures to grams (weight) or milliliters (volume).

STANDARD CUP	FINE POWDER (e.g., flour)	GRAIN (e.g., rice)	GRANULAR (e.g., sugar)	LIQUID SOLIDS (e.g., butter)	LIQUID (e.g., milk)
1	140 g	150 g	190 g	200 g	240 ml
¾	105 g	113 g	143 g	150 g	180 ml
⅔	93 g	100 g	125 g	133 g	160 ml
½	70 g	75 g	95 g	100 g	120 ml
⅓	47 g	50 g	63 g	67 g	80 ml
¼	35 g	38 g	48 g	50 g	60 ml
⅛	18 g	19 g	24 g	25 g	30 ml

Liquid Ingredients

TEASPOON	TABLESPOON	PINT	QUART	CUP	OUNCE	MILLILITER
¼ tsp						1 ml
½ tsp						2 ml
1 tsp						5 ml
3 tsp	1 tbsp				½ fl oz	15 ml
	2 tbsp			⅛ cup	1 fl oz	30 ml
	4 tbsp			¼ cup	2 fl oz	60 ml
	5⅓ tbsp			⅓ cup	3 fl oz	80 ml
	8 tbsp			½ cup	4 fl oz	120 ml
	10⅔ tbsp			⅔ cup	5 fl oz	160 ml
	12 tbsp			¾ cup	6 fl oz	180 ml
	16 tbsp			1 cup	8 fl oz	240 ml
		1 pt		2 cups	16 fl oz	480 ml
			1 qt	4 cups	32 fl oz	960 ml
					33 fl oz	1,000 ml

Cooking/Oven Temperatures

	FARENHEIT	CELCIUS	GAS MARK
Freeze Water	32° F	0° C	
Room Temperature	68° F	20° C	
Boil Water	212° F	100° C	
Bake	325° F	160° C	3
	350° F	180° C	4
	375° F	190° C	5
	400° F	200° C	6
	425° F	220° C	7
	450° F	230° C	8
Broil			Grill

Dry Ingredients

OUNCES	POUNDS	GRAMS
1 oz	¹⁄₁₆ lb	30 g
4 oz	¼ lb	120 g
8 oz	½ lb	240 g
12 oz	¾ lb	360 g
16 oz	1 lb	480 g

Length

INCHES	FEET	YARDS	CENTIMETERS	METERS
1 in			2.5 cm	
6 in	½ ft		15 cm	
12 in	1 ft		30 cm	
36 in	3 ft	1 yd	90 cm	
40 in			100 cm	1 m

INDEX

INDEX

INDEX

INDEX

INDEX

INDEX

Subscribe to Food Network Magazine and save 62% off the newsstand price!

Save 10% at FoodNetworkStore.com!

EACH ISSUE has more than 100 amazing recipes, a pull-out recipe booklet, cooking secrets from Food Network Kitchens, tips from your favorite Food Network stars and much more.

GET 1 YEAR for just $15. Order a subscription online at cookbook.foodnetworkmag.com for your special introductory rate.

FOODNETWORKSTORE.COM is the place to shop for products from your favorite Food Network stars. You'll find our chefs' own products, plus other favorite brands of cookware, bakeware, cutlery, cook's tools, DVDs and more. Take 10% off your entire order*! Use coupon code C99246 during checkout.

INDEX

Subscribe to
Food Network Magazine
and save 62% off the
newsstand price!

Save 10% at
FoodNetworkStore.com!

EACH ISSUE has more than 100 amazing recipes, a pull-out recipe booklet, cooking secrets from Food Network Kitchens, tips from your favorite Food Network stars and much more.

GET 1 YEAR for just $15. Order a subscription online at cookbook.foodnetworkmag.com for your special introductory rate.

FOODNETWORKSTORE.COM is the place to shop for products from your favorite Food Network stars. You'll find our chefs' own products, plus other favorite brands of cookware, bakeware, cutlery, cook's tools, DVDs and more. Take 10% off your entire order*! Use coupon code C99246 during checkout.

*The following manufacturers/brands have requested not to participate in this promotion and are excluded: AeroGrow, All-Clad, Breville, Capresso, Chef's Choice, Emerilware, Global, J.A. Henckels International, Jarden, John Boos & Co., KitchenAid Stand Mixers, Krups, Kuhn Rikon, Le Creuset, Lenox, Musso, Saeco, Screwpull, Shun, Staub, Viking, Weber Grills, Wusthof and Zwilling J.A. Henckels. Excludes cookbooks shipping from Jessica's Biscuit and gourmet foods shipping from igourmet.com. Clearance items, gift certificates and gift cards do not qualify. Cannot be combined with other special offers or promotional gift certificates. Cannot be applied to previous purchases. Limit one use per e-mail address. Offer valid through December 31, 2011. Terms subject to change.